Comhairle Cathrach
Bhaile Átha Cliath
Dublin City Council

First published in 2021 by
Dublin City Council
c/o Dublin City Library & Archive
138-144 Pearse Street
Dublin 2

A catalogue record is available for this book
from the British Library.

ISBN 978-0-9500512-6-0

Designed by Source Design
Printed by Impress Printing Works

Distributed by Four Courts Press
7 Malpas Street
Dublin 8

Building Healthy Homes

Dublin Corporation's First Housing Schemes 1880–1925

Joseph Brady and Ruth McManus

Comhairle Cathrach
Bhaile Átha Cliath
Dublin City Council

Contents

Four Courts Environs

The South-West City

City Centre

Southern Docklands

Northern Docklands

The Suburbs

Foreword – Lord Mayor Hazel Chu

Dublin Corporation had a task of enormous proportions when it decided in the 1880s that it needed to become directly involved in the provision of houses for the working classes. What followed over the next fifty or so years was a series of projects by which it explored the various issues and solutions to housing provision as it attempted to build healthy houses for its citizens. Many of these schemes have stood the test of time and are appreciated and sought-after places to live.

So, I am delighted to welcome this book which aims to re-introduce Dubliners to the many thriving communities, mostly in the inner city, which resulted from its work. The Corporation, both its officials and elected members, was actively involved in trying to meet the needs of its citizens and it is good to be reminded of the importance of a commitment to public service.

The issues it faced were much the same as those faced today. What kind of housing to build – individual family homes or apartments? Should we build in the inner city where people had their networks or out in the suburbs where there was more space? Finance was a perennial problem. Should we build what people can afford, even though that might be sub-standard or should we accept that the city has a duty to provide decent housing for all and share the burden? The book invites us to consider these issues and to reflect on the solutions which were found at the time. Perhaps they offer us pointers for today.

The book makes use of photographs, maps and the city architect's original diagrams, which are part of the wonderful resource that is the City Archive. Together they provide pen pictures of each of the schemes and they invite citizens to walk and appreciate them in real life. The book concludes with a detailed look at Marino and Drumcondra. These schemes show what can be done with the appropriate resources and the political will. These were a great investment by the city and it is wonderful to see them still sought after almost a century after they were built.

This book is a fascinating insight into the work of Dublin Corporation and the creation of the city that we know.

Location of Completed Early Schemes

1. Barrack Street

2. Bow Lane

3 Blackhall Place

4. Lisburn Street

5. Church Street

6. Ormond Market

7. Cook Street

8. Bride's Alley

9. Oblate (Inchicore)

10. Keogh Square

11. Ceannt Fort (Mount Brown)

12. Colbert's Fort (St James' Walk)

13. Spitalfields

14. Boyne Street

15. Trinity Ward (Townsend, Luke, Moss streets)

16. Magennis Place

17. Fairbrothers' Fields

18. Montgomery Street

19. St Joseph's Place

20. Elizabeth Street

1. Location of completed early schemes

Preface

In March 1919, the City Council took the formal decision to proceed with the development of a large suburban housing estate in Marino. The plans, prepared by H.T. O'Rourke, were impressive and showed a highly designed urban environment with a great deal of open space. Central to the scheme was variety in house design with no fewer than 10 types suggested within an overall conception that would put any private developer of the time to shame. It is hard to think that it is a century since this happened and it is wonderful that the houses which were built in the 1920s not only have stood the test of time but are much in demand. Marino is well known but it is important to remember that there had been quite a number of housing schemes in today's inner city before the Corporation embarked on their great experiment in Marino. Because they were relatively small, they are often overlooked and passed-by without a second glance. Yet many of these have also survived into the present-day because they were well built and well conceived.

This book is intended to rekindle interest in these early schemes so that the reader can learn their story and be encouraged to go and look at the many which survive. Their individual stories are also part of the greater story of how the city began to deal with its major housing crisis. The evolution of policy, both as the result of pragmatism and principle, is tracked through these developments and the limitations on what could be done emerge clearly from the discussion. These little schemes have their own individual characters and are an important part of our urban heritage. They have adapted and been adapted to the modern world and continue to serve their original function. They are a lasting tribute to all who had the vision and the energy to create them and for these reasons they deserve to be better known.

One central feature that emerges from this book is that the challenges of one hundred years ago are the same challenges as are being faced today and the constraints and limitations on action are not greatly different. Perhaps there are lessons to be learned from the experiences of the early part of the twentieth century.

We begin our survey with the Corporation's first tentative steps in Barrack Street in the early 1880s. Their earlier co-operation with the Dublin Artizans' Dwelling Company has been analysed in other publications and we wanted to concentrate on what the city had itself achieved. It was more difficult to choose an end point for the book since this was a story which continued into the 1980s. We decided on the middle 1920s and on the Drumcondra scheme because by the time of its completion, many of the important policies and especially the concept of reserved areas had been developed.

This book derives from the many years of research on Dublin which we have undertaken and which is both published and unpublished. It would not have been possible without the help and encouragement of Dr Mary Clark, the former City Archivist and Stephanie Rousseau, Assistant Archivist or without the great working environment which the City Archive provides. Grateful thanks are also due to Paul Ferguson, Map Librarian in Trinity College Dublin for his wisdom and assistance and to Trinity College Dublin for providing us with many map extracts which have added greatly to the production.

Joseph Brady
Ruth McManus

Introduction

The story of Dublin Corporation's involvement in housing provision begins in the last quarter of the nineteenth century, but the origins can be traced further back in time. The crisis in housing provision for the working classes grew slowly during the nineteenth century and it had not peaked by the time the twentieth century dawned. Dublin Corporation laboured throughout most of that century to deal with the issue. The genesis of the problem lay in a complex interaction of a number of forces. Dublin during the nineteenth century grew strongly from immigration from a poor countryside; people who had either the intention but not the means to travel further and people for whom Dublin, though offering very little, promised at least the prospect of a life better than was available where they lived. Birth rates were also high and though so too was the death rate, there was sufficient dynamic in the population to ensure growth.

There was limited demand for a labouring class in Dublin. Dublin never developed the labour-intensive heavy industry of the midlands of the UK. Its main industries were connected with brewing, distilling, food, textiles and linen. These were important, even vital, sources of employment, but were never of the scale needed to provide decent, secure employment to a great mass of the city's population. These subsisted on a variety of insecure and irregular employments often connected with distribution and service provision to the better off (see O'Brien, 1982). For women, domestic service was an important source of employment while prostitution became the fate of many in a city which seemed to have a significant demand for such services.

This population needed housing but their means were very limited. In UK cities, large areas of working class housing were provided by speculators in close proximity to their places of employment. In Dublin, speculators could not see any economic return from such ventures given the depth of poverty in the city. Another source of housing would soon become available.

In the eighteenth century, Dublin had grown eastwards and in the good economic times of the period fashionable districts had grown up on both sides of the river while the western part of the city had became unfashionable and had settled into a slow decline by the end of the eighteenth century. Developers such as the Gardiner and Pembroke/Fitzwilliam families produced urban landscapes in the style that we now call Georgian (see Ó Gráda, 2015) and a sumptuous lifestyle was available to those who had the means to enjoy it (see Boyd, 2005). Two events conspired to make this housing available to the poor. The first were the Acts of Union which joined Ireland to the United Kingdom of Great Britain on 1 January 1801. The upper echelon of society now had no reason to live in Dublin, there was no parliamentary business and the 'season' was greatly diminished. In 1815, the third Duke of Leinster sold his town palace, Leinster House, to the Dublin Society for £10,000 and a yearly rent of £600. This single event, perhaps more than any other, proclaimed the city's diminished status. The second event was more of a trend and perhaps of greater significance. In the UK and Europe generally, a fashion was emerging for suburban living, encouraged by the development of the railway. This allowed people to live at some distance from the smell and noise of industrial centres while enjoying the benefits of a rural and, it was believed, more healthy environment. In the UK, this was encouraged by the Romantic movement in literature which described the city as a place where the spirit could not thrive. Dublin did not have the industry to drive the exodus but people followed the fashion and began to seek housing in the suburbs. This did not involve much of a spatial dislocation since the city was quite small and the legislative writ of Dublin Corporation was essentially encompassed by the canals. Developers were quick to see the advantage of building in the suburbs and, by mid-century, townships developed on both sides of the city and along the southern coast, the attractions of which were enhanced when the railway from Dublin to Kingstown opened in 1834. Not only did the townships remove people from close proximity to the poor of the city, they were also separate legal entities, beyond the control of the Corporation, and therefore immune from having to provide for the city's needs. It was a happy arrangement, the inhabitants of the townships could continue to use the city for business and recreation but leave it and its problems in the evening (Brady, 2015).

This left an oversupply of fine single-family Georgian houses in many parts of the city. Clearly, the poor could not afford to rent these houses on a single-family basis and so began the process of converting these houses for multiple-family occupancy; what became known as tenements. The process was already well advanced in the south west of the city when the Revd Whitelaw conducted his census in 1798 but tenementation spread eastwards during the nineteenth century. Prunty's (1998) map for the city at mid-century shows that tenements were widespread in the city but not yet on the main streets of the once-fashionable eastern city. Only in the south-eastern sector, that under the control of the Pembrokes, were tenements relatively absent and would remain absent. In contrast, there was nothing to control their spread in the north-east of the city, developed mainly by the Gardiners. Following the death of Charles Gardiner in 1829, the fortunes of the family declined and they lost control of their Dublin property. The area gradually declined in status as more and more houses were turned into tenements by their owners.

The city's decline was gradual during the nineteenth century but the research provided for the 1913 Housing Inquiry showed the depth of the problem. It identified three classes of tenements. There were 1,516 houses in the first category, housing 8,295 families or 27,052 persons. These houses were in good structural condition, though with limited facilities but they could be brought to a required standard. The second class were so decayed as to be on or fast approaching the border-line of being unfit for human habitation. There were 2,288 of these with 10,696 families or 37,552 persons in them. The final class comprised 1,518 houses with 6,831 families or 22,701 persons. These were described as being unfit for human habitation and incapable of being rendered fit for human habitation. Combining these categories saw approximately 18,000 families in urgent need of accommodation.

Dublin Corporation had not been idle. By the time of the inquiry they had built 1,385 dwellings directly. However, compared to the need, it was clear that much needed to be done. Prunty (1998, 2001) has provided an excellent account of the growth of the slums and the first measures taken to alleviate them and only a brief summary will be offered here. The Corporation, working within its legislative framework began to be actively involved in dealing with the slum and tenement problems only after the Dublin Improvement Act of 1849 improved the coherence of city governance. Efforts were first directed at improving the sanitary environment but these started to become effective only after 1866. They led to the establishment within Dublin Corporation of the Public Health Committee which was to prove important in developing best practice. A significant moment was the appointment of the city's first Medical Officer of Health, Dr Edward Mapother, in 1864. It became clear very quickly that there was an important relationship between public health issues and poor housing and he, and more especially, his successor Dr (later Sir) Charles Cameron, were vitally important in developing the Corporation into a housing provider. The reader will note the central role of Cameron in many, if not most, of the developments which are discussed here.

The Corporation's first involvement in housing provision came as a result of the Artisans' Dwellings Act, 1875 (amended in 1878). Under this Act, the Corporation could apply to the Commissioners of Public Works in Ireland for loans to undertake slum clearance. They were limited in what they could do and could only acquire the property, clear it and put in the necessary services. It needed the approval of the Local Government Board to undertake any building and, unless the Board decreed otherwise, had to dispose of the buildings within three years of building. However, Dublin Corporation found an enthusiastic partner in the shape of the Dublin Artizans' Dwelling Company (DADC), established in 1876. This was a commercial undertaking, supported by the leading citizens of the city, with the mission of providing good healthy housing for the better-off working classes – the artisans. Among its trustees and directors were Edward Cecil Guinness, Arthur Guinness, Jonathan Pim, William Findlater and Arthur Stokes. The commercial nature of the company was made clear in the prospectus: 'The Directors fully concur in the opinion expressed by Miss Hill in her "Homes of the London Poor," that the work of building for the people must be carried out on "thoroughly sound commercial principles and not as a charitable undertaking."' The company reckoned that it could produce a return of five per cent per annum. A limit of a four or five per cent annual return characterised a number of UK companies which combined a philanthropic intent with capitalist approaches – 'five percent philanthropy'. However, it should be noted that the Prospectus put no such limit on returns, rather it noted that this was what might be expected 'at least'.

Dr Mapother identified a small number of unhealthy areas in 1876 which led Dublin Corporation and the DADC to develop the Gray Street area and later the environs of Plunket Street. While very good housing was built, these developments proved ruinously expensive to the Corporation because of the means whereby compensation was determined for displaced property owners. It was also quickly recognised that these developments did nothing for the very poor, who could not come close to affording the rents to be charged.

It was time for Dublin Corporation to get involved directly in the provision of housing and this it began to do in the 1880s. They had no clear roadmap to guide them in going about this and the legislative framework also needed to develop, so what the reader will find in the pages which follow is that housing policy developed in fits and starts with sometimes contradictory positions being taken.

Public Health Issues

This book is concerned with housing and housing policy but it is useful to include here a short discussion of the development of public health policy since both were intimately related. When Dr Mapother was appointed in 1864, knowledge of the transmission process for infectious diseases still had some way to go. The miasma theory still held sway and had been an important aspect in urban design since the beginning of the Christian era, at least.

Vitruvius, writing on the question of city location in *de Architectura* in the first century (it is believed), noted that the ideal city site would not have marshes in the neighbourhood because: 'when the morning breezes blow toward the town at sunrise, if they bring with them mists from marshes and, mingled with the mist, the poisonous breath of the creatures of the marshes to be wafted into the bodies of the inhabitants, they will make the site unhealthy'. It was still the view in the middle of the nineteenth century when Mapother and Cameron were beginning their promotion of public health policies that poisons of various kinds were responsible for many diseases. These were associated with filth and decay and it is not an accident that the discipline in which they worked was called 'sanitary science'. Cameron, following in the footsteps of Mapother, gave a series of twelve lectures on the subject of Public Health in the Royal College of Surgeons in 1868. These were published later in that year at 'the request of the Municipal Corporation of Dublin, who conceive that their circulation might aid in the wider diffusion of a knowledge of the laws of health, and thereby supplement the good work of sanitary reform, in which the '"public health committee" of the Municipality are now so successfully engaged'. In his first lecture, Cameron stated:

There is sufficient evidence to justify the belief that fever, cholera, whooping-cough, and, in a word, all infectious and contagious diseases, are produced by the introduction of an animal poison into the body – each variety of poison producing a different disease. These poisons are as much entities as are arsenic or strychnine; and as they possess in all probability an organised structure, they are capable of reproducing themselves under favourable conditions – that is, when located in the human body. One the other hand, it is nearly certain that these poisons cannot long exist in air, water, or earth (p.12).

In essence, Cameron was arguing that disease was the result of pollution and the key to its elimination lay in sanitation. He developed his theme in his lecture on water. He commented that 'several maladies are directly produced, and others indirectly induced by the constant use of bad water… There is the clearest evidence that cholera is infectious and that the virus of this disease is frequently conveyed through the medium of water'. (p.37). Writing of the charcoal filter produced by Mr Maguire of Dawson Street, he said:

Some authorities contend that charcoal does not perfectly remove the virus of cholera, nor, probably of other diseases from water; and if zymotic diseases are propagated by low forms of vegetable life, it is most likely that charcoal exercises no effect up such organisms, I believe, however, that there are putrescent animal and vegetable matters in impure water which though not specific animal poisons, are yet capable of inducing disease if permitted to enter the body: these substances are unquestionably destroyed by charcoal (p.38).

Dr Mapother and Dr Cameron's efforts were reported regularly to the city council via its No 2 Committee (Sanitary) and the reports for the 1860s show the efforts made to deal with the issues described above. There was a focus on the conditions within tenement houses, especially the sanitary arrangements. The reports discussed problems with various industries and workrooms and the remedies applied. There were many slaughter houses in the city and their distribution was such as to make inspection difficult but there were concerns that: 'Notwithstanding the best water supply and sewerage, the earth in the neighbourhood of these places becomes imbued with the blood and refuse of the animals, and the air becomes polluted, much to the injury of the health of the surrounding residents' (Mapother, 1866, p.30). An interesting idea promoted by Dr Mapother was of a disinfecting room: 'It has been found that no means for destroying contagious poisons is so effectual, yet so simple, as an exposure to a temperature of 212 degrees, a dry heat equal to that of boiling water. No injury is done to clothes or furniture by such a heat'. He noted that this service was offered free of charge to the poor in Liverpool where their clothes, bed clothes and other items where 'fever poison' might lurk were treated.

The poor quality of housing was identified as a primary cause of much illness. The 1867 report commenting on deaths from bronchitis noted: 'This greater mortality is, no doubt, due in large measure to causes beyond the control of your Committee – such as insufficient clothing, fuel and food – but the dwellings of the poor are often badly protected against the weather, and many of them are so ruinous that they should be demolished. There is need for the erection of comfortable residences for the humbler classes' (p.12). He went to comment that: 'Many rain-spouts discharge over, instead of under the flags, and this circumstance may cause many poor persons, whose feet are badly protected, to catch fatal bronchitis' (p.13).

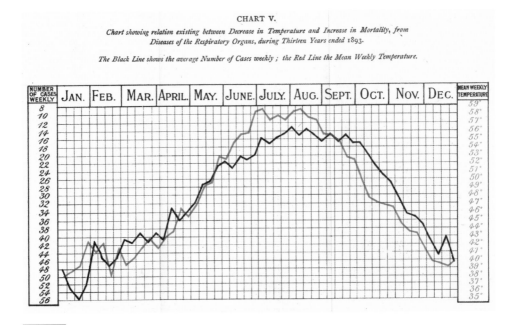

CHART V.

Chart showing relation existing between Decrease in Temperature and Increase in Mortality, from Diseases of the Respiratory Organs, during Thirteen Years ended 1893.

The Black Line shows the average Number of Cases weekly ; the Red Line the Mean Weekly Temperature.

2. Relationship between temperature and mortality for the thirteen years ending 1893.
Report upon Public Health, 1893, Chart V.

By the time of the housing schemes with which this book is concerned, there was a regular inspection system for tenements and lodging houses and they were judged against published standards with fines for breaches. In essence, tenements were required to be clean and in good repair. The roof needed to be sound because leaking roofs induced colds and rheumatism. Floors need to be level so that they could be kept clean. The gutters needed to be clean and to discharge directly into a grating. Particular attention was to be paid to very steep stairs, rooms less than seven feet in height, deficiency of light and ventilation in rooms, halls, stairs or lobby as well as the absence of a yard or garden. It was felt that a minimum of 300 cubic feet of space was required per person. Fines of just under £66 were imposed in 1896, for example, for breaches of these requirements while 48 houses were de-tenanted and closed as being unfit. The total number of houses closed from 31 August 1879 to 31 December 1896 was 2,948.

The state of medical knowledge had also moved on and the role of bacteria in disease was now better understood. However, there was still a general acceptance that the methods and approaches used against 'fever poisons' could also be used against bacteria. By now Charles Cameron was the 'Superintendent Medical and Executive Officer of Health, City Analyst and Inspector of Explosives'. His officers reported regularly to the City Council and his annual report is a detailed examination of myriad matters relating to public health. Reporting was done at different spatial scales from the city to the level of individual houses and reports do not shy from naming infractors. This short discussion here will concentrate on the report for 1893 (Report 136/1894) because it is remarkable for the analysis offered on a surge in typhoid fever.

The report for 1893 show the kinds of illness that Dubliners had to be concerned about. The total number of deaths recorded during the previous year was 7,139, of which 830 were caused by the principal zymotic diseases (the then current term for acute infectious diseases). The previous year had been worse with an epidemic of measles and a bad flu season adding 726 deaths to the overall total.

Causes of death for selected years with the number of deaths per 10,000 persons living in the Dublin Metropolitan Region.

	1883	1887	1891	Average 1883–92	1893	Yearly Average per 10,000	1893 per 10,000
Small-pox	0	1	0	0	0	0.0	0.0
Measles	27	514	5	165	103	4.7	2.9
Scarlatina	179	260	4	141	25	4.1	0.7
Typhus	141	24	8	43	16	1.2	0.5
Ill-defined Fever	37	33	3	23	13	0.7	0.4
Typhoid Fever	132	135	191	187	276	4.5	7.9
Whooping Cough	333	159	159	195	191	5.6	5.4
Diphtheria	14	36	23	24	34	0.7	1.0
Cholera	7	14	5	10	31	0.3	0.9
Diarrhoea, Dysentery	237	460	211	265	447	7.6	12.7
Other Zymotic Diseases	149	220	256	230	397	6.6	11.7
Phthisis (T.B.)	1330	1269	1292	1257	1298	36.2	37.1
Other Constitutional Diseases	846	895	889	882	968	25.3	26.0
All causes	10161	10777	9454	9706	9409	278.9	269.1
Deaths per 1,000	29.1	30.5	25.3	27.9	26.9		
Mean Air Temperature (°F)	47.5	47.5	47.4	47.8	49.5		

Source: Summarised from *Report upon Public Health*, 1893.

The death rate over the decade had remained stubbornly high and this was an increasing cause for concern. Infant mortality was a major problem, especially among the poorer families. As Cameron put it: 'Maladies such as measles and whooping-cough, which rarely kill children who are well fed, housed, and cared for, cause immense ravages amongst the children who dwell in miserable tenements, who are badly fed, and who are insufficiently protected from cold and wet' (p.41). Diarrhoea and dysentery were the most deadly of the zymotic diseases and they were largely associated with poor water. However, while in overall terms, the high death rate was attributed to the large numbers of poor people, diseases such as Phthisis (Tuberculosis) were just as fatal in the suburbs as they were in the city.

It might seem odd that the table above contains the information on the mean air temperature but this was one of the pre-occupations of these reports. Meteorological data were seen as very important because graphs of deaths from a variety of diseases showed an apparent correlation with temperature.

The case of typhoid fever is used here to illustrate this. The map provided with the report, and reproduced here, shows that the disease was widespread across the city and not just in the poorer areas. However, death rates from the disease were much higher among the poorer sections of the population because, as Cameron theorised, they did not have the physical strength to fight off the effects. Typhoid fever is a bacteriological infection from the bacterium *salmonella typhi* and is spread by eating or drinking food or water contaminated with the faeces of an infected person. Poor sanitation and poor hygiene are significant risk factors. When Cameron was writing, it was generally accepted that the cause was a bacterium (though this was not universally accepted) and that faecal spread was important. In Dublin, though, the hangover from miasmatical thinking could be seen in the emphasis on spread via the soil or sub-soil of the city. Cameron was of the view that the bacterium could be made airborne and spread that way. That is why the map shows the distribution of gravel and clay soils. It was the view of Cameron, and others, that the bacterium was endemic in the soil of the city, having been spread by centuries of cess pits and middens. Paradoxically, the improvement in the sanitation of the city had improved things for the bacterium in that it did not thrive in concentrated sewage. As the level of sewage in the soil decreased, so the ability of the bacterium to spread improved. So, it was everywhere in the city. However, since the flow of sewage was easier in the gravels than in the clays, the bacterium did better in gravel soils. Moreover such soils provided greater access to the air and thus enhanced the spread of the disease. This explained why the occurrence was worse in 1893 than it was in 1891. As Cameron put it: 'The number of deaths caused by typhoid fever, recorded in Dublin in 1893,

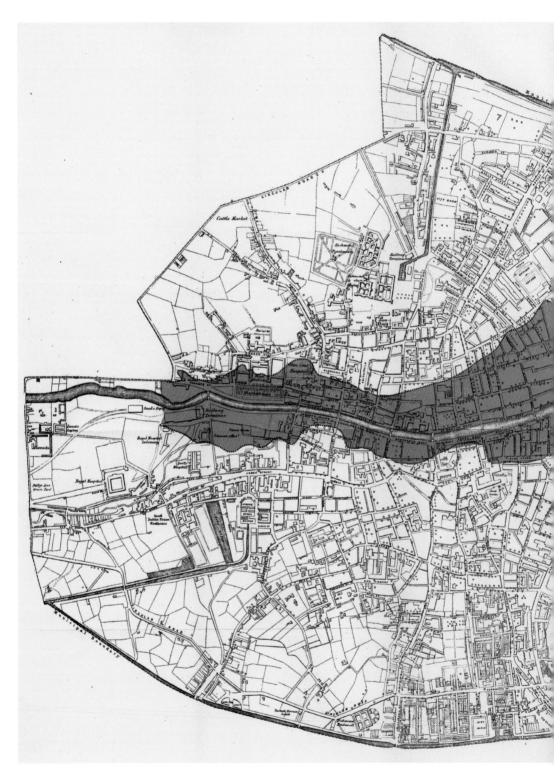

The red marks indicate the places in the city of
Dublin in which cases of typhoid fever
occurred during the years 1892-1893 inclusive.
The portion coloured green is gravel
all outside is clay.

3. Typhoid Fever in Dublin, 1893.
Report upon Public Health, 1893.

exceeded the number registered in any previous year. The rainfall in 1893 was extremely small, and the summer was unusually warm and prolonged meteorological conditions which, probably, were the causes of the excess of typhoid fever' (p. 28). A little further in his report he commented: 'In my present Report I give a map showing the distribution of 3,461 cases. The difference between the gravel and the clays, though shown very decidedly, is not as marked as in the map of 1891. This is probably due to the exceptionally hot and dry year of 1893, in which the superficial layers of the clay dried to a greater extent than usual, and permitted of the escape of the typhoid organism' (p.39).

This analysis is of interest because it explains the focus in his approach on good air, clean water and on the covering of yards and closes with either concrete or tarmacadam.

The death rate in the city did not improve, leading to two inquiries in the early years of the twentieth century. The first was undertaken in 1900 by a committee appointed by the Local Government Board (LGB) and it reported in May of that year. Little seems to have come of its recommendations and a further report was undertaken in 1906 by Surgeon Col. Flinn, the LGB's Medical Inspector. Flinn's report is very useful for a number of reasons. Firstly, he gives a forthright analysis of the progress made in implementing the recommendations of the 1900 inquiry. His analysis of the problem is comprehensive and his view on the need for housing is equally clear: 'I am fully sensible of the difficulties that surround the tenement room question in Dublin, and I am also aware that considerable improvements have been effected in several quarters of the city. The tenement house question is, however, one of ever-pressing urgency, as the habits and insanitary surroundings of the tenement dwellers play a large part in influencing the prevalence of disease' (p.37). He provided a map of the city showing where poverty was most concentrated (shaded brown in Figure 4) and it will be seen that this is where much of the effort of Dublin Corporation, described here, was concentrated. Finally, his report contained a fascinating insight into the life of the Dublin poor by giving the detail of the income and expenditure as well as the dietary habits of individual families in some of the poorest streets. This would not have come as a surprise to Cameron or his staff, or indeed to many in the Corporation, but it provided a useful and succinct justification for the housing agenda which was then developing.

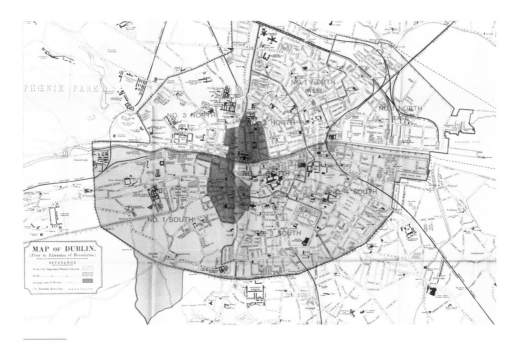

4. Principal areas of poverty in Dublin, 1906. Local Government Board for Ireland (Flinn, 1906).

The 1885 Housing Inquiry

Dublin Corporation was not particularly slow in getting to grips with the housing question in the city. Indeed the fieldtrip undertaken for them by Mr Dudgeon (see Barrack Street) in the 1880s showed that Dublin bore favourable comparison with the efforts in the major industrial centres of the UK. They had already begun contemplating their first direct development before a major inquiry was undertaken during 1884 into the state of working class housing in the UK. This was a Royal Commission with a quite large and varied membership drawn from the upper echelons of the army, church, nobility, science, the law and other important branches of society. The third report of the Commissioners, published in 1885, focused on Ireland and provides a useful benchmark against which to view later progress. The Corporation, especially Charles Cameron, took the opportunity to record their views and it gives a good insight into their thinking at that time. It was a mixed report card, which reflected the scale of the problem. While the Commission noted that very little had happened prior to 1866, they accepted that much had been done in recent times but that because of the scale of the problem, the then current situation had to be described as 'unsatisfactory'. The focus of the problem was the tenements, where poor quality sub-division created bad living conditions. Matters were made worse because the demand for housing put pressure on supply and this resulted in rents being high, to the enrichment of the property owners.

> Notwithstanding the energetic action of the corporation and of private persons and of societies, the condition of things in Dublin is very far from satisfactory. It is said that the great improvement which has taken place in some quarters is counterbalanced by the deterioration which is found in other districts. The evil of tenement houses, which was found to be a source of great misery in the housing of the working classes in London, exists very extensively in Dublin. There are certain portions of the city which were formerly wealthy and fashionable quarters which now are inhabited entirely by the poor. Owing to the large number of houses in Dublin, once inhabited by the wealthier classes, still in substantial repair, and now turned into tenement dwellings, there appears to be here a more than usually favourable opportunity for the conversion of such houses by certain structural alterations into habitations really suitable for tenement dwellings. Much good might be done were the conversion of a house originally used as the dwelling of a single family into a tenement dwelling prohibited until these structural alterations have been made.
>
> ...
>
> One of the chief causes of this state of things is, that the artisan and labouring population of Dublin is abnormally large, and forms an exceptionally high percentage of the population as compared with other towns. However, there seems to be little or no opportunity for the working classes to live in the suburbs. The depopulation of Dublin by the better classes has been going on for some time with the result of the better houses being now tenanted by the working class population. But while this migration is taking place the poor not only remain within the city, but even those whose work during the day lies outside return at night to sleep in Dublin. The usual consequence follows the congestion of population. Although wages are low rents are in proportion high, and the profits in Dublin as in London often go to the enrichment of the middlemen or house-farmers. These evils re-act upon one another.

> The depressed conditions under which the people live lower their wage-earning power, and deprive them of the chance of making for themselves more favourable surroundings (p. vi and vii).

The 1885 report showed that conditions in Dublin were not greatly dissimilar to the large cities of the UK; it was the scale of the problem that marked Dublin as being different. The position in Ireland as a whole was equally bad. Only in Belfast was the position found to be 'satisfactory', though conditions in Londonderry were found to be improving. The sanitary arrangements were good there and many artisans owned their own property. Otherwise the Commissioners came to the view:

> that the poverty of the labouring classes in most of the towns of Ireland is extreme; that nothing could be more miserable than the condition of many of their dwellings and surroundings in the towns; that notwithstanding the adverse influences of their existence their standard of morality is very high; and that the existing evils of administration are not due to defects in but to the failure of the existing authorities in acting upon legislation, which has invested them with ample powers (p.10).

Cork had 1,732 tenement houses, occupied by about 22,000 persons and they were reported to be in a disgraceful state, and that overcrowding had existed for 50 years with scarcely any improvement. The Corporation too had acted under the Artisans' and Labourers' Dwellings Improvement (Cross) Acts and cleared an area of 107 houses which was let to the Improved Dwellings Company. They built for a better class of person but nothing was done for the people displaced, who crowded into the already crowded neighbourhood. This and the cost involved persuaded the Corporation not to proceed with a second scheme. They had not built houses themselves but said that they would if they could get money cheaply enough.

The conditions in Limerick were described as being as bad as possible, while even in prosperous Kingstown (now Dún Laoghaire) the apathy of the authorities allowed bad conditions to persist.

> The tenement house system prevails to a considerable extent, and the condition of these dwellings calls for severe comment. Overcrowding is common, the houses are badly roofed, and the floors are frequently of

earth, with the filth of years accumulated upon them, and there is often no proper separation of the sexes. In the Cottages, also the same state of things is allowed to continue. Privy and ash pits accommodation exists only in name, and it is not remarkable that fevers frequently prevail in town.

The Commissioners found the circumstances in Waterford most remarkable of all. Waterford was a wealthy town and there was no borough taxation of any kind, yet very poor conditions were allowed to persist. The death rate on one occasion reached 42 per 1,000 but no bye-laws had been introduced for the management of the tenements despite the obvious overcrowding. The Corporation were mostly wealthy landowners and while they derived little rent from the tenement property personally, some of the worst houses were built on Corporation ground. They showed no enthusiasm for getting involved in housing the working classes, fearing that adopting any of the legislation would inevitably result in taxation.

Affordability of Housing

One of the recurring themes in the pen-pictures which follow is the question of affordability of housing. There was a great deal of concern expressed in ensuring that the housing being provided to the working classes was made available at reasonable rents. It seems to have been generally accepted that housing was expensive and that the demand was such as to drive prices to levels which did not reflect the quality of the accommodation. Indeed one of the arguments in favour of Corporation building was that it would relieve the upward pressure on rents and permit families with lesser incomes to enjoy better conditions. There are no official statistics on the incomes of the working classes for the time period being considered here. This is hardly surprising given the nature of employment and its often casual nature. There are glimpses now and again and these can be useful in putting the rents demanded into their context.

As previously noted, Flinn's 1906 report provided information on the income and expenditure patterns for people living in a selection of inner city streets for a sample week. The picture is one of great variation between families and great variability from week to week. Thus in Church Street a coal labourer reported earnings of £1 per week, while his son who was a builder's labourer earned 15s.

A painter earned £1 5s. per week while in full employment but in the previous two weeks had earned only 15s. and 3s. respectively. In Francis Street, a bricklayer had no earnings during the survey week but a labourer had earned 15s. while a charlady had taken home 4s. 6d. Labourers on North Anne Street earned between 12s. and £1 but work was variable. A printer on Lisburn Street could earn £1 15s. when in work but that was irregular while a cooper had a more regular income of 21s. per week. A window cleaner might make 15s. per week.

Income data presented to the 1913 Housing Inquiry (Appendix XXIII) shows the following distribution, expressed here as percentages of the total number of households occupying each type of dwelling. It was often suggested that a minimum income of 20s. per week was needed to provide the basic necessities for a family.

Weekly Income of Heads of Households in Tenement and Other Houses

| | Percentage of each class of housing | | |
Weekly income	First Class Tenements	Second Class and Third Class Tenements	Second and Third Class Houses
under 10s.	8.5	11.2	5.0
10s. to 12s. 6d.	2.7	3.8	2.1
12s. 6d. to 15s.	5.5	7.3	6.2
15s. to 17s. 6d.	3.7	5.2	5.4
17s. 6d. to 20s.	23.6	28.2	33.3
20s. to 22s. 6d.	2.6	2.9	3.2
22s. 6d. to 25s.	6.6	6.1	7.9
25s. to 27s. 6d.	1.4	1.0	1.7
27s. 6d. to 30s.	5.8	4.0	4.9
30s. plus	12.0	6.8	8.8
Pensioners, Others, Unknown	27.5	23.5	21.4
Total	**100.0**	**100.0**	**100.0**

Derived from Appendix III, 1913 Housing Inquiry, Appendices, p.347. Note that this does not imply that earnings are constant.

Book structure

The book analyses Dublin Corporation's housing schemes from their first direct building project in Barrack (Benburb) Street until their Drumcondra scheme in the late 1920s. During this period most of the important housing policies evolved and the scale of development moved from tens of dwellings to many hundreds.

The early section of the book explains the legislative background and the development process and this will give the reader the necessary framework against which the individual schemes can be understood. Each scheme is discussed individually, and the analyses are self-contained. The sequence of the discussion is mainly chronological, but schemes are grouped geographically to give a better sense of what was happening to the city. Not every proposal was seen through to completion and in some cases building was spread over many years.

Some terms and explanation

The 'tenement' has already been introduced. From the beginning it was the term most used by Dublin Corporation to describe multi-family dwellings, at first without distinction being made between purpose-built blocks and those created by sub-division. As tenements began to be become more associated with poor quality housing, there was a tendency to call purpose-built multi-family units 'block tenements' or simply 'blocks'. The term 'cottage' was widely used to describe single-family houses of one or two-storeys. It was not a technical term and 'house' is sometimes used in the same sense. A dwelling could be either a tenement or a cottage.

Both tenements and cottages were normally described in terms of 'rooms'. This was a somewhat different usage to the modern one in which houses are often labelled by the number of bedrooms. The 'rooms' referred to here were 'useful' rooms and could be dwelling spaces or bedrooms, depending on the configuration of the cottage. In addition to a certain number of rooms, a tenement or cottage might be expected to have a w.c. and a scullery / larder space. Separate bathrooms were a later addition, the necessity for which was still viewed with some scepticism in the 1920s.

There is variation within Dublin Corporation documents and other sources in the use of 'artizan' versus 'artisan'. The latter is usually used here except when referring to Corporation committees.

In 1924 Dublin Corporation was summarily abolished by the government. The government had been unhappy for some time with the Corporation and on 11 March an inquiry into the 'performance of its duties' was opened in the Mansion House by Mr Nicholas O'Dwyer, Chief Engineering Inspector of the Department of Local Government. The Minister, having received his report, decided on 20 May 1924 to dissolve the Corporation without giving much detail as to his reasoning. From then until 1930, the city was administered by three Commissioners. Two of them, Seamus O'Murchadha and Dr W. Dwyer were Commissioners of the Dublin Union, while the third, P.J. Hernon, was an Inspector in the Department of Local Government and had been chair of the Cork Union. He was later to become City Manager. The Commissioners followed the form of Corporation processes but there was no recorded debate about decisions.

Ordnance Survey plans at various scales are used throughout. The most detailed are the '5-foot' plans where five feet on paper is equivalent to 1 mile on the ground. At a lesser level of detail are those at 1:2,500 or 25 inches to 1 mile. Occasionally it was necessary to make use of the 1:10,560 sheets which are at a scale of six inches to 1 mile.

Units are imperial throughout and the conversions below may be of use. Prices are in pounds sterling.

1 acre = 4 roods = 160 perches

1 acre = 4046.86 sq. metres

1 acre = 0.405 hectare

1 hectare = 2.47 acres

10,000 sq. metres = 1 hectare

1 foot = 12 inches

12 inches = 30.4 cm

1 yard = 3 feet

1 yard = 91.44 cm

£1 = 20 shillings = 240 pence (*d.*)

Developing Policies

The Approach

Dublin Corporation had developed an association with the Dublin Artisan's Dwelling Company in the clearance and redevelopment of unhealthy areas, using the provisions of Artisans' and Labourers' Dwellings Act 1875 (as amended). However, by 1881, the Corporation was considering a different approach by adopting the Labouring Classes' Lodging Houses and Dwellings Act (Ireland) 1866 as a suitable vehicle for providing working class houses. The Public Health Committee prepared a report (129/1881) which set out their thinking. In it, they recalled that the Corporation had considered the 1866 Act when it was first introduced but it was felt that its application was beset with so many difficulties as to be impracticable. Equally, though the Labourers' Dwellings Act, 1868 offered some additional possibilities, it was considered cumbersome and not effective in that it enabled the local authority to deal only with isolated dwellings and not with areas. Any intention of putting the Act of 1868 into practice was abandoned and instead the Artisans' and Labourers' Dwellings Act 1875 was adopted because it allowed for compulsory purchase, something specifically excluded from the Acts of 1866 and 1868, and therefore permitted the clearance of unhealthy areas. The 1881 report noted that the 1875 Act had been practically applied to two areas – the Coombe and Plunket Street. What prompted reconsideration of the 1866 Act was that the operation of the 1875 Act was proving both limiting and expensive. Additionally, the 1866 Act did not limit construction to houses and therefore shops, workshops and other uses could be considered in a development. So, the Public Health Committee recommended to the Council that the 1866 Act be adopted but used only in a limited way. Because there was no power of compulsory purchase, it made no sense for the Corporation to seek to obtain property on the open market, they would have to pay too much. Likewise it did not make sense to acquire houses in the hope of renovating them for working class use because most were constructed as single family dwellings and not at all suited to multi-family living. However, the Corporation did own a lot of property, especially in the Oxmantown Area, and so it could make use of the Act in such areas. Therefore the Public Health Committee recommended as follows:

> That the Labouring Classes' Lodging Houses and Dwellings Act, 1866, affords to owners of premises important facilities for carrying its provisions into effect; and that as the Corporation of Dublin are possessed of lands and premises eminently suited for this purpose, their adoption of this Act, by the erection of dwellings and lodging houses on their property known as the Oxmantown, be strongly recommended to them, as the site not only presents unusual facilities for the purpose, but also because it affords a reasonable prospect of it proving financially successful.

The final phrase is instructive because at this time, there was a belief that an income could be derived from such housing. This will be explored a little below. The report referred to above was submitted in June 1881 but the Council asked for further consideration and by September, the Public Health Committee had revised its opinion and was now prepared to recommend the purchase of land for housing (Report 197/1881). They noted:

> that there are very many vacant spaces in Dublin, especially those reported on in the Annual Report of Dr Cameron for 1880, which might be purchased on reasonable terms, and upon which dwellings might be erected with great advantage. Your Committee are not at present prepared to recommend the purchase of houses with the view of having them repaired under the provisions of the Act, but this matter is at present under their consideration, and they will further report thereon.

There was some debate within the Corporation as to their powers to raise loans from the Local Government Board (LGB) but these were resolved at the meeting of 12 September 1881. The following month, the minutes of 3 October 1881 noted the adoption of the following resolution.

> That this report (197/1881) be adopted; and that pursuant to the 5th section of the Labouring Classes' Lodging Houses and Dwellings Act (Ireland) 1866, public notice shall be given that it is the intention of the Council of the Corporation of Dublin to take into consideration the propriety of adopting the said Act for Dublin, and that they will take it into consideration at a Meeting to be held on Monday, the 7th day of November 1881, at the hour of One o'Clock at the City Hall, Cork Hill, Dublin.

This was duly done and on 7 November 1881, the 'Council of the Corporation of Dublin having this day, pursuant to due notice in that behalf, taking to consideration the propriety of adopting the "Labouring Classes' Lodging Houses and Dwellings Act (Ireland) 1866" for the Borough of Dublin, hereby determine that the said Act shall be and the same is hereby adopted for the said Borough of Dublin'.

Part of the Corporation's investigations involved the commissioning of a report from Mr Arthur Dudgeon, a well known Dublin civil engineer and architect. He visited Glasgow, Liverpool, Birmingham and London and the digest of his report presented to the Corporation by Sir Charles Cameron, then the Executive Sanitary Officer, is a very useful account of what was being done in these locations to build for the working classes and of the financial results obtained (Report 240/1881). The account outlines variable action in these cities with variable results. So, for example, Birmingham had done nothing under the 1866 Act.

> One scheme only, but that a very large one, was put forward by Birmingham in 1876, under the Artisans' Dwellings Act of 1875. The limits included 93 acres, and 43 acres have been acquired at a cost of one-and-a half millions sterling, or £34,884 per acre. The Corporation does not propose to build, as it is estimated there are now 5,000 vacant cottages in and around Birmingham. By purchasing a vacant piece of ground at a small cost within the municipal boundary, the Corporation have been enabled to dispense with the stringent provisions of the 1875 Act, to form new wide streets, and create valuable building frontages, and it is proposed to let a large proportion, if not the whole of the area, for commercial purposes.

He was particularly interested in the work undertaken on commercial principles and he suggested that it was to those efforts that 'we must look for encouragement'. He presented examples of the work of a number of philanthropic and semi-philanthropic organisations.

The Metropolitan Association for Improving the Dwellings of the Industrial Classes was the pioneer of the movement in London. It was established in 1841 and obtained its charter in 1845. The Association had 13 separate blocks of buildings which housed 17 cab-drivers, 32 carmen, 13 charwomen, 23 dairymen,

65 labourers, 53 porters, 66 tailors, and 43 widows and a large number of the tenants earned wages between 15*s*. and 20*s*. The Society for Improving the Condition of the Labouring Classes could claim 'with justice to have shown that the people of the lowest class are not irreclaimable as regards their domestic habits, and that if an opportunity is given them to improve, they are in most instances glad enough to avail themselves of it.' The Improved Industrial Dwellings Company had built 28 groups of dwellings, each group comprising one or more blocks of from five to seven storeys in height and in which were two, four, or six distinct tenements of two, three, four, five and six rooms. This was a profitable operation even though many earned less than 20*s*. per week.

> The number of tenements, consisting of one to six rooms, is no less than 3,949, and they accommodate various classes of tenants, including 29 bakers, 91 bootmakers, closers, &c., 53 butlers, 33 bricklayers, 104 carpenters, 6 charwomen, 84 carmen, 32 commissionaires, 18 dressmakers, 19 engine-drivers, 60 working engineers, 72 labourers, 33 letter carriers, 29 messengers, 60 printers, 211 policemen, 135 porters, 45 painters, and 28 waiters.

As can be seen from the above it was a comprehensive report and his conclusion was enthusiastic. It was possible to provide suitable accommodation for low income families and yet produce a decent return. It was his view that, learning the lessons from these cities, and choosing the right sites it would be possible with almost absolute certainty to get a return of five per cent in Dublin. After further consideration, the Corporation decided on its first scheme in Barrack Street and quickly thereafter in Bow Lane.

New legislation was introduced in 1890. The Housing of the Working Classes Act, 1890 was a long Act but it repealed almost all the Acts in place at that time; only a few sections of the Housing of the Working Classes Act, 1885 were retained. This brought much needed clarity and simplicity to the process of building and development and although the Act was lengthy, it was well arranged into distinct parts. Parts I to III set out different approaches. Part I, that used most often by Dublin Corporation, provided the power to acquire compulsorily any insanitary area and to clear it. Entire districts could be purchased, cleared and ultimately redeveloped. Part II gave power to the local sanitary authorities (Dublin

Corporation in this case) to order the closing and, if necessary, the demolition of any house which was unfit for habitation. It also allowed for reconstruction schemes. Part III had to be adopted specifically by each sanitary authority. On the face of it, it seemed to be rather limited in that it provided for 'lodging houses' for the working classes. However a closer reading reveals that Section 53 includes within that term 'separate houses or cottages for the working classes, whether containing one or separate tenements (see Bolton, 1914). In essence, this allowed the Corporation to build housing whenever it felt that it was appropriate. It did not have to demonstrate a particular need in a particular place.

The Act was amended in 1893, 1894 and 1896 but these were short Acts designed to explain better the operation of particular sections or to remove ambiguity or a lack of clarity. The 1908 Act was of far greater significance. Commonly known as the Clancy Act because of the work of J.J. Clancy, K.C. and M.P. for North County Dublin in getting it through the houses of parliament. Loans could now be for eighty years instead of sixty years. The first two years were free of repayments of the principal and this is why Corporation reports came to refer to the costs in year three. It also removed such loans from the Corporation's balance sheet when it came to borrowing limits imposed by the Public Health (Ireland) Act of 1878. An important improvement which both reduced the Corporation's costs and speeded up the process was that Provisional Orders approving clearance could now be confirmed by the Local Government Board. This removed a requirement for an Act of Parliament to confirm an order. The Act also established a housing fund which was to be used to assist with repayments. However, the amount available under this heading proved to be rather trifling – a total of less than £1,000 up to March 1913.

The Act was also useful in that it provided a definition of the 'working class'. It is one of those generic terms which everyone understands but probably differently. Section 16 of the Act described the working class as including 'mechanics, artizans, labourers and others working for wages, hawkers, costermongers, persons not working for wages but working at some trade or handicraft without employing others except members of their own family, and persons, other than domestic servants, whose income in any case does not exceed an average of thirty shillings a week, and the families of any of such persons who may be residing with them'.

Operating under Part I, Dr Charles Cameron, the Chief Medical Officer of Health, declared that the area in question was insanitary; the formula of words is outlined in the later discussion here. The Artisan' Dwelling committee then considered and usually approved the recommendation and work began on designing a housing scheme. The work of the Artisans' Dwellings Committee was overtaken by an Improvements Committee, following a decision on the type and number of standing committees at the Council meeting of 28 January 1901, and in later years by a Housing Committee. Both recommendation and housing scheme were approved by the Council and a decision taken to raise the appropriate funding. This usually took the form of a loan from the Local Government Board. The Local Government Board prescribed the form of public advertisement that was necessary and the kind of information that needed to be prepared, including maps of the area.

Following Council approval, application was then made to the LGB, accompanied by a range of required documentation that included certified copies of the resolution passed by the Council, the detail of the improvement scheme with maps, including names and details of property occupiers and owners, and estimates of the costs. The Board then held a public inquiry into the making of a Provisional Order declaring the area insanitary and it usually dealt with the proposed housing scheme too. Interested parties could make representations and orders were sometimes opposed. If the LGB Inspector was convinced by the arguments made, a provisional order was made and it was usually confirmed by the Local Government Board. At that point the Corporation had once again to apply for the loan, using a special form. Assuming that the loan was granted, the next step was for the Corporation to seek the appointment of an Arbitrator who would fix the compensation payable to the property owners affected by the scheme. This was an important innovation and it removed one of the major impediments to development. Previously, awards had been determined by juries and they made ruinous (from the Corporation's point of view) judgments about value. With the arbitration completed, the development could begin.

It can be seen that it was a lengthy process, even when it went smoothly, and it was a major effort for all arms of the Corporation for relatively small returns since every individual development, no matter how small, had to go through this process. It was also a very open process. Proposals were presented in public and were subject to formal public cross-examination with public opinion being marshalled whenever one group or another felt it to be to their advantage. It was considered necessary that the views of people being affected by proposals be sought and groups who might otherwise have had little or no influence found themselves being represented by legal counsel. The decision making was generally undertaken in private. The rationale for decisions was not always explained and this was often criticised. It would also be naive to deny that informal contacts played an important role in the decision-making process; Dublin was a small place and the middle classes a small group. Yet, it is impressive to read the accounts in the newspapers of the robust encounters at the public inquiries relating to very small housing schemes.

Standards

The reader will notice that required standards changed over time. In February 1910, the Local Government Board issued guidance for architects who were preparing plans for working class dwellings. The basis for this was the specifications for cottages under the Labourers (Ireland) Acts with provision made for appropriate sanitary arrangements. There was concern that rooms should be big enough and airy and the minimum cubic space for one or two storeyed houses was as follows:

Houses of less than four rooms

Living Rooms	1,200 cubic feet
Principal Bedroom	960 cubic feet
Other Bedroom	610 cubic feet

Houses of four rooms or more

Living Room	960 cubic feet
Principal Bedroom	960 cubic feet
Other Bedrooms (or Parlour)	610 cubic feet

By 1912 there was a strong body of opinion that these capacities were not big enough and that bedrooms should be not less than 1,000 cubic feet in volume.

The height of rooms was to comply with any bye-laws which were in force but were not to have less than 8 feet clearance. Generally 8 foot 6 ins was the norm in Dublin Corporation schemes. Rooms which were partly in the roof could descend to 5 feet but at least one half of the room had to have eight feet. Ventilation was emphasised as being of the 'greatest importance' and it was desirable that every room should have a fireplace because of the ventilation which it provided. Windows were to occupy at least one twelfth of the floor area and every window was to be capable of being opened for at least one half of its total area. In addition, ventilators were to be added to walls and chimneys. Notwithstanding these technicalities, the appearance of buildings was to receive due consideration.

Policy Issues

The policy approach of Dublin Corporation began to evolve gradually. It was an 'evolution', which was sometimes reflective of principle and sometimes of pragmatism. The modern concept of 'town planning' had not been developed at the beginning of the Corporation's journey and the gradual absorption of model village and especially garden suburb ideas can be seen in the changes to plans, especially from 1914 or so.

There was debate about the merits of block buildings (flats) versus houses (cottages). The current inhabitants of insanitary areas lived mainly in multiple-occupancy tenements and rehousing them in individual houses was challenging on small sites. Conversely, there was concern about replicating the existing densities in new flat blocks, sometimes disparagingly referred to as 'barracks'. The question of providing individual sanitation to each dwelling was settled early on and became standard but not before shared facilities had been tried. Because it was related to the question of rent, the size and nature of accommodation varied. Early schemes tended to focus on three-roomed cottages and two-roomed flats but over time the mix changed to include four-roomed and even five-roomed cottages with a gradual diminution in the number of two-roomed units. Five-roomed cottages were the norm at Marino through three- and four-roomed cottages made a return in Drumcondra. Given the size of families that were being housed, it always meant that densities were quite high within the units, even if housing densities on the ground were quite low.

Health officials were always concerned that people would have enough air space and the cubic capacity of rooms received a lot of attention. 'Good air' also required the provision of gardens where possible though some sites were not big enough.

Playgrounds became a feature after about 1912 and it is interesting to compare the early and later plans for the Church Street and Ormond Market schemes. As noted previously, the 'germ theory' of infection had come to replace the idea of spread by miasma by the 1880s but Charles Cameron still believed in the principle of replacing 'bad air' by 'good air'. 'Good air' was healthful and it was something that should be provided in any development.

The virtue of inner city sites versus suburban sites did not became a live matter of debate until the Corporation began to contemplate large scale developments and they became more aware of the developing ideas of garden cities and garden suburbs. These issues will emerge in the discussions which follow and it will be seen that there was not a neat evolution in ideas. Sometimes pragmatism trumped principle and caused decisions to be taken which were accepted as being sub-optimal. This was particularly so when sites were narrow and confined and where the number of people to be rehoused was large. It was usual that those displaced by clearance would be housed on the site in new accommodation. This was not a legislative requirement, except in London, but the LGB Inspector could insist on this or on a specified proportion. If anything, the LGB Inspector sometimes found himself wondering if the Corporation was trying to rehouse too many on the site. There was nothing to prevent people being offered better accommodation elsewhere but this required building on a greater scale and it would be some time before virgin sites would be explored.

One of the perennial issues was the question of rent. The Corporation was conscious of the limited incomes of those in the tenements, though there was considerable variation in ability to pay. At the same time, Dublin Corporation's income was determined by the rates and rates were paid by all strata of society. The Griffith Valuation was becoming less and less reflective of the actual value of property and people could pay significant rates on modest properties. As elected representatives, councillors understood the twin demands of providing good quality housing for the working classes while not alienating the ratepayers.

The question was whether tenants should pay the 'economic rent' or whether the rent should be subsidised to some degree. As will be seen, there was no easy answer to this. If the Corporation built dwellings of a character which came within the income range of the poorer tenants, there was a danger of simply recreating bad housing. Equally, putting a large and continuing burden on the rates was to nobody's advantage. The rates in Dublin were regarded as being very high and were seen as a disincentive to business as well as a burden on ordinary people. There was also the issue of how to present the costs of development to the ratepayers; public perception was an important element even in these early days.

The reader will notice how small were many of the early schemes, yet each required the same process to be followed and the same amount of effort. They were small because that was all that could be afforded at the time and later accounts here demonstrate how this resulted in less than ideal developments. This also helps understand both sides of one of the arguments that characterised the 1913 Housing Inquiry. On the one hand, it is possible to agree with the LGB view that not enough had been achieved while simultaneously understanding Dublin Corporation's view that they had been very active and had acted to the best of their ability.

Early plans favoured regular angular street layouts with little variation. There was concern with the finish of buildings, both inside and out but rent levels were the ultimate determining factor. Thus the inner walls of the more expensive flats in the Montgomery Street scheme were plastered rather than whitewashed while Portmarnock red brick was specified for the Patrick Street flats. As the garden suburb influence grew, there was more effort put into design with curved streets, culs de sac and geometric patterns among the outcomes. This transition is evident after 1914 or so in some schemes where development was delayed and the plan was reconsidered before building.

People

The same people will appear in the discussions which follow and they exercised a notable influence on these early schemes. **P.C. Cowan** was usually the Local Government Board Inspector who assessed the Corporation's schemes. Originally from Dundee, Peter Chalmers Cowan began his association with Ireland when he was appointed county surveyor for the southern division of Co. Mayo in 1886. In 1899 he was appointed as chief engineering inspector of the Local Government Board, a position which he held for twenty years. He was clearly very interested in the housing issue and had definite views on how it should be approached. He exercised a strong influence on the schemes that emerged and was a force to be reckoned with. His appointment did not survive the transition to the Free State and it was abruptly terminated in 1923.

Charles MacCarthy became city architect in December 1893, taking over from Daniel Freeman and held the post until 1921, when ill health forced him to retire but he had not been active for the few years immediately preceding. He designed many public buildings, including libraries, fire stations and the Bolton Street Technical School and was responsible for the design of over 1,700 dwellings. He was one of the assessors for the 1914 competition to produce a town plan for Dublin and he was interested in the emerging ideas of town planning and garden suburbs. He was succeeded by **H.T. O'Rourke** (Horace Tennyson) who was appointed to the permanent staff of Dublin Corporation in March 1916, having previously been working in a temporary capacity. His first appointment was as Clerk of Works on the Lisburn and Lurgan streets scheme in March 1914 but he was quickly transferred to the City Architect's office. O'Rourke was a Dubliner and he played a hugely important role in the development of the city, even after his retirement in 1945. He became Assistant City Architect on 1 April 1918 but though not formally appointed city architect until 1922, he effectively acted in that role due to the illness of Charles MacCarthy. He was a central figure in the production of the Dublin Civic Survey in 1925 and he was one of the officials who travelled to Holland in the same year to view their approach to public housing.

Charles Cameron was another formidable figure for most of the period covered by this book. Though the best-known photograph of him shows him in a kilt, he was born in Dublin in 1830. By the 1860s among his various titles, he was Professor of Hygiene, or Political Medicine, in the Royal College of Surgeons in Ireland as well as being City Analyst. He succeeded Dr E.D. Mapother as Chief Medical Officer of Health in 1876 and continued in that role, though his title and portfolio of responsibilities changed, until his death in 1921. He had a wide brief and was responsible for enforcing the sanitary laws, working to improve public health as well as making decisions relating to clearances. He prepared numerous fascinating reports on public health and was not reticent in letting his opinions be known on what he believed needed to be done. His career as an analyst in food inspection and the Chief Medical Officer of Health in the city is discussed in Carroll (2011) while he published a volume of his reminiscences in 1913.

His key role in the development of any housing scheme was to declare any area insanitary and so set in motion the process of redevelopment. He was careful in so doing not to condemn buildings which were in good condition and this sometimes produced awkward sites. He was criticised in the report of the 1913 Housing Inquiry for what was described as a lax attitude to the sanitary laws by not closing all of the worst tenements. The Inquiry was not convinced by the argument that this was a pointless and even purposeless action when the people who would be displaced had nowhere to go. He was resolutely defended by the Housing Committee in Report 20/1914.

Barrack Street

Having found the advice of Mr Dudgeon useful in relation to the adoption of the 1866 Act, the Corporation decided that they would ask him to design a scheme for their property in the Oxmantown estate. There were two plots available in Barrack Street, one having a frontage of about 240 feet, and the other a frontage of about 160 feet. The land had been leased since the time of Charles II but had reverted to the city estate in 1883 and comprised some very bad housing as well as slaughterhouses and other undesirable uses. Though it was not mentioned in the Corporation or newspaper reports, it was also the centre of one of the red light districts of the city, doubtless because of the proximity of the large Royal Barracks (now Collins Barracks).

5. The Barrack Street and Blackhall Place area at mid-nineteenth century. Ordnance Survey plan, 5-foot, Sheet 18 (12 & 13), 1847 edition.

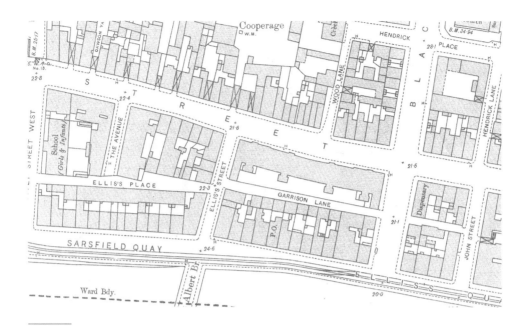

6. Barrack / Benburb Street development. Ordnance Survey plan, 5-foot, Sheet 18 (56), Revised 1907-8, 1909 edition.

The 1847 5-foot Ordnance Survey plan (fig. 5) shows a densely built up area. Barrack Street joins with Tighe Street to form a route parallel to the quays until it meets the cross road of Queen Street. Blackhall Place does not yet reach to the quays and the route is via Hendrick Place and Hendrick Lane.

Dudgeon's report (90/1883) recommended the building of two blocks and that the ground-floor frontages facing Barrack Street, a new street, and Ellis's Street, should be utilized for shops. The tenement blocks would have no basements but would rise to three or four storeys. He noted that there was a perception that the working classes did not like to be housed in tall buildings but he dismissed that as being inaccurate and argued that, on the contrary, people liked the upper floors where they had access to good air. The tenements would be reached by staircases which would give access to galleries that would run the length of each block at every floor, thus giving individual access to the tenements.

The next step under the Act was to appropriate the lands for the purposes of building and so the Finance and Leases Committee of Dublin Corporation offered to sell the land to the Public Health Committee. This Committee, having bought the site, in turn recommended to the Council on 28 November 1883 that the site be developed for artisan housing. The next step was to apply for a loan and Mr Dudgeon compared the various mechanisms available to obtain relatively cheap money from the State.

As in his earlier report to the Corporation, he concentrated on the economic possibilities of the scheme and argued that, if all the elements were built, it would be possible for the scheme to yield an income. The Artisan' Dwellings Committee was not entirely convinced and suggested that 'possibly Mr Dudgeon's estimates are too favourable' but they accepted the general case and took comfort in 'that it cannot involve any substantial loss, and may effect a great benefit'.

They decided now to ask the City Architect to produce the detail of the plan and this was reported on 1 July 1884 with the Artizans' Dwelling Committee recommending to the Council 'to memorial Her Majesty's Lords of the Treasury for leave to appropriate the two parcels of lands for the scheme and to apply to the Commissioners of Public Works for the sum which will be required for the purchase of the sites and the erection of the buildings'.

The City Architect reported that he had made the rooms bigger than in many of the schemes he had visited in the UK and he had improved on the sanitary arrangements. He believed it a major defect in many of these schemes that sanitary provision was too close to the dwellings. So he proposed that 'all sanitary accommodation, water supply, dust shoot, &c., is provided for outside the walls of the dwellings, and are easily approached from the different apartments. This arrangement I consider most desirable, as in the event of any of the sanitary arrangements getting out of order, no foul air or other escapement can affect the dwellings' (Report 89/1884).

The first plot ran from the new street to Ellis's Street and had a frontage of about 250 feet. This was divided into four sections to avoid overcrowding and to assist in infection control, should that prove necessary. The second plot was an awkward site, so he suggested that it was best to divide it in two by running an avenue, 30 feet wide, from Barrack Street to Ellis's Place. This would give him four frontages to build on, two on Barrack Street and two in the proposed avenue, which would not be a thoroughfare but rather a good air space and a playground for children.

The final scheme would include a lodging house, mostly for men but with some provision for women. At this stage, though, there was no mention of the latter. The men's lodging house comprised a separate block and also contained a wash house and two reclining baths each for men and women. In total the scheme would offer 15 shops, 66 double rooms and 50 single rooms at weekly rents that varied from 3*s*. 6*d*. for the double rooms and between 1*s*. 6*d*. and 2*s*. for the single rooms. The report noted that the rents bore very favourable comparison with the prices paid for 'miserable rooms' all over the city. The 72 beds in the men's Lodging House cost 4*d*. per night. All in all, and taking into account the rents from the shops and the wash room, it was estimated that the scheme would yield an annual profit of about £30.

This report was not immediately adopted when it was considered by the Corporation on 1 September 1884 and it was sent back to the Artisans' Dwellings Committee for reconsideration. The problem was that Mr Dudgeon's scheme,

7. One of the surviving blocks on Benburb Street in 1987 before renovation.

even though he provided no drawings, would accommodate 708 people for an expenditure of about £25,000 while the City Architect's plan would accommodate only 600 people but at a cost of £20,000. The Committee was asked to see if the City Architect could meet the accommodation targets of Mr Dudgeon. Their view (Report 136/1884) was that the plans of the City Architect were sound but that they could make some changes that would increase accommodation. They suggested reducing the number of the shops to four, the double rooms to 44 while increasing the number of single rooms to 116. This would produce an annual loss of about £30 but the Committee expressed the view that when the plan was implemented it might be possible to produce further changes and savings sufficient to cover this. In any event, there was a reasonable hope that the scheme would pay its way and it was felt that the scheme should proceed, such was the need. This was an important moment for the Committee as it recognised that the need could justify some modest annual expenditure.

The sanction of the LGB was obtained on 18 August 1885 for a loan of £20,000 to be repaid over 40 years. Tenders were sought and submitted for consideration on 9 November (Report 167/1885). They received thirteen tenders for some or all of the blocks from local builders, five of whom had their offices on Great Brunswick Street. However, the

8. Benburb Street - the blocks on either side of 'The Avenue' in 1987 approximately. Note the railing around the roof space.

building process did not go entirely smoothly. One of the successful builders had to withdraw from the project and there were additional unforeseen costs. During construction the City Architect came to the view that a flat concrete roof should replace the standard slated roof on one of the blocks as he had noted that there was little yard space in the scheme and the roof could serve that purpose. The Artisans' Dwelling Committee thought this was a good idea and decided to do the same with all of the blocks. The original intention was to whitewash the bare brick in the interior rooms. This was a cheaper option than plastering and this the Corporation tended to use for its cheaper rentals. On this occasion, it was decided to change the specification and plaster the interior walls 'to enhance the appearance of the interior of the dwellings and to add to the comfort of the inhabitants'. These changes are set out in detail in Report 51/1888 which sought approval for an additional expenditure of £6,500. This represented an increase of almost one-third on the original estimate and was proof, if proof was needed, that the Corporation had yet to get its costings correct. Similar issues had arisen in its operations in collaboration with the DADC, but this time the process was entirely within their control.

The *Irish Times* described the opening of Dublin Corporation's Barrack (later Benburb) Street scheme in 1888 as a 'ceremony of a most interesting character' (*Irish Times*, 27 April 1888, p.7). The scheme not only involved housing but also the creation of a new street to Ellis's (Sarsfield) Quay, which was named Sexton Street.

The outcome was a development of 144 tenements, five of which were ground floor shops. The tenements were four-storey blocks, with nine three-roomed tenements and the remainder divided equally between one and two-roomed units. There was a complicated schedule of rents which ranged from 4s. 6d. to 5s. for three rooms, 3s. to 4s. for two rooms with the smallest one-room units available at between 1s. 6d. and 2s. The shops cost 10s. per week.

By this point there were also 16 beds in the lodging house for women, also at 4d. per night. It is not explained why the Council made this addition and the newspapers did not feel the need to comment. All the beds in the lodging house were in dormitories on the upper three floors of the building. Lodgers were provided with cooking facilities to cook their own meals and it was possible to rent a storage area for their food. They were admitted to the building after 6 p.m. and they could cook or relax in the reading room until 8 p.m. when they were permitted to use the dormitories. They were required to be up by 8 a.m. the following morning but could stay in the building until 10 a.m. Permanent lodgers were given more leeway and could return during the day to cook their dinner. The lodgers could also make use of the roof space and it was noted in a review in the *Irish Times* that there were fine views over the city and that the lodgers could read, smoke and listen to the army bands in the vicinity. The facilities for women were separate to those for the men and somewhat more cramped. Everything was under the control of the Superintendent, who was paid 30*s*. per week in 1888, with residence, and it was reported that any boisterous or troublesome people were immediately removed (*Irish Times*, 3 September 1889, p.6).

The opening ceremony involved a large attendance of the dignitaries of the city and the making of several speeches in praise of the scheme and those involved in its promotion. One phrase, however, indicated just how early was the scheme in the Corporation's thinking. The Lord Mayor stated that the present scheme was 'merely an experiment, a great experiment – and on its success hinged another important question – namely the feasibility of the corporation furthering the establishment of suitable homes for artisans and labourers at rents within their means and accomplishing that end without further burdening the rates'. It is as well that the Corporation did not rely too much on the experience with Benburb Street because it quickly developed a reputation for being bad housing. The problems had emerged as early as 1892 as the Breviate of the Artisans' Dwellings Committee for 31 January makes clear (Report 16/1892). Dr Cameron reported that:

> At the close of the year 1891, the number of dwellings in occupation in the Benburb Street Buildings was 140, leaving four unoccupied... The number of persons in the buildings were 497, and consisted of 255 males and 242 females. There were nine deaths – one a boy, 14 years, of gastric fever; one woman, 36 years, bronchitis; two women, 56 and 27 years respectively, decline; four children, from 5 to 9 months, convulsions ; and one man, aged 50 years, congestion of the lungs... The Lodging-houses were used by 27,654 persons, 25,208 males and 2,448 females.

The problem lay with the sanitary provision. It was reported that:

> He found several of the passages and corridors in an uncleanly state, and water-closets and sinks which had been broken were yet out of repair. In the two blocks of buildings there are 42 w.c.'s for males, and 22 for females; there are also 22 sinks for the conveyance of slops and refuse-water. On some flats nine families have the use of two male and one female w.c's, while on others accommodation to the same extent is afforded for but five families. It is a general experience that w.c.'s used in common by several families are invariably taken but little care of by those who have access to them.

The Ordnance Survey plan for 1909 (fig. 6) shows the completed development. Most noticeable are the blocks along Benburb Street with Garrison Lane at the rear but there are also blocks on either side of 'The Avenue'. Blackhall Place now runs directly to the quays, bisecting Hendrick Place. The development survived into the 1970s, though the quality of accommodation was increasingly at variance with that generally available and the decision was taken to the demolish the four blocks along Benburb Street in 1975. Some elements remain to the present day. The blocks fronting onto The Avenue (now Ellis Court) survive but best preserved is the block on the corner of Benburb Street and Blackhall Place, which was reprieved.

Bow Lane

The Corporation took its time with the Bow Lane scheme. Part of the City Estate, they had originally intended to continue leasing the site and in December 1885 had decided to lease it to a James McGowan for 99 years. They rescinded that decision in January of the following year, deciding instead on a scheme of 85 cottages at weekly rents of between 2s. and 3s. (Report 188/1886). This would have produced an annual loss but the rents were targeted at the poorest class of people, a group which the Artisans' Dwellings Committee felt had been hitherto neglected. The development was almost ready to begin when the Council decided that it needed to reconsider it. It had already adopted the scheme and authorised an application to the Treasury for approval to use the site as well as an application to the Local Government Board for a loan of £10,325. The LGB held its inquiry on 25 May and approved the loan on 21 June with Treasury approval coming on 30 July 1886. Tenders were then sought but it was at this point that the process stopped. The tenders were much higher than expected and it seems that this caused the Council to take fright and there was considerable debate and recrimination about the site and the process.

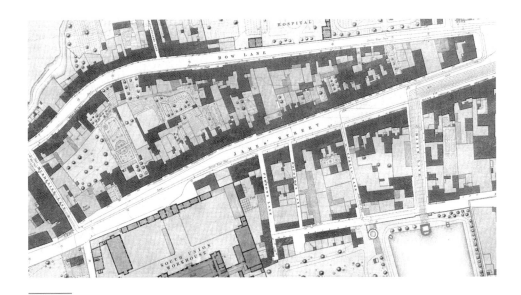

9. Bow Lane in the mid-nineteenth century. Ordnance Survey plan, 5-foot, Sheet 18 (19), 1847 edition.

It seems that the Artisans' Dwelling Committee and the City Architect had not discussed in detail whether the site was suitable. He claimed that he had mentioned its unsuitability in advance of preparing the plans but it seems that he did not carry the implications of this through to the specifications. Having revisited the matter, his opinion was that the site was unsuitable and would cost a lot to get it into a proper 'sanitary condition'. This involved considerable levelling of the site and the laying of a heavy layer of concrete. Taking this more realistic view resulted in a revised estimate of £12,500.

The Artisans' Dwellings Committee felt that the City Architect's estimate of the annual costs was, in fact, too low and their view was that the scheme would cost the Corporation of the order of £166 per annum. On this basis, the recommendation to the Council in February 1888 was to stop the development and wait until they could see how the Barrack Street scheme was working out. The Committee was concerned that if they had to increase rents and build a different sort of dwelling in order to make the scheme more financially realistic, they would end up housing a class of person different to the one they intended (Report 9/1888). The Council discussed the report at their meeting of 26 March 1888 and referred the matter back to the Artisans' Dwellings Committee asking them to consider if another site should be chosen. This decision, in turn, was rescinded at its meeting of 11 June 1888 with the revised view that a special committee, drawn from the general membership of the Council, should look at the question of using the Bow Lane site (Report 69/1888). The view of this committee was not unanimous but the prevailing opinion was that the City Engineer be asked to prepare a revised plan 'such as will secure a reasonable return for the expenditure'. This proposal received broad approval at the Council meeting of 16 July 1888 but the reader will note that the financial considerations were made far more explicit.

> That Report No. 69 of the Special Committee, re proposed Labourers' Dwellings in Bow Lane, be referred to the Artisans' Dwelling Committee with instructions to have amended plans prepared of such a kind as will ensure that the Corporation will be at no pecuniary loss in the event of this Council adopting the amended scheme presented for their approval or otherwise.

The Committee decided to approach Mr Dudgeon again and get him to produce a scheme, largely it seems because he had a track record of keeping costs down. The original proposal was for 85 tenements in 61 cottages and 12 two-storey houses. Mr Dudgeon's alternative (Report 87/1888) was for 86 tenements arranged in two-storey blocks of four tenements each. Most of the units had a living room, bedroom (some with a bed recess in the living room), scullery and separate w.c. and were of a size which Mr Dudgeon deemed suitable for six persons on the basis of the bye-laws. He reckoned that 2,000 cubic feet overall in a tenement would be satisfactory. Because the buildings would not use all of the site, the difficult portion could be left undeveloped and this would reduce the total cost by almost 20 per cent. The rents varied from 2s. to 2s. 6d. for the standard tenements, the more expensive had a bed recess. The greater cost of others was justified by the garden which averaged 45 feet in twenty four units and 88 feet in fourteen units. The scheme had five shops at between 5s. and 5s. 6d., fronting Bow Lane West, with additional accommodation overhead.

Number of units

Weekly Rent	City Architect	Mr Dudgeon
2s.	24	19
2s. 6d.	24	19
3s.	37	19
3s. 6d.		19
4s.		2
4s. 6d.		3
5s.		3
5s. 6d.		2

The Artisans' Dwellings Committee noted that most of the rents were within the original range and this plan was recommended on the basis that it would achieve a good sanitary outcome and did not *seem* to involve any loss, indeed Mr Dudgeon suggested a surplus of about £24 per annum but the Committee did not rely on that. It was noted that the area had a special claim to development since twenty one houses had been demolished to provide the site, as had a further sixteen adjacent to it. The revised scheme was naturally commended to the Council.

Tenders were sought in March 1889 and eight were received. The additional financial control this time was that no tender was to be accepted which exceeded the estimate of Mr Dudgeon. This was taking a chance since the Artisans' Dwelling Committee had previously taken the view that his estimates tended to be optimistic. On this occasion it worked out. The lowest tender was comfortably below the estimate (Report 33/1899) and the scheme was delivered for less than the loan. The dwellings were available on 13 April, and 41 tenants immediately moved in while all 86 dwellings were occupied by the first week in May. Careful vetting of the tenants took place to ensure that they were people whose income would not sustain higher rents elsewhere and the list of occupations is interesting for that reason. There were 47 labourers, 12 goods porters, 1 shop assistant, 2 cabdrivers, 5 draymen, 1 boatman, 1 plumber's assistant, 1 gatekeeper, 2 vanmen, 1 shoemaker, 1 barman, 1 bagmaker, 1 postman, 2 charwomen, 1 dressmaker, 1 needlewoman, and 1 nurse. The five shops were leased to a milk purveyor, green grocer, stationery, bread shop and huxter (Report 72/1890).

There was an official opening ceremony on 15 April, attended by a large number of the dignitaries of the city (*Irish Times*, 16 April 1890, p.3). It was quite an event, new housing schemes were still clearly a novelty, and there were speeches, dedications, the presentation of an ornate key, followed by lunch in the Mansion House. During the event, it was announced that the buildings would be called Kennedy Villas.

There was much praise for the fact that the scheme had been completed for less than its projected cost and it was noted that: 'viewed financially, the scheme which your lordship today inaugurates is distinguished from other improvements introduced by the Corporation, notwithstanding their utility and the great boon they conferred on the citizens of the Dublin, have yet entailed a pecuniary loss. This scheme, on the contrary, will yield an increasing profit, and will afford a remarkable example of the manner in which the question of providing healthful homes for the people may be solved with advantage to them and without loss to the general community' (*Irish Times*, 16 April 1890, p.3). The Lord Mayor responded that 'he also hoped that the Corporation would continue to construct such buildings as those around them, and they could do this without involving any extra charge on the rates of the city. ... At the same time, the Corporation did not desire to make a profit out of these houses, being satisfied if they got sufficient to repay the outlay, and to provide for the necessary repairs'.

The *Irish Times* was enthusiastic and suggested that 'a visit to Bow Lane, West, which runs off James' Street, cannot fail to afford pleasure to all who desire to see the honest working poor of the Metropolis comfortably housed at rents within their reach'.

Unfortunately, it was found that Mr Dudgeon's drive for economy stored up problems for the future. The budget for 1925 contained a significant increase in the allocation for repairs. The buildings in Benburb Street had subsided considerably causing problems not only to the walls but also the flat roof, which needed to be replaced. The position was even worse in Bow Lane. The estimated cost of repairs was £10,000, far in excess of their value so the minimum necessary would be done, costing £2,000. The report to Council noted that the scheme was 'badly designed, constructed with poor materials and bad drainage and erected on made-up ground' (*Freeman's Journal*, 16 April 1924, p.7). Notwithstanding the comment above, the buildings were occupied into the 1980s. Minutes from 2 April 1984 show that the process of redevelopment was underway when it was noted that 33 of the 56 flats had been detenanted.

10. Bow Lane flats in the 1960s.

Blackhall Place

The urban environment in Blackhall Place and its immediate environs was generally good (see map in Barrack Street discussion) but the City Estate had a plot which was quite ruinous and the Corporation decided to redevelop this, creating a new street as well as renovating existing tenements. As with the earlier developments, this involved the Finance and Leases Committee selling the property to the Artisans' Dwellings Committee. The site was bounded by Blackhall Parade, Blackhall Street, Blackhall Place and North King Street, while the upper (northern) part of the block was occupied by St Paul's church yard. The block diagram shows the layout very clearly together with the location of the various types. The plan was initially for 59 new houses, some multiple occupancy, which were divided into four different classes, A-D. Of these, eight were of class A, six of class B, 15 of class C, and 30 of class D (Report 64/1891). It was intended to build a new road that would run from North King Street to the lane at the rear of Blackhall Street and fronting on this road, there would be 29 two-storey tenements containing four dwellings each (Class A). The 29 ground floor tenements would be rented at 3s. 6d. per week, while the 29 on the upper floor would cost 2s. 6d. per week. Each tenement had its own w.c. and the ground floor ones had a garden which was 19 feet by 17 feet.

Fronting onto North King Street, the Committee wished to erect five two-storey houses, the ground floors of which would be shops with a living room, bedroom, scullery, w.c., coal bunker, meat safe and yard and available for 6s. 6d. per week (Class B). The upper floor dwellings, reached by a staircase common to every two dwellings would have similar provision at a weekly rent of 3s. 6d. per week. The plan for Blackhall Place involved 15 two-storey houses in single occupancy (Class C), each with a hall, parlour, living room, 2 bedrooms and a scullery, w.c., meat safe and yard. These would be rented at 7s. 6d. per week.

There were derelict yards and stables within the plot and there the Corporation wished to build eight one-storey single occupancy houses (Class D) at a weekly rent of 4s. 6d. which would offer a porch, living room, two bedrooms and the usual facilities.

The Class E dwellings were unusual in that the proposal was to renovate these pre-existing four-storey houses on Blackhall Street. These were already in five tenements per house and the renovation envisaged an annex which would contain the sanitary provisions for each tenement. The rents here would vary from 2s. 6d. for the basement tenements to either 4s. or 4s. 6d. for the ground and upper floors.

Sir Charles Cameron, the Superintendent Medical Officer for Health, was asked for his views and these were reported in Report 102/1891. He felt that the proposed range of rents was beyond the reach of many people who needed assistance. In his view, rents in this scheme and others should not exceed 3s. 6d. per week and the need was for accommodation at 1s. and 1s. 6d. per week. He felt that the tenements which the Corporation proposed to be renovated should instead be converted back to the single family homes they once were and disposed of. However, he also made the point that the conversion of the basements into tenements would be at variance with both the spirit and the letter of the Public Health Act of 1878. This was not to be the last time that Cameron demonstrated his independence of thought. He was never a mere functionary who went through the motions of his office. In this case, and in others, it seems clear that he made personal representations to the Local Government Board, something he should not have done. Yet, his reputation within the Corporation was high and his opinions carried weight.

Whatever about the objection about rent levels, the issue with the basements caused the Corporation to pause. However, it soon came up with a solution which seemed to them to meet the objections to the basement tenements and Report 108, a conjoint Report of the Finance and Leases Committee and Artisans' Dwellings Committee, recommended that the project proceed and a loan be sought from Her Majesty's Treasury for the scheme. The Minutes of the Council Meeting on 14 September 1891 record the following motion:

> That this Council, having considered the Reports Nos. 102 and 108, relative to proposed Dwellings for the working-classes at Blackhall street, Blackhall Place and North King Street, approve of the proposed buildings as comprised in Report 64 of this year-subject to the ground at rere being excavated so as to give more light and air to the basement.

It seems that the Treasury was well briefed on Cameron's objections, for they too asked the Corporation about rent levels. They noted that the intention was

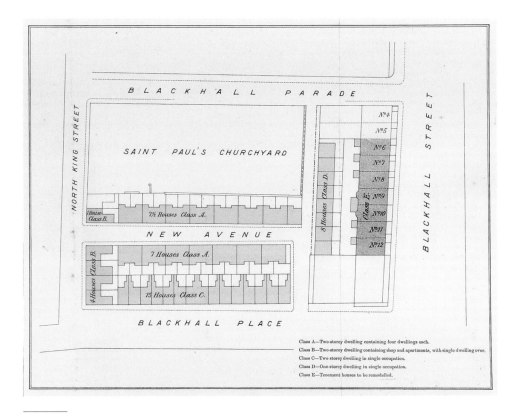

11. The Blackhall Place Housing Scheme as planned. Report 64/1891, Volume I, p.432. Note that the orientation of the plan has West at the top.

to charge rents of between 2s. 6d. and 7s. 6d. but that Cameron had suggested that lower rents were appropriate. The Treasury agreed with lower rents though they were prepared to raise the limit to 4s. 6d. They suggested that fifteen Class D dwellings be substituted for the 15 houses in Blackhall Place. This would give 30 tenements at 4s. 6d rather than houses which would cost 7s. 6d. per week.

The City Surveyor, Spencer Harty, responded that he had deliberately chosen to build houses at 7s. 6d. along Blackhall Place as it was a respectable neighbourhood. This was the Corporation as developer being conscious of the impact of its developments on the private owners around. The LGB retorted by asking what class of artisan could afford the 15 houses at 7s. 6d. This was responded to on 26 August saying that it would be the class of artisans who currently inhabit 'houses build by the Artisans' Dwelling Company, and which are let at a weekly rent of 7s'. The Corporation provided a fascinating list which contained employments which might not immediately come to mind as being within the category of 'working class artisan': cooper, carman, tailor, milliner, brass finisher, silversmith, dressmaker, bank porter, police constable, carpenter, soldier, plumber, bricklayer, railway policeman, engraver, van driver, school teacher etc. etc.'

The Report (116/1893) did not endorse the LGB's suggested changes to the scheme and it was approved at the council meeting of 11 September 1893. There was further correspondence but the Council noted the approval of HM Treasury for the scheme in a letter dated 4 January 1894 at the council meeting of 15 January 1894. Report 107/1894 (dated 30 June 1894 and approved on 13 August 1894) removed the controversial element from the scheme. It was found that the cost involved in converting the seven houses in tenements and the stables and coach-houses into eight cottages was not value for money. No other action was suggested in relation to the houses. The concern expressed by Spencer Harty to

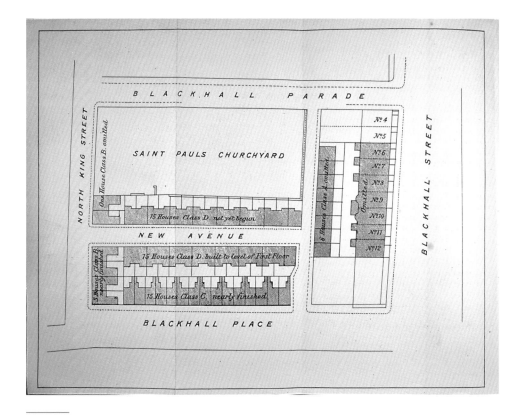

12. The Blackhall Place Housing Scheme under construction. Report 30/1895, Volume I, p.259.

13. The Blackhall Place Housing Scheme as built. Ordnance Survey plan, 5-foot, Sheet 18 (46 & 56), 1907 revision, 1909 edition.

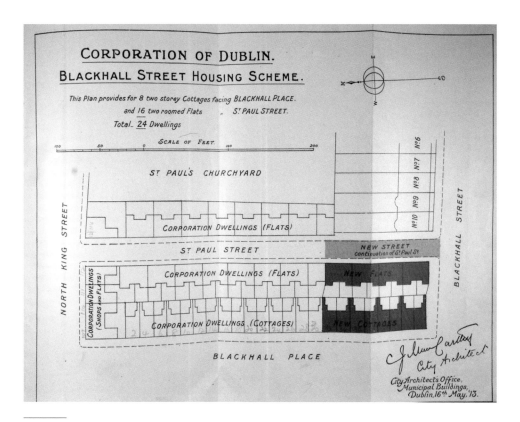

14. The Blackhall Place Housing Scheme reconsideration (1913), infill and re-orientation of the roads. Report 143/1913, Volume II, p.396.

15. The present-day class C houses on Blackhall Place.

16. Class B houses on North King Street (flats over flats with shops). The shops have been incorporated into the flats. The remainder of the scheme has been extensively redeveloped.

build respectable houses caused the Council to decide to build in brick rather than in breeze concrete, even though the latter was cheaper. The contractor was told to use the old bricks retrieved from the demolition of older buildings in so far as this was possible. When he ran out, he was authorised to construct the rere and interior walls of the class D houses of Tullamore bricks, faced on the outside with Mount Argus bricks, at an additional cost of £438 18s. This report (30/1895, dated 26 February 1895) noted that the dwellings were now in the course of erection.

Both Blackhall Place and St Joseph's Place were officially opened on the same day, 3 October 1896 at a ceremony in St Joseph's Parade. There was still a degree of pomp and ceremony about the event but perhaps not of the same order as the earlier ones and there was no formal lunch in the Mansion House at its conclusion. There were many speeches congratulating the Corporation and the various officials for the work that they had completed and two themes were strongly articulated. The first was a concern with cost but an acceptance that these schemes could run at a small loss as long as this was justified. The High Sheriff commented that 'it was the duty of the population of Dublin, especially the wealthier section, to provide dwellings for the poor, and if there was a slight loss, in his opinion it was money well spent. The second theme was a favouring of individual houses over tenements. Mr T. Lenehan T.C. was but one of a number of speakers who advocated single family dwellings. He that: 'it was his conviction that if they gave the working classes a fair chance with neat and comfortable houses, they would respond to it with

17. Housing in Blackhall area prior to redevelopment, 2002.

habits of tidiness and thriftiness. He thoroughly agreed that it was better that each family should have a house of their own, for by the other method of several families in one house he thought they were only perpetuating the tenement scheme' (*Irish Times*, 5 October 1896, p.6). This did not mean that the Corporation was done with block building, as will emerge below, but it shows that even after only three schemes, there was a strong view that such should be avoided.

The Council returned to the scheme in 1913 and built on the unused portion of the site, replacing Nos. 11 and 12 Blackhall Street, and taking the opportunity to re-orient the roads by extending St Paul Street to Blackhall Street (Report 143/1913). The addition involved 8 two-storey cottages, maintaining the line of Blackhall Place, and 16 two-roomed flats facing onto St Paul Street. The development was approved in January 1914 by the LGB on condition that the size of the bedrooms be increased to not less than 960 cubic feet (Report 87/1914).

The area was redeveloped on a number of occasions afterwards (fig. 17). The Blackhall Place and North King street frontages have survived to the present day and are good examples of the single occupancy houses and the shops with flats. Recent redevelopment of the entire northern side Blackhall Street, replacing earlier flat blocks along Queen Street, used a very striking design.

18. Modern redevelopment on Blackhall Street as it looked in 2005.

Mary's Lane

This proposal arose from the decision to construct a new Corporation Fruit and Vegetable Market, which was opened on 6 December 1892 (Report 165/1892). The road network in the area was deemed unsatisfactory for business and the improvement plans involved the widening of Mary's Lane and the creation of a new road from St Michan Street that would cut through the Ormond Market area and link with Ormond Quay (Report 114/1901). The Mary's Lane scheme would increase the width of the road from 20 feet to 46 feet. Not only would access be improved but the clearance of the present decayed buildings would also improve the air space and thereby improve the hygienic conditions of the locality.

The clearance would leave enough ground on the site of the old vegetable market and on the frontage of the new roadway to provide accommodation for 82 families or about 400 persons. Of these 82 families, 60 would be housed in ten blocks of two-roomed tenements, six in one block of three-roomed tenements, similar to the two-roomed and three-roomed tenements in the Bride's Alley scheme while 16 families would be provided for in four blocks of similar tenements to St Paul Street, in the Blackhall Place scheme. These four blocks of smaller two-roomed tenements would be two storeys high and the remaining blocks would be three storeys high. Each tenement would be self-contained and provided with its own water closet, scullery and water supply. It was noted that no portion of any of the buildings would be used in common except for the staircases and landings, still a relatively new concept and important in signalling a difference to what obtained in most tenements. The plans provided for the buildings to be made from stock bricks, without internal plastering but with whitewashing of the internal walls. The final cost, including the tenements was estimated at £37,000 (Report 114/1902).

The rents for this kind of accommodation were quite high. The City Architect, Charles MacCarthy, assuming that the scheme was a 'self-paying' one, suggested weekly rents of 5*s.* for the three-roomed dwelling, 3*s.* 6*d.* for the larger two-roomed dwellings with the smaller available for 3*s.* The scheme would leave a small strip of land, which was unsuitable for housing but which could be used as a playground.

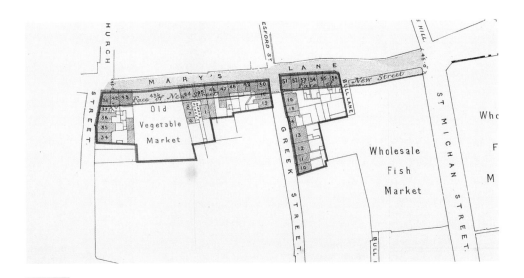

19. The Mary's Lane scheme as proposed in Report 114/1901, Volume II, p. 210.

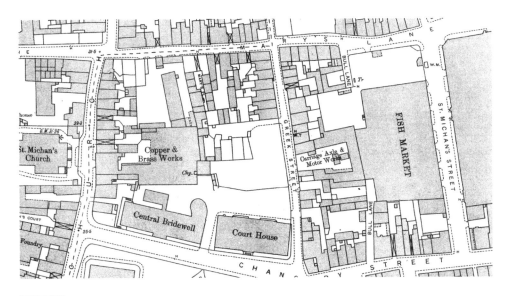

20. Mary's Lane area. Ordnance Survey plan, 5-foot, Sheet 18 (56), 1907 revision, 1909 edition.

Nothing came of this project but it remained on the Corporation's agenda until it was revisited as part of the developments around Ormond Market and Beresford / Church Streets.

St Joseph's Place

St Joseph's Place dates from 1896 but it had been in planning for a number of years. The scheme comprised 80 units, at a quite high density of 30 per acre (c.75 per ha). Later developments such as Marino would be built at a maximum of 12 dwellings per acre.

The report discussing the development makes clear how important the 1890 Housing of the Working Classes Act was in encouraging Dublin Corporation to build outside the narrow confines of the city estate. The Corporation's experience with the Dublin Artizans' Dwelling Company in their Coombe and Plunket Street schemes was an important influence. It had been an expensive experience, where costs, largely compensation to land owners, soared above what had been expected. As Charles Cameron put it, 'The costly experience which the Council had in the promotion of the Coombe and Plunket-street Area Improvement Schemes would not encourage a repetition of such undertakings if no reasonable prospect could be shown that more equitable results might be attained. The law has since undergone a radical change; the carriage of proceedings has been greatly cheapened, and the conditions under which excessive sums could be given as compensation for the compulsory acquirement of property which the neglect of its owners has rendered a danger to the health of the community, vastly modified' (Report 19/1892).

The area chosen for 'improvement' was a small area just off Blessington Street – Upper Eccles Lane, White's Lane and Blessington Place. As described by Cameron, using the required formulation, they were 'unfit for human habitation by reason of the narrowness, closeness, bad arrangement, and bad condition of the streets or alleys and houses and groups of houses within each area, and the want of light, air, ventilation, and proper conveniences, and other sanitary defects; that they are dangerous and injurious to the health of the inhabitants of the buildings in the said area, and of the neighbouring buildings; and that the evils connected with the houses, streets or alleys and the sanitary defects in such area cannot be effectually remedied otherwise than by an Improvement Scheme for the re-arrangement and re-construction of the streets or alleys and houses therein'.

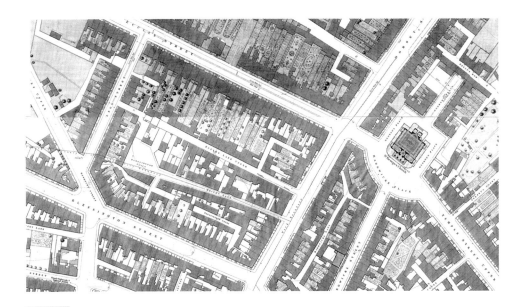

21. The 'White's Lane' area at mid-nineteenth century. Ordnance Survey plan, 5-foot, Sheet 18 (3 & 8), 1847 edition, 1866 revision.

With an eye to prudence, it was explained that with an entire cost of £5,000 for site acquisition and £12,000 for building, the estimated annual revenue of £850 would ensure that it was not a burden on the ratepayers.

It seems that the area was not just one of bad housing and that it had quite a negative reputation. The *Evening Herald* applauded its clearance and described the area as 'the resort of the most degraded of mankind and womankind, it was a foul stain on the name of on the city'. It had fed 'the newspaper columns with items of outrage and robbery' (*Evening Herald*, 24 October 1894, p.2).

Acting under the Housing of the Working Classes Act, 1890, the necessary announcement of the improvement scheme for the unhealthy area called White's Lane was placed in the newspapers on 11 and 18 October 1892 (see *Evening Herald*, p.3). The required inquiry by the Local Government Board took place in two stages. The first, undertaken by Mr Cotton, Chief Engineering Inspector for the LGB, took place on 2 February 1893. This also considered the application for the required loan of £17,000. The Board issued provisional approval for the scheme on 14 March and the Corporation was informed of parliamentary approval on 12 June (*Freeman's Journal*, 25 August 1893, p.2). There was only partial approval of the loan. Approval for £5,000, which was for the purchase of the land was given immediately. Approval for the remainder was withheld until the LGB was satisfied that the people to be displaced by the scheme approved of the arrangements made for them. This resulted in a second inquiry held by Mr O'Brien Smith, LGB Inspector, in February 1894. The hearings were at night to facilitate the people involved and at that time it was estimated that there were 644 people living in 289 rooms in the area. Police-Sergeant Thompson, who was a Sanitary Inspector for Dublin Corporation read out a list of vacant rooms within a one-mile radius and stated that there were 84 rooms available with good sanitary arrangements and capable of housing about four persons in each in Lurgan Street, Linenhall Street, Church Street and nearby streets at a rent of between 1*s*. 6*d*. and 2*s*. per week. Mr Keane, described as a 'sub-sanitary officer', gave evidence that he found 74 rooms in Tyrone Street, Gloucester Street and nearby streets which had good sanitary arrangements and which were suitable for a family at rents of between 1*s*. 6*d*. and 2*s*. 3*d*. Mr James Keane, another sanitary inspector, reported that there were 79 rooms in Lower Abbey Street, Marlborough Street and surroundings of good quality for rents not in excess of 2*s*. 3*d*. On cross-examination it was agreed that these rents were dearer than those generally in White's Lane. Those being displaced had legal representation at the inquiry and they complained about the lack of information from the Corporation prior to the inquiry. They also requested compensation for their displacement, something which they said was in the power of the Corporation to offer but otherwise they were well disposed (*Freeman's Journal*, 15 February 1894, p.7).

The inquiry gave the opportunity to Mr Harty, the City Surveyor, to outline the scheme. The proposal was for the land to be cleared and an entirely new scheme constructed. A system of streets (or avenues!) was envisaged, each 30 feet wide with the roadways to be asphalted and the paths concreted. There would be 80 cottages, one storey high, each with a living room (average length 16 feet 3 inches and width 10 feet) and two bedrooms: one 9 feet 9 inches square and the other 11 feet x 7 feet 8 inches. Each cottage was to have separate concreted yard, some 12 feet 3 inches x 18 feet 3 inches with a water closet, scullery and coal bunker. A site was to be provided for a boys' national school.

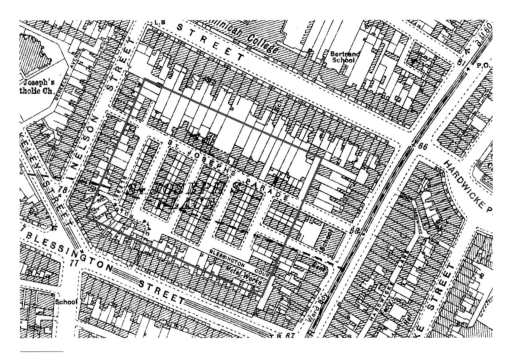

22. Layout Plan of St Joseph's Parade. Ordnance Survey plan, 1:2,500, Sheet 18 (VII), 1939.

The arbitration process took place during 1893, following the approval for clearance, and it took some time as there were quite a number of landowners in the area. The reports give further insight into the ruined state of the area as well as to the capacity of owners to try to swindle the Corporation. No. 82 Dorset Street was described as having 13 rooms and 38 people living in it with one water closet. The Corporation's Valuer, P.F. Leonard, stated that he was afraid to visit the top floor because of the shaky state of the stairs. That house alone yielded an annual income of £71 10s. and the valuer was suggested that the compensation should be £179 18s. 6d. A claim by Michael Hunt was thrown out when it was demonstrated that the leasehold income he claimed to be receiving was almost double what he was in fact getting. The arbitration process also indicated that weekly tenants were left in a difficult position being subject to dislocation but without being eligible for compensation (*Freeman's Journal*, 5 October 1893, p.2).

Advertisements seeking tenders to build were sought in spring of 1894. Five were received, one was disqualified and in June 1894, the tender from Wm Connolly and Sons for £10,720 was recommended to the Corporation. Although reported as 'Connolly', the correct spelling of this builder's name was 'Conolly'. Demolition was well underway by September 1894 (*Irish Times*, 24 September, p.3) but the arrangement with Mr Connolly seems to have been somewhat fraught. The old houses on the site were cleared and the materials sorted into that which could be sold and general rubbish. Much to the annoyance of the local parish priest, Revd Francis Ryan, Connolly piled the rubbish onto the school site where it remained, despite demands and even a Corporation resolution to remove it, until matters were brought to a head in November 1894. A special meeting of the Artisans' Dwellings Committee of Dublin Corporation, attended by Mr Connolly, and involving a visit to the site, considered a cranky letter from the parish priest. Mr Connolly suggested that it would take six months to clear the rubbish but after some discussion he agreed to do it within a month. This was only after it was pointed out to Mr Connolly that he had obtained 'a good deal of work for the city and it would not be wise for him to throw obstacles in the way of the present work' (*Evening Herald*, 10 November 1894, p.3). Mr Connolly understood this reference

23. Present-day housing on St Joseph's Parade.

and it seems to have ended the dispute. The list of subscribers to the new school project was published in the *Freeman's Journal* on 1 December 1894 and it was noted that work would commence shortly with the expectation of having the school completed by the following September (p. 3). It was reported in the Breviate for the quarter ending 31 January 1895 that the 'process of clearing the ground on the site made considerable progress this quarter. The plot sold for the purpose of erecting a school thereon has been cleared and handed over to the purchaser, Rev. Francis M. Ryan' (Report 31/1895).

A letter to the Corporation from the Local Government Board and dated 25 July 1896 noted that their inspector had visited the development and 'the inspector informs the Board that the 80 one-storey cottages and out offices proposed in the scheme are now fully completed and tenanted and that the works have been completed in accordance with the plan and specification' (Minutes 10 August 1896, p. 239). Certainly, life seemed to have developed its own rhythm in the area by 1899 with lodgings, with or without board, being offered at 4 St Joseph's Parade, with a suggestion that they might suit 'couple men' (*Evening Herald*, 18 March 1899, p.5).

Despite being so centrally located, the housing has not changed greatly since it was first completed, though there have been significant changes to neighbouring locations. The little development nestles between the main roads of the locality and though St Joseph's Parade can be quite busy, no houses from this scheme open onto it. It is high density and the locality lacks open space though the recent enclosure, by narrowing of Blessington Court when it joins St Joseph's Place, has resulted in a tiny green oasis.

Bride's Alley (Patrick Street / Nicholas Street)

The distinctive streetscape of the east side of Patrick Street from the top of the hill at Christchurch Place to St Patrick's Park is often assumed to form part of the Iveagh Trust development. In reality, two distinct but not entirely separate developments took place side by side at the same time. The more ornate structures with their distinctive copper domes were built by the Iveagh Trust, while their slightly more austere neighbours to the north comprise a Dublin Corporation flat scheme, begun slightly earlier. While the exteriors of both developments are relatively unmodified, though their interiors have been modernised, their urban context has changed dramatically due to the widening of the west side of Patrick Street during the 1990s as part of the tangent road scheme extending along Clanbrassil Street to the South Circular Road; the legacy of the various traffic consultants who arrived during the late 1950s and the 1960s.

The area between Christchurch Place and St Patrick's Cathedral had fallen into decay by 1890 and was a matter of concern to the Wood Quay Ward Ratepayers Protection Society. As businessmen, they were concerned at the impact of the dereliction on business by virtue of the loss of a population with some income and their replacement with those who had none. A small group of them got together in December 1891 and the report of their meeting in the *Irish Times* (11 December 1891, p.6) set out the problem very clearly. In the Bull Alley area houses were either collapsed or in decay. One side of Wood Street had lain demolished for years and Golden Lane, Ross Lane, Kennedy's Lane were in a similar condition. It was reported that there was a willingness by 'influential gentlemen' to assist the Corporation in any measures they might take and there were calls for the Corporation to get involved. The Corporation got involved to the extent of clearing many of the ruined buildings but they took the view that they did not have the money to do any building. This resulted in a further meeting of ratepayers that, supported by the local public representatives and the clergy of both denominations, resolved to send a delegation to Dublin Corporation to state their case. The motion declared that 'the present condition of the west area between St Patrick's and Christ's Cathedrals to be a continued eyesore to the residents

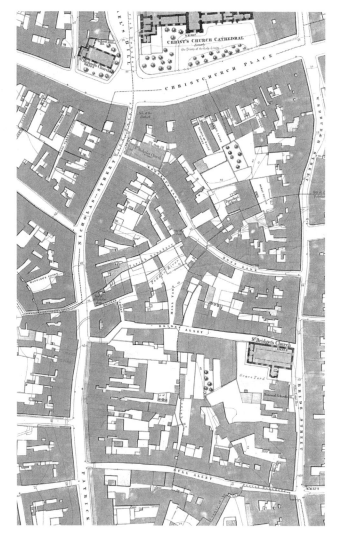

24. Bride's Alley (Patrick Street / Nicholas Street) area. Ordnance Survey plan, 5-foot, Sheet 18 (56), 1847 edition, 1866 edition.

of the surrounding districts and a disgrace to the city. We demand that steps be taken at once to acquire ... the derelict ground for the erection of dwellings for artisans and labourers' (*Freeman's Journal*, 29 January 1892, p. 6). Though plans were made and adopted by the Corporation, the perceived lack of progress resulted in another public meeting in 1895. Some speakers felt that there were elements within the Council who were reluctant to proceed with the redevelopment of the area. Others were less critical of the Corporation's intentions but felt that they needed a spur to get on with the task. The debate resulted in a motion being passed which urged the Council to proceed quickly with the scheme they had adopted. In order to keep the pressure on the Corporation, the meeting agreed to the establishment of a permanent committee (*Irish Times*, 28 June 1895, p.6). There was also a brief mention of a park as part of the development. This had been in the air for some time and was an element in a short but lively correspondence in the *Irish Times* about the nature of the proposed development. Thomas Drew RHA, who was the consulting architect for both St Patrick's and Christchurch cathedrals, with an eye to the developing idea of town planning had suggested that the entire area needed to be planned comprehensively and not in what he called 'hole and corner' planning (*Irish Times*, 3 February 1892, p.6). He also advocated what he called 'Poddle Park' to be provided adjacent to St Patrick's, a feature which was not immediately appreciated by the ratepayers' association but which later became an important part, not only of the Corporation's development, but also that of the Iveagh Trust.

To be fair, Dublin Corporation had not been idle. The first consideration of the development of the area, which became known as the Bride's Alley scheme, was in a report from the Artisans' Dwelling Committee (Report 111/1893) presented to the Council in 1893 which considered the 'extensive tracts within the Wood Quay Ward which been rendered vacant or become derelict, dilapidated, and uninhabited through a combination of influences frequently described' (p. 723). The area under consideration was bounded by Christchurch Place, Patrick's Close, Bride Street, Werburgh Street and Nicholas Street / Patrick Street. Ideally, the area stretching to St Patrick's Cathedral was in need of clearance but compensation would have to be paid to the owners and the feeling in the Corporation was that it was beyond their resources. So they contented themselves with the area to the north.

A report to the Artisans' Dwellings Committee was adopted on 13 April 1896 (Report 33/1896). This recommended the development of an awkward site bounded on the north by the Church of St Nicholas, the rears of premises facing onto Christchurch place and Derby Square, on the south by Bride's Alley, on the east by Werburgh and Bride streets and on the west by Nicholas and Patrick street. For reasons of cost, the small lane of Derby Square was omitted; the houses there were in reasonably good condition and the compensation that would have to be paid would be significant. The entire cost was estimated at £68,000 and the rental was estimated in gross terms of £1,903, 4s. per annum. This left an annual deficit of £1,212 14s. per annum with a loan from the LGB being paid off over 50 years. Seven different classes of houses were suggested; a total of 60 dwellings, housing 128 families. From the beginning there were reservations about what was being proposed. It is very unusual to find comments in a Corporation report which suggested that the scheme being proposed was not necessarily the best and that reconsideration should be allowed for. The Council voted to remove this paragraph from the adopted report No. 33 but a similar sentiment was retained in the further report No. 65 (adopted on 1 June 1896). It seems that they were still not sure about what kind of accommodation was most appropriate. They had built cottages in Blackhall Place and St Joseph's Parade but also had experience of building flats in two storey and higher blocks in Benburb Street. The DADC Plunket Street cottage development was across the road. This first draft plan suggested a mixture of both and it was a complicated mixture (see figure 25).

- A – 15 Self-contained houses of three storeys with a shop on the ground floor. These were big houses with seven rooms in addition to the shop.

- B – 16 Buildings in flats, each of three storeys with three families in each building, two rooms per family.

- C – 10 buildings in flats, each of three storeys with shops on the ground floor, three families per building. A shop and two rooms on the ground floor, 2 rooms on the first and second floors.

- D – 2 buildings in flats of two storeys each with two families in each house, two rooms each.

- E – 9 self-contained houses with one family and four rooms each.

- F – 6 buildings in flats, each of three storeys with three families and three rooms each.

- G – 2 buildings in flats, each two storeys with two families and three rooms each

   All tenements (flats) were to contain a scullery with sink, coal box, meat safe and shelving.

The proposed rents varied with the size of the property and the floor on which it was located; ground floor locations cost more. The range was from £1 per week for type **A** while type **B** cost 3s. 9d., 3s. 3d. and 3s. A '**C**' flat varied from 7s. 6d., 3s. 3d. and 3s. while a '**D**' cost 3s. 9d., 3s. 3d. The **E**-type was 7s. 6d., **F** cost 5s., 4s. 6d. or 4s. while **G** was either 5s. or 4s. 6d.

The plan was reconsidered in 1898 (Report 129/1898) and simplified considerably. The houses were replaced by flats for reasons which were not entirely clear. The redesign was the result of 'taking into consideration the requirements and surroundings of the residents lately occupying the premises upon the cleared area, that houses of a more suitable character should be erected, and which would, at the same time, largely augment the estimated income therefrom'.

They had another look at the plans in March 1899 (Report 43/1899) because they had learned of Lord Iveagh's plans for the lower part of the site on Bull Alley. Having 'waited' upon his Lordship, they were able to readjust the boundaries of their plot and make it more coherent.

> By Lord Iveagh's Scheme, Bride's Alley will be converted from a tortuous, narrow lane into a straight and wide street 45 feet in width, the south side of which will be in Lord Iveagh's Area and the northern side of which will form the southern boundary of the Bride's Alley Area. This new arrangement has enabled the City Architect to do away with the awkward, angular street shown on his plan which accompanied 129–1898 and allowed him to provide a straight street parallel to the straight new street which is to replace Bride's Alley (p. 393).

Cost remained an important consideration. One 'political' way of presenting the costs, with a view to making projects appear less expensive and therefore more palatable to the ratepayers, was to separate the costs of clearance from those of development. The Committee reasoned that since this was a clearance area, the costs of acquiring and clearing the site and providing services would have to be met regardless of whether any subsequent building took place on the site. Although the cost of the scheme was presented as amounting to £91,000, this did not include the £35,000 required to acquire the site, nor the £9,000 necessary to clear and service it. In many ways this was simply an

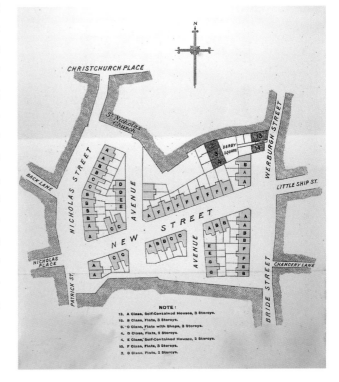

25. The first proposal for the site. Report 65/1893.

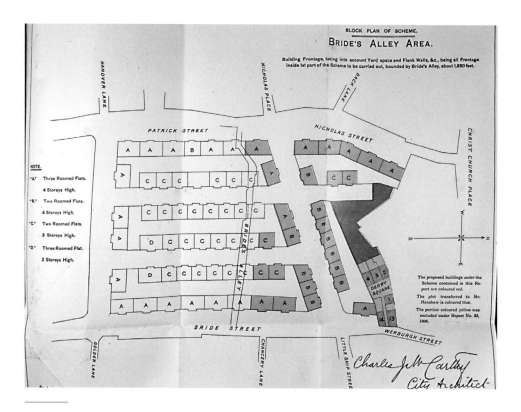

26. Bride's Alley scheme as envisaged in 1898. Report 129/1898, Volume 3, p.396.

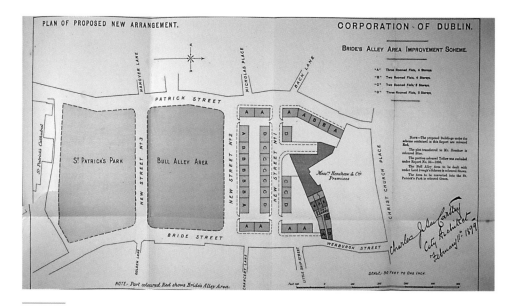

27. The Bride's Alley scheme as modified in 1899. Report 43/1899, Volume 1, p.406.

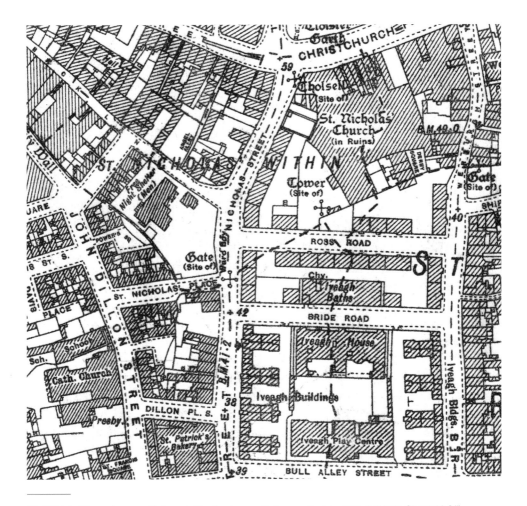

28. Bride's Alley scheme with Iveagh Trust scheme. Ordnance Survey plan, 1:2,500, Sheet 18 (XI), 1939 edition.

accounting exercise, since all of the costs would ultimately be paid for via the rates. However, this reduced the apparent subsidy that would be required to keep rents at a reasonable level. The rents proposed were between 3s. 6d. and 6s. per week, yielding £2,633 per annum. This was a significant increase on the first plan due to the increased density of development. If development costs were limited to the building, rather than also including the site acquisition, clearance and servicing, then the annual deficit would be £463. This was based on the assumption of a 50-year loan from the LGB.

29. Aerial view of Dublin Corporation and Iveagh Trust developments.

While the buildings in the new scheme would be four storeys high, there would be no shops because the LGB now refused to sanction any loans for the erection of buildings other than dwellings. Fortunately, Lord Iveagh included a row of shops in his scheme. In additional, it was decided not to divide the space at the rear of the buildings into separate yards but to create a common space for the tenants of all the houses facing onto such spaces. With a concern for the overall appearance, they specified that the buildings should be of a somewhat ornamental character. The gables were decorative, reminiscent of Dutch Billy gables, and the façade was faced with Portmarnock red brick, which seemed to be in fashion at the time; the red colour was judged to be particularly fine. It had been the brick chosen by Trinity College Dublin for a series of improvements in 1894 (*Irish Times*, 19 June 1894, p.4) as well as for the new Fire Station at Lower Buckingham Street (*Irish Times*, 12 October 1899, p.6).

The former plan had provided for 26 distinct houses or blocks containing accommodation for 198 families of which 80 were to have three-roomed flats with 118 in two-roomed flats. The new plan provided for 29 houses or blocks containing accommodation for 210 families of whom 112 were to be in the three-roomed flats, and 98 in the two-roomed flats. Of these 29 houses, seven fronted onto Nicholas

30. The entrance to Derby Square in 1990 before it was lost to redevelopment.

Street, four onto Bride Street, 11 onto New Street 1 (Ross Street) and seven onto New Street 2 (Bride Road). As decided, they were four storey except for those facing New Street 1 (Ross Street) which were three storey.

This arrangement produced four types of flats, each with a water closet and scullery. A separate entrance for each house by means of an open doorway was provided with either granite or concrete stairs.

- A – 11 blocks, each of four storeys with eight families in three-roomed flats.
- B – 7 blocks, each of four storeys with eight families in two-roomed flats.
- C – 7 blocks, each of three storeys with six families in two-roomed flats.
- D – 4 blocks, each of three storeys with six families in three-roomed flats.

   These edge Ross Street.

As will be seen in the discussion which follows below, the question of cost was perennial. Fears that advantage could be taken of the Corporation was clearly to the fore when the Council passed the following motion at its meeting on 7 December 1903.

31. Patrick Street, 1990 before renovation.

32. Ross Road, 1990 before renovation.

33. Looking north from Bride Road, inner courts, 1990 before renovation.

34. The Iveagh Baths, 1990.

That, before any scheme for the better Housing of the Working Classes in this City be promoted or carried into effect by this Council, or any negotiations or agreements entered upon or come to by this Corporation, or any Member or Members thereof, with the Landlords or owners of any Houses or Premises or slum property in any unhealthy areas for the purpose of any such scheme, including the widening of any thoroughfare or street in connection there with, the provisions of the Housing of the Working Classes Acts shall first be enforced with respect to all such property, and the Landlords or owners thereof compelled to make same sanitary and fit for human habitation, and if they fail to do so, that said houses and premises be closed and demolished at the expense of such owners or landlords, so that for the benefit of the ratepayers the enormous costs, expenses and other outlay hitherto incurred by the Corporation in connection with such schemes may be avoided.

A final change to the plan was agreed in 1903, whereby the Corporation gave up the site intended for 5 type B blocks on Bride Road to Lord Iveagh who proposed to build a swimming baths. The proposal was enthusiastically taken up by the Corporation who did not seem concerned at the loss of accommodation (Report 68/1903). The Breviate of the Improvements Committee for the quarter ended 31 March 1905 noted that the sale had been completed (Report 81/1905).

The availability of money dictated that larger schemes be undertaken in phases, as will be seen time and time again in the schemes that followed. This sometimes also resulted in parts of the site being left undeveloped. In this case, the first two sections of the scheme were approved speedily. The Council at its meeting of 13 August 1900 approved the tender for the first section (Report 118/1900). Approval for the second section followed on at 1 April 1901 (Report 43/1901) but this left some undeveloped ground. It remained that way until 1908 when the Improvements Committee considered the feasibility and desirability of building on the vacant ground as well as on undeveloped land at the Oblate site and Mooney's Lane (discussed below). The committee's analysis suggested that the latter two could be completed to advantage but that building on Bride's Lane would cost more than could be recouped in rents. However, they recommended that the Corporation proceed to build on Bride's Lane because the accommodation would be useful and they had paid a lot to obtain land which was lying idle (Report 81/1908). The recommendation for five blocks, containing 36 two-roomed tenements was considered on 1 June 1908 and despite an attempt to have it postponed for six months, it was adopted by the Council. The costs were outlined in Report 145/1909, tenders were sought for this third section on 2 May 1910 and Messrs Martin were chosen from the three received (Report 113/1910) at the Council meeting on 6 June 1910. Report 145/1909 is also significant because of the comments of the City Treasurer and Law Agent in relation to block buildings. They suggested that though flat blocks had social benefits, rents could never match the required outlay and they were expensive to manage because tenants got out of them as soon as they could become tenants of cottages. The advice was not immediately heeded but this was part of a growing acceptance that flat blocks were not as attractive an option as cottages.

Reflections in 1903

By 1903, Dublin Corporation had been directly involved in housing provision for twenty years, and indirectly, through its work with the DADC, for even longer. Given the experience gained during that time, it is unsurprising that there were varying opinions among both elected members and officials of the Corporation as to how best to proceed. The Corporation met a deputation from the Dublin Trades' Council on 4 May 1903 and it was agreed to hold a conference between the parliamentary representatives of the City and County of Dublin, the members of the Corporation, and the members of the Trades' Council. This meeting took place at the Mansion House on 12 September, 1903, under the presidency of T. C. Harrington, M.P., Lord Mayor, and it established a committee to investigate the various issues. Their work formed the basis for Report 176/1903, which is useful not only for the assessment of the legislative and administrative framework within which housing development took place but also because it provided a summary of the then-present state of working class housing.

The following is a list of the Corporation schemes, including those they had inherited from the townships with the average rent, though there was considerable variation in some schemes.

Benburb Street	139 dwellings	2s. 9d.
Bow Lane	81 dwellings	2s. 10d.
Blackhall Place	80 dwellings	4s. 3d.
St Joseph's Place	80 dwellings	4s. 6d.
Bride's Alley Area	138 dwellings	6s. 7d.
Clontarf		2s. 6d.
Donnycarney		2s. 0d.
Montgomery and Purdon Street Scheme (underway)		2s. 11d.

The Clontarf and Donnycarney schemes were inherited upon the extension of the boundaries of the city in 1901, following the absorption of the townships.

There were other providers of dwelling houses for the working class and the report noted that 'fairly good dwellings' for the working classes had been provided by

private individuals with 581 tenements on the south side at rents that varied from
1s. 6d. to 14s. per week and 254 tenements on the north side with rents that varied
from 1s. 6d. to 11s. per week.

- Dublin Artisans' Dwelling Company had accommodated 266 families and
  were in the process of building 249 cottages at Arbour Hill. The rents varied
  considerably from 1s. 9d. per week to 14s. per week but with the greatest number
  in the 4s. to 8s. range. The report noted that the Company would soon house
  2,910 families, comprising about 13,500 persons though this apparent surge
  was not explained.

- The Association for the Housing of the Very Poor, with which Cameron was closely
  associated, had 36 tenements with rents from 1s. 3d. to 3s. per week but they had
  acquired a large site on John Street on which they proposed to provide 338 dwellings.

- Guinness had built 87 dwellings for their employees at rents from 3s. 6d. to 8s.
  per week.

- The City and Suburban Artisans' Dwelling Company had 250 dwellings at Cork
  Street and 38 in Inchicore. While these ranged from 3s. 6d. to 7s. per week, by far
  the great number were rented at 3s. 6d.

- The Industrial Tenements Company was the oldest company of this type and
  its Meath Street building housed 52 tenements at rents from 1s. to 4s. per week.

- The Great Southern and Western Railway Company had built 148 houses,
  accommodating 865 persons at rents that ranged from 3s. 6d. to 7s. per week
  with an average of 5s.

- The Midland Great Western Railway Company had built 82 houses for its
  employees at rents of 7s. and 3s. 6d. per week.

- Watkins Brewery had provided 87 dwellings for its employees at rents of between
  2s. 6d. to 6s. 6d. per week.

- In addition, the Iveagh Trust had intensified its building and they now housed
  325 families at New Bride Street at rents that ranged from 1s. 9d. to 2s. 6d. for
  one room, 3s. 3d. to 4s. for two rooms and 4s. to 5s. for three rooms.

In total, the report noted that the number of families provided for or soon to
be provided for was 5,394. The breakdown indicated that the Corporation had

provided 1,041, the companies listed above had provided 4,028 with an additional 325 by the Iveagh Trust. No details were given of the privately-owned tenements. When this was viewed against demand, it painted a grim picture. The city had a population of 292,000 in 1901, comprising 59,263 families, having 4.6 members on average. Some 36.6 per cent (21,702) of these families occupied each only one room, and 13,620 (23%) occupied two rooms each. 'No such state of things, or anything approaching to it exists in any other town in the United Kingdom'.

Insanitary Locations

A list of locations which had been declared insanitary was also provided. It was also noted that more than 3,000 houses had been de-tenanted and closed since 1879. While many had been refurbished, others were now in ruins. There were 302 derelict houses, 148 houses in complete ruins and derelict sites on which 82 houses had previously stood. On the south side of the city there were (at the time of the report) some 786 houses in a very defective condition housing 2,149 families in 2,982 rooms. On the northside there were 700 houses in a similar state with 1,496 families in 2,401 rooms. The total population which would be affected by clearance was 12,926. It was the view of the report that these should be de-tenanted 'if there was sufficient and proper accommodation for their denizens'. The locations mentioned were:

Nerney's Court and Kelly's Row	100 families
North Gloucester place and adjoining places	150 families
Moore Market and adjacent alleys	50 families
Beresford Street	70 families
Ormond Market and adjacent alleys	100 families
Pigtown Lane and neighbourhood	90 families
Irwin Street	550 families
Part of Marrowbone Lane	40 families
Cook Street and Michael's Hill	100 families
Ash(e) Street and neighbourhood	130 families
Hackett's Court Kevin Street	40 families
Aungier Court and Digges Lane	45 families
Townsend Street	80 families
Leeson Lane and adjacent courts	60 families
Newmarket	60 families
Total Number of families	**1,665**

Changes to the law

The discussion also turned to the question of what changes to the law would be required in order to facilitate or even permit the required housing programme. It was noted that any housing scheme was a costly business, involving all sorts of legal expenses and that the ratepayers did not understand the scale of expenditure necessary. They made the point that the process for each scheme cost more or less the same regardless of the number of houses in it.

Compensation payable to land owners remained a concern and they wanted it limited to the value of property in its derelict state. While Dublin had managed to get legislation to control excessive compensation payments under Part I and II of the 1890 Act, there was no such limitation on Part III, which could be a useful provision in that it allowed for dwellings to be provided on vacant land and to house people displaced by other improvement schemes. To improve matters, the report asked that local authorities be given power to acquire land outside their legal boundaries and to use land which they already owned in such districts for housing. To do this, they needed to have the provisions of the Acts extended to such transactions, especially the 80-year loan term and capacity to keep such loans off their balance sheet.

They asked for a streamlining of the process of declaring a house unfit and they asked that they should have flexibility in the timing of orders and not to be always bound by the law terms. The Corporation also wished to be able to acquire land which had lain unused for three years at its current market value only while they wished to provide incentives to builders of housing for the working classes by being able to remit all or part of the rates for a period of up to ten years.

In all, 'the recommendations do not by any means exhaust those which might be made to render less difficult by fresh legislation the great problem of housing in such a place as Dublin, but they are put forward as likely to be of at least considerable use and as immediately practicable in view of the fact that they are mainly based on the law as recently amended in England, and now actually in force in that country.'

In conclusion, the report was of the view what while there had been progress, much remained to be done. A key conclusion was that they needed to build in suburban areas, not only because this was more economical but also because this would reduce the pressure on rents in Dublin, which were scandalously high. They felt that their clearance schemes were actually rewarding the owners of poor housing since they received high compensation when their property was condemned. Rather they felt the incentive should be re-oriented so that the owner would see it to be more beneficial to improve the property or to risk losing it.

At this early point therefore, the mind of the Corporation had turned to suburban, even semi-rural, building with subsidised transport. This was not to be the final word – schemes would continue to be inner city – and it would be some considerable time before the suburbs materialised, while the subsidised transport costs remained always a dream.

> It was the unanimous opinion of the Committee that it would be a fatal mistake to continue to put a premium on bad sanitation and improper housing by purchasing up, at a ruinous rate, insanitary areas and rebuilding them. The most desirable remedy for the state of things existing in the city is to build, at first, on the outskirts cottages or self-contained dwellings, and to procure cheap means of transit to and from the city for workers, which the Committee believes will not be difficult to arrange with the Tramway Company and Railway Companies. The providing of these semi-rural dwellings will lessen the congestion in the older parts of the city, and, when this has been done, and the pressure on the tenement houses relieved, the law can be strictly enforced for the condemning and demolition of houses which are not fit for human habitation, unless same are forthwith put into a perfectly sanitary condition and the Committee believes that, once it becomes clearly understood by owners of tenement property that they must carry out to the full the duties toward their tenants which the law imposes on them, and that neglect on their part to do will entail the demolition and confiscation of their property, the Housing Question will be in a very fair way towards solution.

Montgomery Street and Purdon Street

The area around Montgomery Street and Purdon Street (later Foley Street) was notorious as the one of the main red-light districts in Dublin though one would never glean that from the Corporation reports or from the newspapers of the time. While the police courts were regularly reported, and assaults and robberies were covered, cases involving prostitution were scarcely mentioned. The reader was invited to infer from reports such as 'Lousia Mervin of Purdon Street was charged in custody of Constable 123C with having, while in a house in Purdon Street, stolen 2s. 6d. from the trousers of Private Hopkinson (*Evening Herald*, 23 June 1900, p.5). The area was to figure strongly in Joyce's *Ulysses* as 'Nighttown' and the reputation lives on in popular history as 'the Monto'. It was also an insanitary area but there seemed to be a reluctance on the part of the Corporation (as a whole) to do anything that would associate them with the place, to the point of not always referring to the area by name in their discussions. The local conditions bothered the Public Health Committee and their report in 1900 noted that it had long been advising that a scheme be progressed (Report 179/1900). They also suggested that this did not need the full application of the housing acts because the lands could be obtained by negotiation rather than compulsory purchase. It was believed that this would be far cheaper because of the ruinous nature of the houses and the owners seemed anxious to sell. The Corporation eventually listened and a proposal from the Public Health Committee (not the Improvements Committee) was approved at a meeting on 20 November 1900. The text noted that they (the Corporation) 'hereby approve of, and adopt, the Scheme framed by the Public Health Committee for the acquirement of the several houses, lands, and premises comprised in the Montgomery and Purdon Streets Area Improvement Scheme, 1900'. By 3 June 1901 the Corporation had the provisional order from the LGB empowering them to acquire the necessary property. Despite the advice of the Public Health Committee that NOT going to arbitration would be more cost effective, an arbitrator was appointed, and his report was complete by September 1902. This led to a Council decision on 12 September to raise of a loan of about £11,000 (Report 141/1902).

35. Montgomery Street and Purdon Street in the mid-nineteenth century. Ordnance Survey plan,
5-foot Sheet 18 (9), 1847 edition.

Getting the property was only the first step, the scheme had to be agreed. This
posed a difficult problem, one which was recognized in the title of the Public
Health Committee's report to the Corporation. They proposed a scheme for
'providing dwellings for the working class and the 'very poor''. The problem was
that the very poor could not afford very much but Dublin Corporation had yet to
accept the necessity of substantial subsidies. The categories of employment falling
into this description were enumerated in Report 183/1902 as labourers, the lowest
paid class of porters, small dealers, pedlars, hawkers, charwomen, rag-pickers,
night watchmen, the inferior class of seamstresses and sandwich men. This was a
category of people who might be expected to earn less than 16s. per week and who
could pay rent of the order of 1s. to 3s. per week. In fact, as the data for the 1913
Housing Inquiry would show, many would have earned a lot less than 16s. per week.

It was recognized by the Corporation that they could simply clear the area or they could put it profitably to artisans' dwellings but they accepted that they needed to do something for the class of people described above. This was going to be their first experiment in trying to house the very poor and they recognised that to this point they had been housing artisans or tradespeople. They suggested funding it with a 60-year loan, which, at the time, was longer than would be granted by the usual funding sources and would have to be from an outside source. If this could be done it would keep annual repayments to a minimum. However, though the scheme would not pay for itself, it was felt that the deficit could be contained to between £125 to £290 per annum, depending on what had to be paid for the loan.

As Report 183/1902 put it 'The Clearance Scheme, one to improve the public health, and to remove an eyesore from our midst, must necessarily be unproductive from a financial point of view; but a scheme for supplying municipal dwellings for the most dependent class of the people, following on a clearance scheme, need put little, if any, cost upon the ratepayers, while it is calculated to do much good directly and indirectly'.

Keeping costs down had consequences and this led the Corporation to approve a scheme which had some elements of the tenements that they were knocking down. What proved most controversial was the provision that only one water-closet and one scullery, with scullery trough and water supply, would be provided for every four of the cheaper tenements. Granted, this was better than the families would have previously experienced but it still represented a departure from what had been built elsewhere and there was unease in both the Local Government Board and within elements of the Corporation. Indeed Sir Charles Cameron voiced his objections and these were heard by the Local Government Board. This led the LGB to make a formal objection to shared facilities and in a letter to the Council which was read on 7 September, they commented that they were unable to withdraw their objections to certain sanitary defects in the scheme as pointed out by the Medical Officer of Health and the LGB Inspector. In fact, the Council had drawn breath and the Public Health Committee made much the same point in their Report 117/1903 which was accepted by the Council on 7 September 1903. In this, they noted the views of the LGB and reminded the Council that the Medical Superintendent Officer of Health (Cameron) had repeated advice (first given in relation to Barrack Street) that sanitary accommodation used in common by several families would never be kept in proper order. Even in the case of the most modest rental accommodation in Bow Lane, each tenement had its own sanitary accommodation. The outcome was that the w.c. was now in the same room in the one-roomed tenements but this too was less than ideal. It caused Anthony Roche, MRCPI to write complaining that 'living in air so tainted is universally accepted to be a cause of ill-health' (*Irish Independent*, 11 September 1906, p. 6).

The scheme now moved to implementation and the Public Health Committee reported in July 1904 (Report 103/104) that they had completely acquired the Montgomery Street and Purdon Street area and in pursuance of their Report 183/1902, dealing in detail with the scheme, they had 'laid full particulars before and have obtained the formal sanction of the Local Government Board to carry it out to completion in its entirety'. Following a public process, ten tenders were received

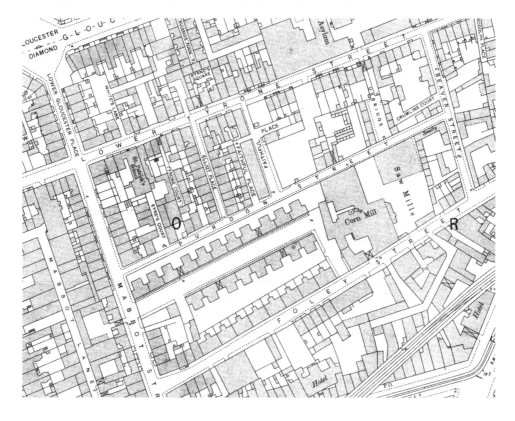

36. Montgomery Street and Purdon Street scheme, as completed. Ordnance Survey plan, 5-foot plan Sheet 18 (48), 1907 edition.

(Report 176/1903) and it was awarded to Mr Thomas Mackey (8 May 1904) with the usual condition that 'those employed on these works under the contract shall be paid the standard rate of wages paid in Dublin and district, and that regular tradesmen only shall be employed to do tradesmen's work, and that the hours and conditions of employment recognized as proper in the district shall be observed.'

The scheme involved the clearance of the existing buildings and their replacement with 25 blocks, five stories in height, facing a new street. In essence, this was a private road allowing the tenants access to Foley Street but keeping them away from Mabbot Street. The construction was described as being 'of the plainest' though of a most substantial character. The walls were built with Co. Dublin common stock bricks, without any internal plastering while the floors were breeze concrete, supported on steel joists on expanded metal, and laid with deal floorboards. All the tenements (except those on the ground floor) would be accessed by external balconies of steel and concrete. They provided 484 single-roomed dwellings at rents varying from 1s. 3d. to 2s. 6d. per week, 16 two-roomed dwellings at rents varying from 2s. 3d. to 3s. per week.

In addition, and to improve the social balance somewhat, facing Montgomery Street there would be eight, five-storey blocks containing 64 two-roomed dwellings at rents varying from 3s. 6d. to 4s. 6d. per week as well as 16 shop-tenements, each consisting of a shop with two rooms attached which were proposed to be let at 12s. 6d. per week, clearly aimed at better off artisans. There was no change to the external appearance of the buildings but the inner walls were plastered.

The *Irish Independent* reported that Foley Street was nearing completion in June 1906 (p.6). Montgomery Street had become Foley Street, commemorating the celebrated sculptor, among whose works was the O'Connell monument. Whatever the Corporation intended by this name change, which is seen on the Ordnance Survey extract (Figure 36), it did not change the nature of the environs.

The scheme was not a success and the Corporation struggled to find tenants, notwithstanding the housing crisis. At its meeting of 13 March 1911, the Council approved the following motion.

That as the Corporation Buildings in Foley Street are now almost completely unlet, representing a loss to the City of about £6,000 per year, this Council hereby instructs the Estates and Finance Committee to consider and report upon the advisability of reducing by one-half the rents of all the rooms the rents that have not already been reduced, as this would be the only means of inducing the Working Classes to dwell in the property.

The problem continued into 1912 and the minutes of the meeting of 9 December recorded the following approved motion.

That as there are 90 back rooms at present unlet in the Foley Street buildings – some of them never opened since they were built – owing to the exorbitant rent asked for them, the Estates and Finance Committee is hereby requested to consider the advisability of further reducing the rents of all the back rooms to one shilling per room; by so doing it would be of great benefit to the poor, and a source of increased revenue to the Corporation.

While councillors identified rent as the main disincentive they were well aware that there were other considerations but were reluctant to state them openly. An acknowledgement of the particular circumstances of the area was made in a reference to the tenements that they proposed to build in the Trinity Ward scheme. Noting their policy to build cottages they wrote that: 'This Course has been pursued in accordance with the experience which has been gathered from the Foley Street experiment, where a large proportion of these block tenement dwellings remains unoccupied. There may be other circumstances, however, operating against the successful letting of the dwellings in this locality into which we do not desire to enter'. When the successful tender had been announced back in 1904 a reporter from the *Irish Daily Independent* had asked the Chairman of the Public Health Committee, Alderman McCarthy, how they expected to get respectable tenants to live in the new dwellings or whether they will be deterred from going there by the 'undesirable character of the neighbourhood'. The Alderman's reply showed that the Corporation had considered this question carefully. He replied that the Corporation would be able to deal with any 'disorderly houses' remaining on Montgomery Street and the new houses would be cut off as far as possible from the 'restricted area in which the undesirables still lived'. The City Architect, Charles MacCarthy, explained further that 'everything possible will be done to protect the families of the prospective tenants of the new dwellings from the contaminating influences of such hideous spots as Elliott Place, Faithful Place etc. None of the new houses would be closer than 20 feet to Purdon Street and a twelve-foot wall would separate them from that street. There would be no direct access onto Purdon Street from the new houses and none of the windows will overlook it, except for the scullery windows in one row and even these could be provided with obscured glass. A new street would be constructed from Mabbot Street and round at the end of the tenements to Montgomery Street'. This satisfied the *Irish Daily Independent* and its report ended with 'these rough outlines of the great clearance scheme now in hands show that the Corporation have taken every precaution to safeguard the tenants from the contaminating influences of the adjoining dens of iniquity, and to give them ingress and egress to and from the new dwellings without being brought into contact with the wretched sisterhood of the streets' (*Irish Daily Independent*, 7 October 1904, p.5).

Eventually, the Corporation managed to find the appropriate rent level at which tenants were prepared to discount the reputation of the area and (Housing) Superintendent Verschoyle reported in Spring 1914 that all dwellings in Foley Street were let (Report 183/1914).

Trinity Ward, Townsend Street

Dublin Corporation tended to give the generic label 'Trinity Ward' to a number of small schemes in the south inner city. The 'ward' was the electoral area which had Trinity College as its focus and was a very mixed area. The fine Georgian houses of the Pembroke estate still retained their character and status. There were tenements but their greatest concentration was in the blocks between Great Britain Street (Pearse Street) and the river. As far back as the middle of the nineteenth century, the docklands and warehousing district on the southern side of the Liffey, east of Carlisle Bridge, had comprised a narrow belt of poverty in this otherwise prosperous part of the city. The parish priest of St Andrew's, Westland Row, writing to the Archbishop in 1861 noted enclaves of squalid poverty within this 'the richest parish in the city', with two, three, sometimes more families in one small room, 'the bed, straw or shavings, sometimes neither, the clothing, the rags they have on them during the day' (Dublin Diocesan Archives, file 1340 no. 78). These enclaves included all the lanes off Townsend Street, the streets between Townsend Street and the quays and the lanes off the quays. Not surprisingly, matters had not improved by the beginning of the twentieth century and the area was ripe for improvement. The difficulty was that though poverty was widespread, the worst manifestations were dispersed.

In 1905, the attention of the Improvements Committee was drawn to a block of houses on Townsend Street (nos. 179–190) in the block defined by Great Brunswick Street and Tara Street as being ripe for development. Thom's directory for that year shows all in tenements. Charles Cameron was particularly enthusiastic about an improvement scheme because being ruinous, they spoiled the streetscape and by building the Corporation could both provide housing for the working classes and improve the urban landscape. Trinity College owned nos. 185–189 but they refused to sell and the Corporation were not moved to use a compulsory purchase order. The other part was owned by a Miss Bowen who, being keen to facilitate working class housing, gave the land on a 500-year lease. It is odd that the Corporation decided to proceed with such a small scheme but an important consideration may have been that it was believed that the scheme would be financially self supporting

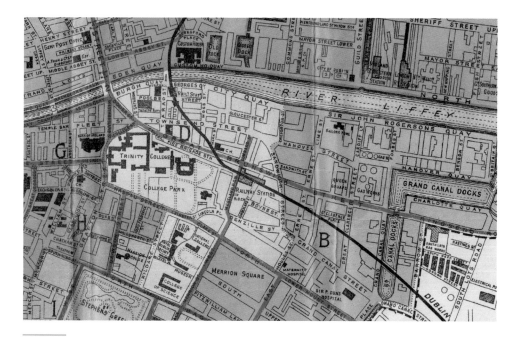

37. Trinity Ward, coloured yellow. Thom's Directory, 1911.

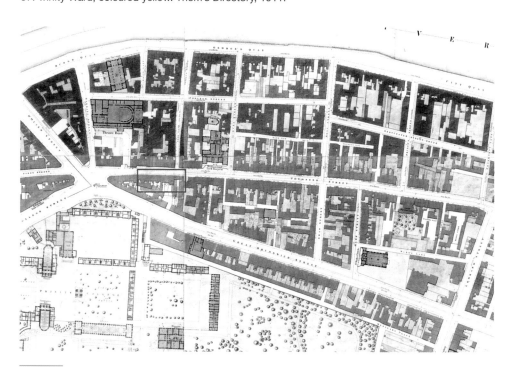

38. Western side of Trinity Ward in the mid-nineteenth century. The houses in question are on the southern side of Townsend Street to the west of the Lock Hospital. Tara Street has yet to be created. Ordnance Survey plan, 5-foot, Sheet 18 (14,15,21,22), 1847 edition.

39. The docklands of Trinity Ward. Extract from a 'Bird's eye view of Dublin'. Supplement to the *Illustrated London News*, 6 June 1846.

40. Dublin Corporation Buildings, Townsend Street, Summer 2020.

and might actually make a profit. The plan provided for three blocks four storeys high, containing 5 three-roomed tenements on the ground floor, and fifteen two-roomed tenements on the upper floors. The rents were 10*s*. 6*d*. for the ground floor, 4*s*. 6*d*. for the second floor, 4*s*. 3*d*. for the third floor and 4*s*. for the heady air of the fourth floor (Report 154/1905). These were rather expensive and were referred to as 'artisans dwellings' by the Corporation; they were clearly not aimed at the very poor of whom there was a large population in the area. It makes it more difficult to understand the enthusiasm for such a small scheme, though the Improvements Committee suggested that seeing this development completed might make it easier to deal with Trinity College in the future. The report was approved at the Council Meeting of 2 October 1905 and tenders were considered and decided upon on 5 November 1906 (Report 204/1906). The 1909 edition of Thom's directory notes nos. 180–88 as 'Corporation Buildings'. The buildings have been boarded up for some years but plans have been approved for the Peter McVerry Trust to refurbish the buildings, including the retail units, as apartments (An Bord Pleanála, PL29S.307790).

Cook Street

Cook Street was another awkward site, this time on the river side of Christchurch Cathedral and it proved difficult and controversial to complete. The Ordnance Survey plan shows how it was located adjacent to the old city wall but what it does not convey is the steeply sloping nature of the site. It rises very rapidly from Cook Street to High Street, the ridge on which the city was originally developed. Its development generated a great deal of debate around the question of whether it was worthwhile to engage with such sites when the results were going to be sub-optimal.

Attention was first drawn to the area in July 1904 by an influential deputation of the clergy of both denominations, several of the prominent merchants of the district as well as local Poor Law and Municipal representatives. Cameron undertook the required investigation and reported on the insanitary condition of the area in September 1904. It was going to be a messy scheme on a bad site. The

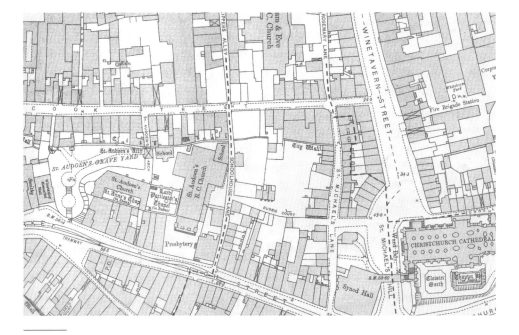

41. Cook street and environs before development. Ordnance Survey plan, 5-foot, Sheet 18 (56), 1907 revision, 1909 edition.

Improvements Committee pondered as to whether it was an unhealthy area (Part I) or whether there were just unhealthy buildings which could be dealt with under Part II of the legislation and would more properly come under the remit of the Public Health Committee. This was seen to be a simpler and cheaper approach. The Corporation soon took it back to the Improvements Committee but the Public Health Committee was reluctant to let it go and for a while two parallel processes were undertaken but with the knowledge of the Council who seemed to be able to cope with the potential for confusion.

The Public Health Committee obtained Council approval in 1907 to undertake a survey and valuation of the area (Reports 159/1907 and 281/1908). While this was going on a further deputation urging action was received. One member, Mr James Talbot Power, noted that as a large employer that there was a need for cheap, local dwellings in this locality. 'He instanced the case of his own firm having a considerable number of houses close to the distillery, which the employees were always most anxious to secure'.

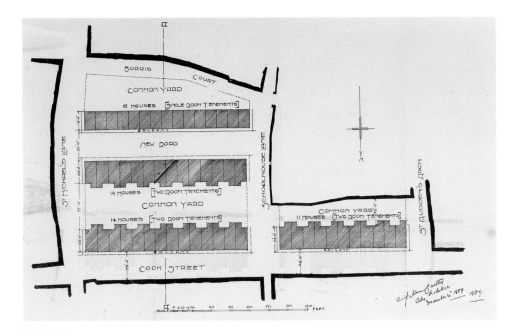

42. First thoughts on the scheme for Cook Street, 1909. Report 273/1909.

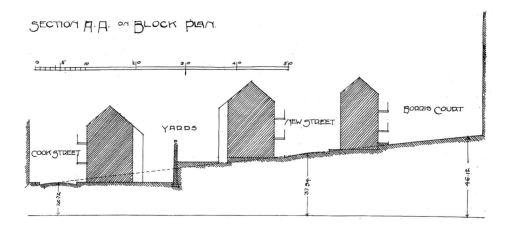

SECTION A.A. on BLOCK PLAN.

COOK STREET
YARDS
NEW STREET
BORRIS COURT

43. Difficulties of the Cook Street site, 1909. Adapted from Report 273/1909.

Eventually, the Council decided, having considered and approved Report 281/1908, to give the matter back to the Improvements Committee and told them to proceed with a redevelopment scheme. However, the Law Agent advised that Cameron needed to prepare another statutory representation and this was provided on 21 September 1909.

Consideration of the issue took some time and a number of meetings but the proposals for Cook Street were set out in Report 273/1909 (dated 14 December 1909) from the Improvements Committee which provided for 39 three-storey two-roomed flats, a total of 117 tenements and 15 three-storey one-room flats, a total of 45 tenements. The cost of the scheme was estimated at £18,207 with rents of 3s. 6d. for the two-room tenements and 2s. for the one room tenements, leaving an annual deficit of £40 6s. The difficulty of the sloping site is clear from the block plan and there was little room for anything but the housing. There was an area on the east side of Michael's Lane which was equally insanitary but the Committee proposed to leave it out of the scheme because the plot was too awkward to use for housing. They suggested that it be acquired at some future time and perhaps used as a play ground. It did not become a playground but it was ultimately incorporated in the reconstruction project of St Audeon's and the city wall. The area on which they proposed to build contained 83 families or 272 people. However, it was assumed that the people then living in Michael's Lane would apply to be housed bringing the total to be housed up to 105 families or 356 persons. On the site at the time were 29 tenements, 5 cottages, 4 houses in ruins, 4 workshops, 1 stable yard, 1 marine store and 4 waste sites.

The concept of an 'unhealthy area' was still sufficiently novel that the Improvements Committee thought it useful to include an explanation in its report. The principle that once it was decided that an area was unhealthy, there was an obligation on the Council to act was an important one and one that would prove useful to the Corporation in dealing with the Ormond Markets and Spitalfields schemes some years hence.

> The law respecting "unhealthy areas" is, that if the Corporation has before it in legal form an official representation from the Medical Officer of Health that any particular area is an unhealthy one, the Municipal Council is bound to take into consideration such representation, and if satisfied of the truth thereof and of the sufficiency of its resources to declare by resolution the area to be an unhealthy area and that an improvement scheme ought to be made in respect of same.

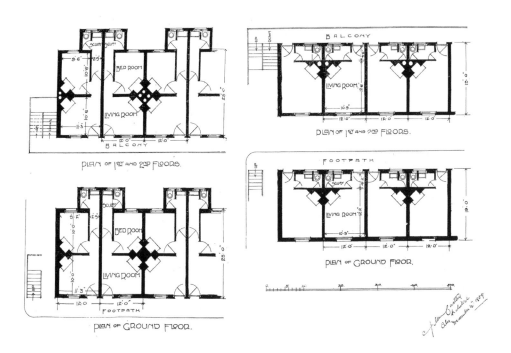

44. Proposed layouts for Cook Street, 1909. Adapted from Report 273/1909.

After passing said resolution the Council must proceed to make a scheme for the improvement of the area. Having regard to all the circumstances which have been brought before us, we are thoroughly satisfied that the conditions of the Cook Street area is such that, in the interest of public health, the clearing of it should not be any longer deferred.

It was also intended to widen Cook Street, Michael's Lane, Schoolhouse Lane, St Audeon's Arch and Borris Court, and to create a new road running east to west parallel to Cook Street (93 feet south thereof) from Michael's Lane to Schoolhouse Lane.

In the notes on the scheme, the Committee explained that their aim was to meet the needs of a very poor class of population who were paying on average *2s. 6d.* per week. Central to the Corporation's thinking in this was the desire NOT to put a burden on the rates. Their scope was rather restricted since they also needed to build decent housing and they were rather pleased with themselves with the solution that emerged.

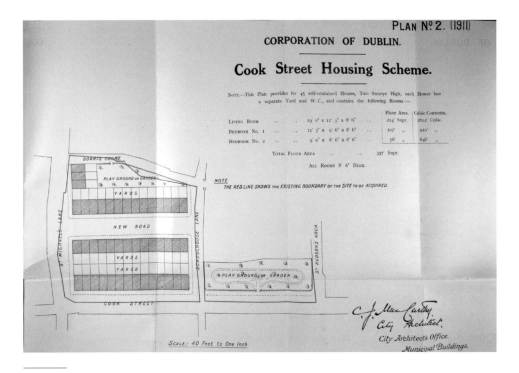

45. Modified plan for Cook Street, 1911 - 45 self contained houses, living room, two bedrooms. Report 178/1911, Volume 3, p. 164.

46. Cook Street development in 1987.

We have experienced some difficulty in formulating a scheme which, while suiting the requirements of the poor people in the district in the matter of accommodation and rent, would not entail any appreciable loss to the rates. Almost at every meeting since the Council remitted the matter for our consideration we have had the subject before us and plans for various schemes submitted'.

There was, however, a substantial loss on each scheme, with one exception, where the loss was set out at £1 per annum, but in this case we considered that an all-round rent of 4s. for each two-room tenement, which would have to be charged to produce this result, would be in excess of the rent-paying capacity of the people for whom we are to provide. As we were thus nearing the solution of the difficulty, the Deputy Borough Surveyor and Mr. Tallon (by direction of the Chairman and in the absence of the City Architect on annual holidays) continued to develop the matter on lines which the Committee laid down, viz. : reduction in constructional cost, so as to have the rents as moderate as possible consistent with the financial success of the scheme.

...

> The part of the scheme which provides for the two-room dwellings has been designed on similar line to that recently completed by the Kingstown Urban Council in Glasthule with the approval of the Local Government Board.
>
> We are strongly of opinion that if this scheme meets with the success which we anticipate there is no reason why, under our existing limited powers, a number of slum areas could not be similarly dealt with.

Consideration of these plans took time and came in for some criticism during the discussion in the Council, who though they approved the scheme in general outline wanted some reconsideration of the small size of the rooms without adding to the loss on the scheme. In any event, the Improvements Committee already had a new proposal and they prepared Report 26/1910 in January 1910. This offered a re-orientation of the blocks so that they could increase the number of two-roomed units while decreasing the number of one-roomed units but the scheme was still one of tenement blocks. The new arrangement also allowed for an increase in the depth of each room by 3 feet. 'The result of this re-arrangement will be the reduction in the one-room tenements, which, while desirable in a limited way, are not considered to be popular with the working classes or remunerative to the City'.

The reports indicate that as the Improvements Committee struggled with their approach to the development, the question of balancing costs with provision never being far from their minds.

> It should be mentioned that your Committee from the start were anxious to have the rooms as large as possible, consistent with cheap rents, and entailing no loss to the ratepayers. The scheme originally recommended by the officers and Committee appeared to be the best that could be made in the circumstances. Your Committee are, however, glad to be able now to recommend the re-arrangement suggested, which, while leaving the rents as before, increases the size of the rooms and reduces the estimated loss to the rates.

The annual subsidy required was now £23 per annum in a scheme that would house 174 families in 45 units of two-roomed, three-storey tenements and thirteen units of one-room, three storey tenements.

The Public Health Committee prepared a report at the same time (13 January 1910) which recommended an increase in the area to be cleared (Report 27/1910).

Report 26/1910 was first considered at the Council meeting of 7 March 1910 when it was decided to refer it back to the 'Committee for further consideration and a plan submitted to Council at next meeting'. That consideration took place on 21 March 1910 at an ill-tempered meeting when the Council approved the plan without modification. The motion demonstrated a degree of exasperation. They had considered two plans within a period of three months but they were still no nearer getting anything built.

> That the report be adopted, and that the Law Agent be instructed to bring the proposed re-arrangement before the Local Government Board Inspector at the Inquiry, and to inform him that the Council, while prepared to carry out the scheme as originally adopted, is equally prepared to carry it out in the modified form mentioned in the report, provided the Inspector approves of same.

Immediately afterwards during that same Council meeting came consideration of the report of the Public Health Committee. They wanted the site extended so that they could build a proper scheme. It would have been chaotic had this plan been accepted so the Council voted to send it back to the Public Health Committee for more consideration.

This was not to be the end of the matter. The required LGB Inquiry began on 14 June 1910 with P.C. Cowan in the chair. On the second day of the inquiry, Mr Cowan expressed the view that the Corporation was trying to fit too many houses on the site. He felt that they would be better to go for a large scheme rather than piecemeal ones. The City Engineer in reply said that the Corporation was trying to save the rates. Mr Cowan said that he would report that the houses were cleverly designed but they were too small. He proposed to adjourn the meeting to a yet-to-be-agreed future date and he asked the Corporation to prepare a report on the entire area, including the parts which they had omitted. However, there must have been discussions in the background because the Inquiry resumed on 18 June for a session which the *Freeman's Journal* referred to as 'exciting' (*Freeman's Journal*, 20 June 1910, p.4). At that meeting, Mr Cowan made it clear that he was going to adjudicate only on the scheme as proposed, which prompted a cranky response from the Corporation's counsel about the work which had been involved in getting Mr Cowan the information he had requested. Mr Cowan replied that 'there appeared to be a little heat, which he regretted'. With some further discussion the Inquiry was concluded, and the provisional order was sent to the Corporation on 12 October 1910.

The final shape of the scheme was still not decided. Just as Mr Cowan was considering the scheme as outlined above, the Improvements Committee was having a further reconsideration which was discussed at the Council Meeting of 26 September 1911 and duly approved. They decided not to build on the entire site but to leave an area between Schoolhouse Lane and St Audeon's Arch as an open space. This they hoped would go some way to meeting the views of a considerable group of citizens who favoured having the entire area as an open space. Moreover, this plot adjoined the back wall of St Audeon's which 'would overshadow the building, shut out light and air, and annul the cheery aspect and comfort of the dwellings generally'.

At this point in policy evolution, the Council had come out against flat blocks and the language of Report 178/1911 is similar to that used in other reports. It was reported that

> The City Treasurer has advised us that the block system of dwelling has proved most objectionable, and that a very strong feeling exists among the working classes against such style of dwelling. Besides, they are more expensive to maintain, and vacancies are more frequent and numerous. Self-contained cottages on the other hand are rarely vacant, and the demand for the vacant ones is always very great. It was also contended that the housing of such a number of families in block dwellings on this area would make the place too congested, and ultimately develop unhealthy conditions, and eventually tend to produce the evils which the Corporation are endeavouring to eradicate (Report 178/1911).

The report offered three approaches but did not suggest that the project be discontinued. The first suggestion, made by the City Engineer, kept the flat blocks but reduced their number. There would be two rows of 14 blocks, each containing two roomed-flats over three storeys and providing accommodation for 84 families. This does not appear to have been even considered by the City Architect, who instead concentrated on the two proposals for cottages, also suggested by the City Engineer, in his report. The first was for twenty-eight three-roomed cottages 'precisely similar' to those then being erected at the 'Oblate' site and which would cost £130. Under this plan, only a small proportion of the area would actually be covered with buildings, the greater portion would be converted into a playground or garden for the use of the public. The City Architect suggested to the Improvements Committee that they might like a greater density of development on the site and the third idea (and ultimately the one favoured) was for forty-five two-storey houses of the same type. The parlour was spacious with a capacity of 1,812 cubic feet while the bedrooms were a standard 910 cubic feet and 646 cubic feet respectively. A comparison of this plan with the earlier 1909 (figures 42 and 45) one shows that the site to the west was now reserved as a playground or garden. The suggested economic rent (based on what a landlord might get) would be 4s. 6d. per week. It was pointed out that this was the same as the charges in St Joseph's Parade where the houses were significantly smaller whereas the houses in Elizabeth Street which were of similar size to those now proposed (though still smaller) were let at 5s. 6d. per week.

P.C. Cowan's report gave the Dublin Citizens' Housing Committee, an enthusiastic lobby group, the opportunity to express again their concerns. Making the point that their views were not specific to Cook Street, they wanted Dublin Corporation to reconsider the use of Part I rather than Part II of the Act. Part I invariably involved a cost on the rates while Part II, theoretically at least, involved forcing the property owners to undertake the necessary renovations. The Committee felt that the Corporation was too negative about the quality of its powers to force such action and was too ready to undertake the work itself (*Irish Times*, 9 July 1910, p.8).

The Local Government Board approved a loan of £9,650, in a letter dated 5 January 1912. The Council moved quickly and at its meeting of 1 April 1912 approved the housing, subject to the work not beginning until the Corporation had full possession of the site and had levelled it (Report 66/1912). Building soon followed and the City Treasurer was able to report in Spring 1914 that so satisfied were the tenants that he had no difficulty collecting rent. Both the City Engineer and the City Architect were of the view that Cook Street did not need to be widened, as had been suggested. They felt that the condition of the footpaths was good and that the volume of traffic did not justify the significant expenditure that would be involved (Report 87/1914). However, the report of the City Treasurer to the Housing Committee was more persuasive. He argued that the environs badly needed a clean up. It seemed that there was a ready supply of stones which the local urchins used with great effect against the windows of the houses. He also argued for the widening and the Housing Committee instructed the City Engineer to have it done (Report 183/1914).

The Cook Street scheme survives intact to the present day, though Cook Street itself never generated the volume of traffic its widening expected. This gives a great deal of light and air to the houses that front onto the street. It remains a small enclave of individual houses in an area of mixed land uses where the 1930s flat block of St Audeon's House is the main housing component.

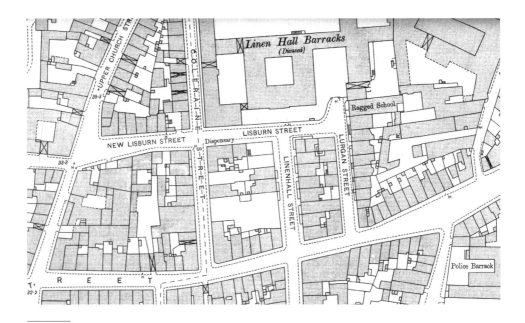

47. Lisburn Street and Linenhall Street and environs. Ordnance Survey plan, 5-foot, Sheet 18 (46), 1907 revision, 1909 edition.

Lisburn Street/Linenhall Street

The area between Capel Street and Smithfield had many sites in need of redevelopment. There has already been discussion of Barrack Street / Benburb Street, Blackhall Street and Mary's Lane. Plans were in hand for larger developments on Church Street and around the Ormond Market and these are discussed in detail a little later here.

The clearance of an adjacent insanitary area bounded by Coleraine Street, Lisburn Street, Lurgan Street, and North King Street was recommended late in 1911 (Report 177/1911). The proposal in the report was to acquire all property within the block except for 1 Lisburn Street and 24–30 North King Street. The intention was to construct 48 three-roomed, two storey cottages on the cleared site at a weekly rent of 4s. 6d. A large portion of site was to be retained as a playground. The space for the playground can be seen clearly on the 1939 Ordnance Survey plan and it and the houses retain their original character today.

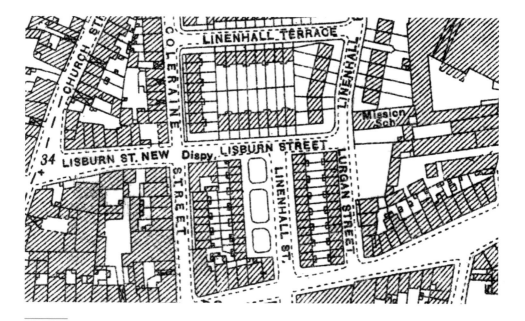

48. Linenhall Street and Lisburn Street as developed. The area set aside for a playground is clearly visible. Ordnance Survey plan, 1:2,500, Sheet 18 (7), 1939 edition.

49. Present-day Linenhall Street.

The estimated cost was £6,690 with expenditure of £130 per cottage. This was sufficient to yield a profit of £15 2s. 4d. Each of the cottages would have a separate yard and w.c. The dimensions were within the normal range. The living room had a fairly common dimension of 19 feet x 11 feet 3 inches (1,812 cubic feet) while the bedrooms offered 901 cubic feet and 646 cubic feet respectively. The standard high ceiling of 8 feet 6 inches was once again provided because of the superior air circulation it allowed. The site was commended to the Council as being easier than the Cook Street scheme and the report was adopted by Council on 13 November 1911.

Inherited schemes

The boundary of the city was extended in 1901 as a result of the Dublin Boundaries Act, 1900, to encompass what had been the independent townships of Clontarf, Drumcondra and (New) Kilmainham. It would be not until 1930 that Rathmines and Pembroke were finally absorbed. The townships had been undertaking social housing projects of their own and Dublin Corporation now inherited a number of projects in different states of completion.

Elizabeth Street, Drumcondra

Drumcondra Urban District Council had obtained a lease from Mr Francis Butterly from 25 March 1900 for 177 years on Elizabeth Street, Drumcondra. They had planned to put twelve cottages on the site but it fell to Dublin Corporation to build the scheme and they decided on (Report 194/1901) 14 two-storey cottages with gardens at a cost of £2,700. The ground floor would have a living room 16 feet

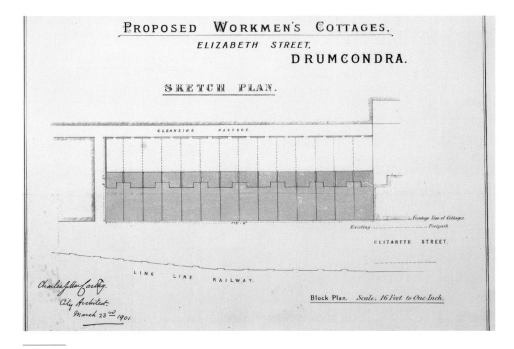

50. Elizabeth Street planned development.

x 11 feet 7 inches with scullery and w.c. and two bedrooms on the first floor. The living room and larger bedroom would have fire places. There would be a concreted yard of 10 feet and a garden with a total depth of 32 feet. The plan placed the cottages in line with the existing street, fronting onto the Link Line Railway but it was noted they could be set back some 7 feet with either gardens to the front or wider footpaths. This was perhaps because the railway embankment rises to the upper storey at least, diminishing natural light and also giving the street a somewhat confined air. However, this option was not taken and the existing street line was maintained.

The report was considered at the Council meeting of 6 January 1902 and referred back for further consideration of costs. This was interpreted by the committee as meaning that a reduction in costs was needed. This was done in Report 43/1902 but without changing the basic nature of the scheme, they managed to increase the profit to £47 17s. 11d. This report was approved on 5 May 1902 and tenders were accepted on 2 November 1903 (Report 122/103).

Rent was set at 4s. 6d. per week which would yield a profit of £42 14s. 8d. However, the rents were soon increased by 1s. per week without the formal approval of the Council. This generated protest in the Council Chamber but the City Treasurer retorted that it had proved impossible to raise money on the basis set out in the original report and he did not believe that it was the intention of the Council to provide a substantial subsidy to the tenants. It is a measure of what the Council thought that no further comment was made on the increase.

Oblate

The site known as the 'Oblate', located in Inchicore, was purchased by the Corporation in 1901 for £4,000. A housing development to cater for the large local working class population was provided for in the legislation dealing with the absorption of the (New) Kilmainham township (Report 81/1902). The Corporation had inherited a site on St John's Road of a little more than 1 acre but it was seen as being both too small and too far removed from the main centres of employment to be useful. Consideration instead moved to two sites – the 'Oblate' and 'La Barte'. Both were deemed suitable but the Oblate site was chosen.

This was a site of about 12.5 acres and was part of the property of the Oblate Fathers. It occupies an excellent position between the ground immediately adjoining the Oblate Church and the Great Southern and Western Railway Works, 'from the employes (*sic*) of which the great majority of the tenants for the proposed dwellings would be drawn, besides which the site is most healthfully situated, and is within convenient distance of the churches and schools in the district. The ground contains ample space to provide a scheme of dwellings, capable of meeting the fullest demands for proper housing accommodation for the artisan and workingman population in the Kilmainham and Inchicore districts'.

The City Architect suggested that there would be space for 350 houses on the site, 47 of which would be four-roomed houses, two storeys high, 210 would be three-roomed houses, two storeys high, and 93 would be small two-roomed cottages. (Report 81/1902).

The scheme which was agreed by the Council at its meeting of 1 February 1904 and set out in Report (178/1903) was somewhat different and involved only about one

51. Recently completed Dublin Corporation Housing in Inchicore at the junction of Nash Street and O'Donoghue Street, 1911. DCLPA.

third of the site, reflecting their view of the immediate need. The plans were for three classes of dwellings. The 14 Class A houses would cost about £245 to build and would be rented at 10s. per week. These would have five rooms, a bathroom and utilities. The 55 Class B houses would have four rooms, a bathroom and utilities and would cost £175 to build. These would be rented at 7s. 6d. The 55 smallest houses, costing £120 to build, would have three rooms and would be rented at 4s. 6d. per week.

The required inquiry was held by Mr. P. C. Cowan on 21 July 1904 and the decision of the LGB was communicated by letter on 5 November 1904. Mr Cowan did not approve the proposal and sent it back to the Corporation for further consideration. He was of the view that it was a good site and he noted that Dublin Corporation would be building both to meet local needs and to relieve congestion in the centre; both aims of which he approved. At the same time, the rates were high in Dublin city and the Board did not approve, at that particular time, of building at a scale which was in excess of the statutory obligations which Dublin Corporation had acquired as a result of the boundary extension.

Equally, he could not see why they wished to build houses which would command a weekly rent of 10s. He pointed out that good houses in the private sector were available for between 5s. and 10s. and he wondered how houses of the class that the Council was contemplating could be seen as meeting the needs of artisans. Indeed,

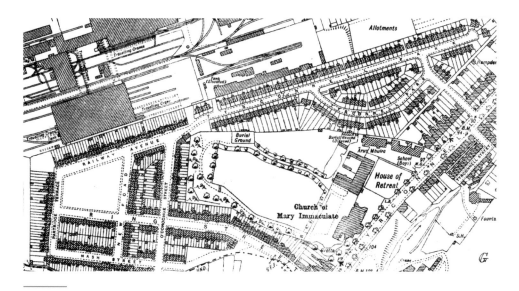

Oblate development. Ordnance Survey plan, 1:2,500, Sheet 18 (IX), 1943 edition.

he reminded Dublin Corporation that they had objected when Kilmainham UDC had sought in 1900 to build houses with rents of 7*s*. Therefore, his decision was that he would not approve funding for any houses at rentals in excess of 7*s*. 6*d*.

The reconsideration involved the elimination of the Class A houses and meeting an objection of Mr Cowan to the location of the w.c. within the Class C houses by moving it outside. The Corporation hoped that this would be enough to get the LGB on side and that they would not press their view on the scale of the development. In that regard, the Report (22/1905) made the point that they had the land and keeping it idle cost money. In addition, it made more sense to build in larger units than piecemeal. The revision proved acceptable to the LGB and an invitation to submit tenders was published in early July 1905 (*Irish Times*, 6 July 1905, p.11) and ten firms submitted bids. The tender required that the builder would use local labour, unless excused, and would pay the minimum standard rates for the Dublin and District area with the usual conditions of employment. The tendering process raised a new issue for the Corporation and one which would recur from time to time; the question of direct labour. Up to this point, the Corporation had made use of private contractors but the suggestion was that the Corporation should employ the necessary workmen directly and so exercise total control over the process. The law agent expressed the view that there was no legal requirement for the Corporation to build via contract and that, as long as they could be assured of getting value for money, there should be no issue for the Corporation in using direct labour. The City Architect commented that he did not have the resources directly under his control to do this but that since the houses were simple to build, it would be possible to employ a Clerk of Works who would do the recruiting and management of the project. The joinery would have to be outsourced to the one of the large firms in the city and the Corporation would have to expend some money on items such as scaffolding and other plant. He felt that in such circumstances that it could be done but not otherwise and he suggested that the approach should be tested with the 22 B houses on the north side of the entrance road (Report 129/1905).

Report 238/1906, adopted on 3 December 1906, noted that the first section of housing was complete and recommended that the streets be named O'Donohoe Street, Ring Street and Oblate Street (amended to Nash Street at the Council meeting). There was still a lot of ground available and in 1908, the Council approved a proposal (Report

91/1908) to build 110 Class C (3-room) houses on the site. The Corporation had come to the view that the three-room house was more popular than the larger one. These would be let at 3s. per week, rents for the first phase having been reduced from the initial intended amount of 4s. 6d., with 6s. per week now being asked for the larger houses. The application was considered at an Inquiry, under P.C. Cowan, which began on 21 June 1909. The Corporation was seeking money to do mains drainage, extend the electricity grid, buy a rubbish 'destructor' and the proposal for just over £17,000 for housing was a relatively low-ticket item. The Dublin Citizens' Association took an active interest in all of the proposed expenditure and in addition to the presence of members of the Executive Committee, had formal representation. Alderman Vance sought to replay the Council discussion by stating that he objected to the scheme on the basis that it involved a continuing loss, year after year (*Irish Times*, 24 June 1909, p. 9). However, the scheme was approved and following a tendering process in March 1910, that of George P. Walsh for just over £13,000 was accepted (Report 81/1910). This was almost £5,000 less than the tender of one of the more established companies G.&T. Crampton. The following year, as Mr Walshe (*sic*) was completing the 110 houses, it was decided that there was space for some additional houses on some angular plots which had been left out of the plans; six in Ring Street, five in Nash Street and three in O'Donoghue Street (Report 12/1912) – note how the Council had already confused the spelling.

This left a plot of about 4 acres which some tenants used for growing vegetables until the Corporation decided in 1913 that housing would be a better use and approved the construction of 113 cottages at a cost of £160 each. Because they would be slightly bigger in area than the more recent cottages in the scheme, though not with more rooms, the Housing Committee report to Dublin Corporation (208/1913) recommended a rent of 5s. per week. The development was approved in January 1914 by the LGB on condition that the size of the bedrooms be increased to not less than 960 cubic feet (Report 87/1914). It will be seen below that the Council itself soon decided on a minimum of 1,000 cubic feet.

Mooney's Lane / Conquer Hill, Clontarf

Report 57/1901 noted that a 'very influential delegation' had waited on the Improvements Committee at their meeting of 28 May 1901 'for the purpose of directing attention to the pressing need which exists in the neighbourhood for

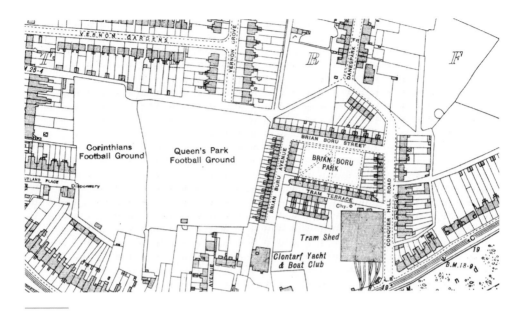

53. Conquer Hill development. Ordnance Survey plan, 1:2,500, Sheet 19 (V), 1938 edition.

providing additional accommodation for the Working Classes living in the Clontarf District'. A housing development had been commenced in the final days of the township and the delegation was anxious that Dublin Corporation would take up the reins. The site, originally obtained from Colonel Vernon, was 2 acres and 16 perches and 10 working men's dwellings had been completed. The Improvements Committee was supportive and recommended that building be continued.

A complication arose in that Councillor Judge attended a meeting of the Improvements Committee and made an assertion, which he later confirmed in writing, that it would not be necessary for the Corporation to proceed any further with the work because a bequest had been received from the late Mr Allingham of Dublin. The nature of the bequest was not described but it seems to have removed the need for any funding. This was noted in the Committee's report (157/1901) which came to a Council meeting on 3 March 1902 and the Council voted to delay consideration of the scheme for three months. An additional six months was voted on 2 June 1902. Clearly there were discussions in the background because the same Councillor Judge proposed on 12 August 1902 that the six month delay be rescinded and that the report recommending building be adopted. This was agreed and led to the following motion on 6 April 1903.

> That owing to the present condition of the working classes in Clontarf, and the consequent urgent need for the erection of suitable dwellings for them it is hereby resolved that immediate action be taken by this Council to carry into effect the scheme already adopted, and that the Town Clerk and Law Agent take all proceedings as at be necessary for that purpose.

However, some more reconsideration was required on foot of the Local Government Board Inquiry. The original scheme provided for 9 two-storey houses, having gardens attached, 9 three-room cottages, similar to those on the site which had been erected by the Clontarf Urban District Council, and 64 two-room cottages (Report 157/1901). As part of his inquiry, which he held on 21 April 1903, the LGB Inspector, A.D. Price on this occasion, visited the houses already constructed and came to the view that two-roomed dwellings would be too small and asked that the plan be reconsidered. This left the Improvements Committee in a quandary since they were concerned that those whom they were housing would not be able to afford three-roomed accommodation. The idea of a Corporation subsidy did not immediately enter their considerations and they asked the Council for direction (Report 80/1903).

The Council decided at its meeting on 10 August 1903 to ask the Improvements Committee to work out the cost implications of the Inspector's recommendations. The reconsideration appeared in Report 116/1903 which was considered and approved by the Council on 7 Sept 1903. In the meantime, the area had been renamed to Conquer Hill Road.

The revision provided for 49 three-roomed cottages and 9 four-roomed two-storey houses. It was noted that the cost of this revision would be £1,300 less than the previous scheme but the profit would be reduced to £51 9s. 2d. It was also noted that rents at 4s. 6d. and 3s. 6d. were considerably lower than the market but in fixing these rents initially, the Committee was influenced by the fact that the cottages built by Clontarf Urban District Council had already been let at 2s. 6d. Further reconsideration was contained in Report 126/1903 and this was discussed and approved at 5 October 1903.

This was the result of a rather odd circumstance. The Council was invited to a meeting of local interests in the local Presbytery on 14 September. This resulted in a proposal for a reduced scheme of 9 four-roomed two-storey houses at 4*s*. 6*d*. per week, 14 three-roomed cottages at 3*s*. 6*d*. per week and 24 two-roomed cottages at 2*s*. 6*d*. It seemed that while working class accommodation was required, the demand was not as great as suggested by the Council.

The Improvements Committee Breviate for quarter ended 30 June 1905 (Report 130/1905) noted that they had 'received a report, dated 2 June, from the City Architect that the 9 A class houses (four rooms) facing Conquer Hill Road were now complete and ready for occupation, and the nine B class houses (3-roomed cottages) will be ready for occupation in a few days'.

Leaving some ground unbuilt did not sit well with the Council and they returned to the scheme in 1908. They decided that there was room for either 36 two-roomed or 20 three-roomed cottages. The recommendation, approved by the Council on 1 June 1908, came down in favour of the 36 two-roomed cottages (Report 81/1908). This was despite the previous rejection of such housing by the LGB.

The houses were never built. The City Treasurer reported that there was no demand in the district for two-roomed dwellings and that any people occupying such moved to three-room dwellings whenever the opportunity presented. He advised further that there no demand for any cottages at that time and that it would be advisable to wait for some time until demand picked up. This was recommended to the Council and approved on 9 August 1909.

Time for Reflection 1913–1915

The period between 1913 and 1915 was a time of major reflection and set Dublin Corporation on the path it would follow until 1930. A new Housing Committee was established in 1913 and they took the opportunity to produce a digest of the what had been accomplished. Even before the Housing Inquiry which would take place later in the year, it seems that there was considerable criticism of the Corporation's impact on the problem, in this case from the Recorder of Dublin, the chief magistrate for the city.

On 10 March 1913, the Council agreed to a motion by Councillor Partridge and Councillor O'Hanlon:

> Having regard to the oft-repeated-and fully reported-complaints of his Honour the Recorder of Dublin about the manner in which the housing of the Working Classes of this City is neglected by this Council, the Town Clerk be, and is, hereby instructed to submit to this Council a report showing what this Council has attempted or achieved in the matter of providing proper housing accommodation for the working classes of Dublin in the past, and what they contemplate doing in the immediate future: and, that the first copy of the report printed be immediately dispatched to His Honour the Recorder.

This was done and appeared as Report 90/1913 from the Housing Committee, another in a very useful series of occasional summaries. This also gives a snapshot of rents. Rents were fixed for each scheme by reference to the ability to pay of the tenants, the nature of the accommodation, the official view of what constituted an economic rent and the voting strength of the various groups within the Council. Comparisons between new and older schemes were constantly being made and there was pressure to modify rents. The following two tables summarise the position.

Development Costs and Number of Units

Development Costs	£	Units
Coombe	24,817	216
Plunket Street	29,479	138
Benburb Street	27,920	144
Bow Lane	10,325	86
St Joseph's Place	26,219	80
Blackhall Place	12,070	85
Bride's Alley	99,721	174
Elizabeth Street (Drumcondra)	2,227	14
Mooney's Lane (Clontarf)	6,946	57
Oblate (Inchicore)	35,489	220
Foley Street	63,607	460
Townsend Street	3,612	20
Cook Street	9,650	45
Donnycarney		8
Total	**352,082**	**1747**

Notes

The Coombe and Plunket Street developments were built by the DADC with the Corporation's involvement limited to providing them with a cleared and serviced site. The Donnycarney cottages were completed by the North Dublin Rural District Council before the city boundaries were extended in 1901. The cost was not known.

Housing Schemes, Type of Accommodation and weekly rents

Number	Type	Rent Shillings	Rent Pence
Benburb Street			
5	Shops with four rooms	10	0
4	Three-room tenements	5	0
3	Three-room tenements	4	9
2	Three-room tenements	4	6
8	Two-room tenements	4	0
19	Two-room tenements	3	9
16	Two-room tenements	3	6
10	Two-room tenements	3	3
12	Two-room tenements	3	0
28	Single rooms	2	0
14	Single rooms	1	9
23	Single rooms	1	6
Bow Lane			
3	Shops with two rooms	5	6
2	Shops with two rooms	5	0
2	Three room tenements	4	6
3	Three room tenements	4	0
19	Two room tenements	3	6
19	Two room tenements	2	6
19	Two room tenements	2	0
St Joseph's Place			
80	Three room cottages	4	6
Blackhall Place			
15	Four room cottages	7	6
5	Shops with two rooms	6	6
5	Two room tenements over shops	3	6
14	Two room tenements	4	0
14	Two room tenements	3	9
14	Two room tenements	3	3
14	Two room tenements	3	0

Number	Type	Rent	
		Shillings	Pence
Bride's Alley			
22	Three room tenements, ground floor	6	6
22	Three room tenements, first floor	6	6
22	Three room tenement, second floor	6	0
14	Three room tenements, third floor	5	6
28	Two room tenements, ground floor	4	0
28	Three room tenements, first floor	4	0
28	Three room tenement, second floor	3	9
10	Three room tenements, third floor	3	6
Elizabeth Street			
14	Three room cottages	5	6
Mooney's Lane			
10	Original three room cottages	2	6
9	Four room houses	4	6
14	Three room houses	3	6
24	Two room cottages	2	6
Oblate			
55	Four room houses	5	6
220	Three room	3s. to 4s.	
Foley Street			
110	Single room tenements	1	0
270	Single room tenements	1	6
16	Three room tenements on ground floor	4	6
16	Two room tenements on first floor	3	6
16	Two room tenements on second floor	3	6
16	Two room tenements on third floor	3	0
16	Two room tenements on fourth floor	3	0
Townsend Street			
5	Three-room tenements, ground floor	7	6
15	Two room tenements, ground floor	3	6
Cook Street			
45	Three room houses	4	6

The report uses 'houses' and 'cottages' inconsistently; there does not appear to be any difference.

Report 83/1913 was yet another synopsis for the Housing Committee of much the same data as Report 90/1913 and presented at the same time. The format was somewhat different and deals more with potential schemes and there are some small inconsistencies between the two reports. Report 83 describes a growing difference with the LGB over rent. The Council noted that they (the Council) had introduced a new policy which both increased the size of accommodation and reduced the rent. Thus the schemes for Church Street, Ormond Market and Weavers Square would have bedrooms of 1,000 cubic feet capacity (see discussion below) as against 910 and 646 cubic feet in the two-roomed dwellings which they previously provided. They had also fixed the rent at 1s. per room or 3s. per tenement.

The Local Government Inspector, P.C. Cowan, had not been impressed. While his concern to provide good housing was not in doubt, he always looked for value and was concerned about the impact on the rates of the city, which were generally agreed to be very high.

> The Chief Engineering Inspector of the Local Government Board found himself unable to coincide with this new departure of the Corporation, and suggested that it would be well if the Corporation would re-consider whether, by approaching the housing problem on such revolutionary lines – producing large deficits on each scheme – it would not be paralysing its efforts to deal with the problem on a large scale, and which will meet the requirements of a city like Dublin, where there is so much tenement overcrowding. Mr Cowan has since been interviewed by the officers with a view of getting some more definite information as to the particular class of scheme he would be prepared to recommend.

The schemes which were underway at the time included Lisburn Street and Lurgan Street, Church Street and Beresford Street and Ormond Market while the Corporation felt that they would be allowed to proceed with Trinity Ward and Weavers Square. Other sites under consideration, some more advanced than others, were included in the discussion.

- Spitalfields and Ash Street
- Francis Street
- Mountjoy Street
- Southern Side Mary's Lane
- St James' Walk
- Marshalsea Barracks
- Marrowbone Lane
- McCaffrey Estate (South Dublin Union)
- Mrs Ryan's property, Dolphin's Barn
- Fairbrothers' Fields

The concept of town planning was still relatively new but people in Dublin were well aware of the idea and of its potential. Councillors had read of and visited model villages such as Port Sunlight and Bournville as well as the garden suburb at Hampstead in London. One of the outcomes of this growing interest was a Civic Exhibition in 1914. It was seen as an opportunity where all interested in the question of municipal housing and planning, among other interests, could gather and discuss the issue with international experts. One of key elements was an international competition for a town plan; a plan which would set out the opportunities for the expansion and development of the city. A substantial prize of £500 was provided by the Lord Lieutenant and the adjudicators were Professor Patrick Geddes (Edinburgh), Mr John Nolen (USA) and Mr Charles MacCarthy (City Architect). The winner was Patrick Abercrombie and this set up a personal relationship between him and the city which would last the remainder of his life and an institutional arrangement with the University of Liverpool which would persist into the 1960s. Despite its unofficial status the plan (*Dublin of the Future*) set the agenda for the next twenty years. It also brought Patrick Geddes, already a major force in planning and regular visitor to the city, into close contact with the officials of the council. Raymond Unwin was another regular visitor to the city and the Corporation seized upon the opportunity in 1914 to draw on the expertise of both.

Another major happening, which might not have been seen so positively, was the inquiry into the housing of the working classes which took place under the aegis of the Local Government Board in late 1913 and which reported in February of 1914. It contained a robust assessment of the Corporation's approach to the housing issue and of the performance of both councillors and officials. Many of its conclusions were challenged equally robustly by the Corporation but whatever about the apportioning of blame, the report was important in setting out clearly what needed to be done. It prompted another stock taking in 1915 and brought much clarity to future directions. Though the decision to hold an inquiry was quickly made and the inquiry equally quickly conducted, it could not have come entirely as a surprise. For some time, various interest groups had been concerned about how the housing question was progressing. The apparently slow rate of progress bothered many while the cost of what was being done bothered others. Those with a particular interest in town planning were concerned about the piece-meal nature of the developments. There were also voices which claimed that Dublin Corporation was an unfit body to deal with the problem having so many slum landlords and publicans on its Council. For its part, Dublin Corporation felt that it was not receiving enough support from the State but that it was doing rather well considering all the obstacles in its path.

1913 Housing Inquiry

The decision to hold a housing an inquiry was prompted by two particular happenings. The first was the labour unrest that characterised 1913. Observers were concerned with the syndicalism which they detected in elements of Larkin's organisation. Poor housing and bad working conditions provided the energy for this and there was fear that it might lead to revolution if handled badly. This and the other concerns, already mentioned, were given keener focus when two tenement houses, nos. 66 and 67, in Church Street collapsed during the night of Tuesday 2 September. Seven people were killed and others injured. The death toll would have been much higher, both houses were fully occupied, had the residents not had some notice of the imminent collapse and evacuated the building. It seems that those killed were caught in the hall of No 66, just as they were about to get out.

The Church Street area was subject to an Improvement order and Dublin Corporation had a new housing scheme in development. This, of course, brought into focus the whole process of tenement management, inspection and closure as well as the pace of redevelopment. It emerged at the inquest that the houses had been inspected by the Corporation, that defects had been noted and brought to the attention of the landlord. Repairs had been undertaken and the Corporation's inspectors were satisfied with the outcome. Though the houses were old and clearly had some problems, it was the firm position of the Corporation, the landlord and of the workers who undertook the repairs that the houses were basically sound and that their collapse was not foreseen. The Coroner's Jury agreed but noted that they were unable to determine the cause of the collapse (*Irish Times*, 20 September 1913, p.14).

This both reassured and worried commentators. There was no obvious dereliction of duty by anyone involved but the failure to predict the collapse raised the question of how many other such houses were there in the city.

The editorial in the *Irish Times* for 20 September summed up much of the thinking in the city. They were not entirely sure about the verdict, feeling that the best that could be said about Dublin Corporation was that they had received a 'Not Proven'

129

verdict. The editorial writer suggested that even if Dublin Corporation had acted to the best of its ability, that 'the problem of the slums had grown too big for it'. They suggested that what was needed was a coming together of the various interests in the city and the pooling of resources and skills. There was a need to involve both business and philanthropy because 'our large employers of labour have still much to do for their workers. That fact has been brought home to them disagreeably by very recent events'. The trades unions would be involved and funding would come both from the rates and from private capital. It would be a committee of citizens. The key role of delivering the housing would still be the Corporation's responsibility, a position which was widely accepted by commentators though not by everyone.

It was one thing to write in such terms, it was another thing entirely to get it to happen. An inquiry was being suggested in many parts and the *Irish Times* agreed that this could be useful as long as Dublin Corporation did not do it. Others felt that an inquiry would be perfect for prevarication and allowing the heat to dissipate. The idea of a Viceregal Commission was in the air. It would have the status necessary to both determine the facts and to impose the solutions.

This idea quickly gained support and the Chief Secretary Augustine Birrell came under increasing pressure to establish one. The Dublin Diocesan Synod of the Church of Ireland passed a resolution at its meeting of 20 October calling for a Viceregal Commission (*Irish Times*, 21 October 1913, p.10). The Association of Municipal Authorities held its second annual meeting in Dublin with a focus on the housing problem. They decided against a Viceregal Commission and agreed that they would send a deputation to the Chief Secretary asking for increased State aid. This produced an infuriated response from the *Irish Times* which was labelled as 'mischievous' by the Lord Mayor of Dublin (see 16 October 1913, p.4 and 17 October p. 3). This editorial writer who was not as well disposed to the Corporation as was the writer of 20 September, stated that Dublin Corporation was not a fit body to be entrusted with a large scale housing programme.

> In the meantime the Dublin Corporation remains a body which scarcely loses a single opportunity of demonstrating its utterly unbusiness-like character... Our housing problem consists in the existence of an enormous number of rotten tenements, and it is aggravated at every turn

> by the drink question. So long as the Dublin Corporation is controlled largely by members representing slum-owning and liquor interests, so long it must be an improper and incapable body for dealing with the housing problem.

The editorial was just as dismissive of the Corporation's chances of getting State funding. They added the imminence of Home Rule into the equation and argued that there was no chance of the remainder of the UK taking on additional liabilities in Ireland at this point and that the Home Rule Bill was going to provoke national bankruptcy.

Notwithstanding these comments, the Association's delegation met the Chief Secretary and the Lord Mayor briefed the Council on the meeting on 20 October 1913 (*Irish Times*, 21 October 1913, p.5). They had been received politely but got no commitments. The Chief Secretary took the opportunity to let it be known that he was not in favour of a Viceregal Commission but that he would set up a Local Government Board Inquiry which would meet in private. The Lord Mayor seemed happy enough with an inquiry which would look at the scale of the problem, the nature of housing to be provided and what sites to use. He also gathered that it would cover Ireland, so Dublin would not be particularly exposed. His only disagreement was with the idea that it should be held in private. It seems he was of the view that the Corporation had a good story to tell.

Mr Birrell had some formidable deputations to meet before he could dispose of the Viceregal Commission. Two such were received on 31 October. The first was led by the Countess of Aberdeen, the President of the Town Planning and Housing Association. As the wife of the Lord Lieutenant and the founder of the Association, she had at least to be listened to and she secured the presence of both the Lord Lieutenant and the Chief Secretary. Her delegation argued strongly for a Viceregal Commission. It would look at the housing question and prepare a comprehensive scheme to tackle it. A focus on Dublin only would ensure that the business could be done expeditiously and a comprehensive scheme would ensure that it was not done 'in little pieces'. They also received a detailed answer from Mr Birrell who explained that, though he had not yet made up his mind (he had!), he favoured a departmental inquiry over a Viceregal Commission Essentially he felt that a departmental inquiry would do everything that a Viceregal one could do but would do it faster and better, since it had the power to examine witnesses under oath.

The second delegation was from the Dublin Citizens' Association, essentially a business-focused organisation. They had taken considerable interest in the various inquiries undertaken by the LGB into Corporation housing schemes with a keen focus on costs. This too was the focus of their deputation. They wanted a Viceregal Commission which would focus on Dublin and be complete within six months. They wanted it to inquire why it cost so much to undertake housing schemes and why it cost half a million pounds to run Dublin Corporation. They wanted it to look at the question of suburban sites, what kind of housing to provide and whether buildings could house more than one family. They got somewhat less time than the previous delegation, but the position was of Chief Secretary was unchanged.

The *Irish Times* was not impressed, especially as it suggested that a local government inquiry, comprising four members, had already been set up and waited only for the announcement. They dismissed Mr Birrell's arguments and said that 'Mr Birrell's public case against a Viceregal Commission is so emphatic, and at the same time so weak, as to make us curious as to the nature of his private objections to it'. While they acknowledged that Mr Birrell had given way on his intention to hold the inquiry in private, they questioned the suitability of the Local Government Board to conduct what would essentially be a trial of Dublin Corporation because they reckoned that they were 'acclimatized to the methods of the Dublin Corporation' (*Irish Times*, 8 November, 1913, p.10).

The *Irish Times* was correct. The Local Government Inquiry, a four-person committee, had been formally established on 3 November with these terms of reference.

I. How far the existing accommodation for the housing of the working classes is inadequate in view of the ordinary requirements of the working classes in the city.

II. The general circumstances of the working classes in Dublin with special reference to the amount of rent they can reasonably be expected to pay for suitable accommodation.

III. To what extent, it is possible by the exercise of the powers granted by the existing law to remedy the housing conditions of the working classes in the City.

IV. The finance of housing schemes which have been carried out by the

Municipal authorities or other agencies for the city workers, and the class of accommodation provided by such schemes.

V.   What measures (including any legislative amendments) you would suggest for dealing with the housing problems in the City and the probable cost of any of the schemes so suggested.

The inquiry members, Charles H. O'Conor, S. Watt, J.F. MacCabe and Alfred P. Delany, examined 76 witnesses, under oath, over 17 days from 18 November to 23 December. This evidence was augmented by the use of published research and that conducted by their own team. The report was published on 7 February 1914, which must be acknowledged as a remarkable achievement. The minutes of evidence, which ran to 393 pages, was published at the end of March, much to the annoyance of members of the City Council who wished to challenge statements.

It was an important report, especially because of the wealth of factual material, not only for Dublin, which it gathered. The *Irish Times* was correct, though, when it said that it would be a trial of Dublin Corporation. The report was quite tough in its assessment of the Corporation. It recognised the work done but also made it clear that what they had achieved was nowhere near what was needed. They accepted that the Corporation had made good use of the legislative framework in the provision of housing but they were very critical about their application of the sanitary laws. They felt that the failure of Dublin Corporation to ensure rigid enforcement of these regulations had made matters worse and had allowed poor housing conditions to thrive. They were particularly critical of Sir Charles Cameron for effectively turning a blind eye to many houses that should have been closed. Cameron had argued that rigid enforcement would have caused great hardship by making homeless people for whom there was no other provision. The report would have none of this.

> In extenuation of the want of rigid enforcement of the laws, it was put before us by Sir Charles Cameron and others that the stringent enforcement of the sanitary laws might inflict great hardship, as it might lead to the eviction of a number of people. While we cannot dispute the truth of this plea were the enforcement of hitherto dormant powers suddenly and drastically exercised, we cannot help coming to the

conclusion that had a judicious but firm administration of the powers already given been exercised during the last 35 years since the passing of the Public Health Act, 1878, it should have been possible without any undue hardship being inflicted to have produced a better state of affairs than exists at present, and especially as at one time during this period the population of Dublin reached the lowest point it has touched for 60 years.

While they did not hold the Corporation directly responsible for Cameron's actions, it was the want of 'firm administration' that allowed him to act as he did. That lack of 'firm administration' was responsible for other problems.

(33) Before concluding this aspect of the question, we must state that in our opinion the low social conditions among the poorer classes in Dublin are in some measure due to the failure to enforce stringently the sanitary laws, though we do not suggest that this feature is peculiar to Dublin. While we say this, we are aware that there are other contributory causes arising from the past history of the country, and the tendency of the rural population to come into the cities and urban areas. A firm administration would, however, in our opinion, have deterred the rural labourer from coming into the City and the absence of such administration must therefore be held to have produced a converse result, and to have had the indirect effect of keeping wages at a low level.

We suggest also that the non-enforcement of the sanitary laws has permitted dwellings which are not fit for habitation to be inhabited by the poorer classes at rents which though in some cases low in themselves are altogether excessive for the class of accommodation provided.

Further it would seem to us that the want of a firm administration has created a number of owners with but little sense of their responsibilities as landlords, and that it has helped much in the demoralisation of a number of the working classes, and increased the number of inefficient workers in the city.

We suggest also that the provision of sanitary dwellings by private enterprise has been to some extent handicapped by unfair competition with insanitary dwellings which could be let at rents that would not pay for the provision of decent homes.

It was quite damning in that the Corporation was accused of creating, even fostering, an environment which was a lot worse than it needed to be, regardless of their efforts in providing good housing. The report did not expand on what caused the lack of firm administration, except to draw attention to a number of councillors who owned tenements or second class housing. A total of seventeen members of the Council owned 91 properties with special attention given to named individuals. The reader was left to draw his or her own conclusions.

> The principal owners of tenement houses sitting as members of the Corporation, are Alderman H. O'Reilly, Alderman Corrigan, and Councillor Crozier, who are returned to us in the evidence as either owning or being interested in 9, 19 and 18 tenement houses respectively, and in 4, 13 and 1 small houses, while ten other members of the Corporation own or are interested in one to three tenement houses, and Alderman O'Connor owns or is interested in 2 tenement houses and 6 small houses.

> (30) We regret to have to report that some of the property owned by the three first named gentlemen, and from which they are deriving rents, is classed as third class property by the Sanitary Staff, or in other words that it is unfit for human habitation. A feature which makes this all the more discreditable is that actually on some of this class of property, both Alderman O'Reilly and Alderman Corrigan are receiving rebates of taxes under Section 75 of the Corporation Act, 1890. Councillor Crozier is also receiving rebate on property which, though not classed as being unfit for human habitation, is not, however, in our opinion in such a condition of repair as to warrant a rebate being given, and does not comply with the express conditions required by the Corporation.

The report was more positive about the housing schemes undertaken by the Corporation, though it was noted that they tended to be small and scattered. They also accepted the fact that the Corporation should be the agency to undertake the necessary housing development: 'The housing question is so intimately bound up with many other questions over which the Corporation have and must continue to have control, that the creation of another body would only add to the difficulties which already surround the problem'. There was a role for private enterprise and they made suggestions as to how incentives might be provided.

Specific Proposals

The Report made it abundantly clear that the housing programme needed to be accelerated and operated on a scale previously not considered possible. There was an urgent need for 14,000 houses to replace those already unfit for human habitation or which soon would be. This meant that housing had to be provided on virgin land in the suburbs. Therefore they disapproved of much work being undertaken at the start of the process in the inner city. They did not, as some commentators have suggested, disapprove of *any* inner city redevelopment. They wanted a quick win and that required scale that was only possible in the suburbs. Later on, the question of inner city sites could be considered. It was accepted that the scale of development required planning and schemes needed to be seen in the overall context of the city; a civic survey was needed. This was all going to be very expensive and it was estimated that, at current levels, the annual deficit that would result from economic rents not being charged would be of the order of £100,000. Clearly this could not be raised from the rates, so it was suggested that the State would fund £60–70,000 of this cost. This would be a very tall order indeed.

Though the Council hated much of the report and their response will be dealt with below, they accepted the need for planning, scale and a concentration on suburban development. They also came up with a creative solution to funding.

Corporation's response

The first opportunity that the Corporation had to respond formally to the report came at its meeting on 23 February 1914 (*Irish Times*, 24 February 1914, p.5). The main business of the evening was to inaugurate the Lord Mayor and the new High Sherriff but the opportunity was taken to comment on the report. The Lord Mayor, Mr Sherlock commented that he was not going to offer an analysis of the report since the Housing Committee was going to do that. In fact, he offered much the same analysis that the Housing Committee would later publish. He was displeased that commentators and the newspapers had chosen to focus on the failings of the previous 30 years rather than on the recommendations that the report had made to solve the housing crisis.

He then provided his analysis of the complaint against the Corporation which, he said, could be summarised in broad terms that they had allowed houses to be inhabited which were unfit to be occupied, that they had not asked for the powers they needed, that overcrowding had been allowed, that tax rebates had been improperly given and that they had made a mistake in concentrating on small schemes.

His response was that the Corporation had been required to proceed with caution because every time they proposed a scheme, the consideration that seemed uppermost in the newspapers, the ratepayers and the Local Government Board was cost and not considerations of decency and public morality. He expected that the Housing Committee would deal with the accusation of laxity in the enforcement of the sanitary laws (see below) but he gave a brief summary of what had been achieved under the direction of Sir Charles Cameron. They had built small schemes because the Local Government Board had advised them not to close houses until the replacements had been built. Moreover, they had been accused of not doing enough to deter rural-urban migration. The Lord Mayor pointed out that the Corporation had tried to introduce a requirement that nobody be employed on a Corporation housing scheme with less than two years residence in the city but the Local Government Board had prevented this. He dealt with a variety of other aspects of the report in what was a good summary and justification of the Corporation. It also laid many of the criticisms made by the LGB firmly at the door of the same Local Government Board.

He also provided an analysis of what needed to be done. It was his opinion that the Corporation should not build any more in the old city until they had undertaken significant building in the suburbs. He recognised that this was a debateable point but he wanted that debate to take place. It was also necessary to decide on the style of dwellings – cottages, flats or the tenements which they were building in Foley Street or Digges Street (see below). They had to decide on a system of rents which was independent of the district in which the houses were located and they had to decide on housing density. He finished with a rousing invitation which was met by applause.

The duty of the hour and of the year is to concentrate not in wordy battles as to what has been and is, but as to what should and shall be. Let there be united effort on the part of all sections and classes to determine general lines of policy, full and free discussion to what was best and feasible; pressure on the Government for financial assistance and other suggested changes, and elimination of all party spirit and controversy. Let them in this year of 1914 recognise their responsibility not only to the city but to the nation. Let no words or acts here be open to use by Ireland's enemies to create public opinion against Home Rule. Let them show by their calmness, moderation and business capacity that they could face and deal with an abnormal situation mainly caused by the abnormal position of the country in being deprived of the right to govern itself.

The Housing Committee did indeed produce its Report (20/1914) and expounded at length on the various criticisms. They quoted extensively from the evidence presented to the inquiry to show that the conclusions were irrational and unfair. The general tenor of their comment was that the Corporation had been the victim of a process which was destined from the outset to show them at a disadvantage. They took particular exception to the attack on Sir Charles Cameron, noting that they had accepted his advice because of the esteem in which they held him and because of the evidence he presented. The cynic might suggest that they also recognised that an attack on him was an attack on them. The members, Thomas Kelly (Chairman), Charles Murray, William Cosgrave, Peter O'Reilly, W.J.M. Coulter and Alfred Byrne were particularly annoyed that the report's conclusions were available some time before the evidence was published.

They had concerns from the beginning, especially when the committee was named and it was seen that only one member had direct experience of the housing issue. They also disliked the fact that while the evidence was taken in public, the deliberations of the committee were held in secret.

When the personnel of the Departmental Committee of Inquiry was communicated, the Housing Committee, after careful consideration, decided to forward a protest to the Local Government Board against the composition of the Committee of Inquiry. We would naturally expect that, for the purpose of inquiring into such a complex and far-reaching problem as the housing of the working classes in Dublin, men of large experience – either as experts in dealing with social problems or eminent sanitarians – would have been appointed. On the contrary, of the four gentlemen who comprised this Committee of Inquiry, one only had in any way come in contact (and that merely in a remote capacity) with the housing, sanitary, and general work of the city. It was therefore, apparent to us when entering this protest, that officials devoid of any experience of the general administrative work of the Corporation, could not take that wide and sympathetic view of the origin and advancing stages of this great social problem, and the numerous difficulties which lie in the path of the Local Authority in endeavouring to solve it. The fact it was evident to us at the outset that the Committee of Inquiry had set its face against taking any broad or comprehensive view even of the Corporation's activities in other departments of public work and the many great schemes for the improvement of the city which have been carried out in recent years, all of which are associated, in one way or another, with the housing and sanitary conditions as they exist at present. We were glad, however, to observe that, on the occasion of the recent debate in the House of Commons on this question, the Chief Secretary for Ireland (Mr. Birrell), who is also President of the Local Government Board, gave full credit to the Dublin Corporation for the great municipal undertakings which it has successfully carried out, while at the same time, with its limited resources, providing to a greater extent proportionately for the housing accommodation of the working classes than any other city in the Three Kingdoms (p. 156).

They felt that they were being criticised for NOT doing the impossible. If they had evicted the 14,000 people found to be living in unfit housing, housing them would have cost £3.5m, a sum which clearly they did not have. The Commission exceeded its brief in that the Housing Committee believed that the job they had been given was to take evidence as to how much additional accommodation was needed and how this could be obtained. Instead, much of the report is a 'general attack on the Corporation of Dublin in its Public Health administration, which was proved to be without foundation by witness after witness. We say the report is discounted, so far as that attack is concerned, by the fact that in no single instance is that testimony of efficiency once referred to'.

It was also an issue that photographs had been included of poor housing areas but without noting that these were the subject of schemes being considered by the Housing Committee.

They complained that Cameron had been unfairly treated and they provided detail on how the death rate had reduced in Dublin since he was appointed. They also noted that the governance structure of the city conspired to make the death rate look worse since it left out the wealthy townships. In overall terms they made the point that Cameron had closed as many tenements as might be expected. 'The easiest way for a sanitary officer to close an insanitary house is to get a closing order. That wipes it off his books and saves him further trouble. It is far harder to get the owner to make it sanitary and keep it so. If all the tenement houses that were unfit at any one period since 1878 were closed, or even half or one-fourth of them, there would be a house famine in the city among the working classes.'

They were particularly annoyed at the charge that Cameron had been lax and they went into considerable detail, quoting from the evidence, to demonstrate the opposite. The Report should, they believed, have taken into account the reasons advanced by Sir Charles Cameron. The Corporation's Housing Committee was 'disposed to regard the view of an eminent sanitarian of his reputation as likely to be the more reliable in an issue of this kind, apart altogether from the fact that in his evidence he fully justified his action'. In overall terms, the Housing Committee's view, supported by the evidence in the report was that:

> The allegation that the sanitary laws were not strictly enforced in reference to insanitary houses is unfounded and absurd. In Sir Charles's period of office after repeated efforts to get 4,313 houses put in repair closing orders were obtained. No closing order can be obtained until the notices, and the issue sometimes of two or three summonses have been

ineffectual. There is no city in the United Kingdom in which so many insanitary houses have been compulsorily closed without compensation to their owners.

In addition to the Committee's formal and closely argued viewpoint, there was a personal memorandum by the Chairman of the Housing Committee, Alderman Thomas Kelly. This was a more reflective and philosophical piece in which he defended the Corporation, teased out the reasons for the present crisis and mused as to the way forward. He argued that the biggest problem was the depth of poverty among the working classes. If work was plentiful and wages were good, then it would be easy to solve the problem of housing. Until that was solved he could not see a solution to many of the social evils in the city.

> The great difficulties which have to be overcome in dealing with the problem of housing in the City of Dublin compel me to wish that a better spirit had shown itself in the various discussions in the Press and on the platform that have taken place in the past nine months. Without in any way doubting the bona fides of those who took part in them, I must say that the constant and persistent reflections on the capacity of the personnel of the Corporation, the continued iteration that 'out of Cork Hill nothing good can come,' leaves a suspicion that those who write and speak thus are not entirely actuated by a desire for reform, and that personal and political bias may provide a motive as much as the public good.

Turning to the recommendation of the report that housing be concentrated in the suburbs, he wondered how a population living on the minimum subsistence wage would be able to survive in the suburbs where prices were higher.

> I wonder if those theorists who gave evidence before the Commission, or who have written letters, or have made speeches on the housing question, will undertake the practical experiment of living on 18/- per week, with their families in suburban residences, and then tell us how it was done. Must also the small traders, who cater for the wants of the workers, migrate and open new shops near the proposed cottage dwellings, and pay increased rents and expenses – though where the capital is to come from to do it I don't know – but if the proposal is to be carried out they must move or starve.

He also wondered what was to happen to the land in the city made vacant by the migration of the population. Perhaps they might be left as open spaces or used for factories or public buildings in some uncertain future. He finished with a plea to the citizens of the city.

> I do not want to convey that the present policy of the Corporation regarding the housing of the working classes is the ideal one, but I do say that it is the best and most practical, having regard to the present circumstances and conditions. The Corporation propose to vastly improve localities now decayed or decaying. They propose no words or lip-sympathy or sentiment, but bricks and mortar and laths and plaster. They propose to give decent, clean dwellings where such do not exist to-day, and if the Corporation's policy is prevented from being carried out, it is certainly up to those who prevent it to show that they are able to do as well within as reasonable a time. If they are not able to show that they can do so, it is the duty of every citizen to maintain and uphold the Corporation's efforts.

The year had certainly been tempestuous for Dublin Corporation. They had started off with a measured assessment of what they had done and what they were going to do. They had an ambitious programme and they felt that they could deal with the criticism that came their way. Within months they found themselves and their housing programme on trial and they emerged somewhat bruised and battered. The level of personal criticism in the report is astonishing by today's standards as was the willingness of people to debate it without immediate resort to injunctions and judicial review. Yet, by early 1914, the Corporation had much to be pleased about. They had survived the inquiry and were validated as the appropriate agency to undertake the badly needed housing programme. They now had clear goals and it was admitted that they could not be expected to fund the programme entirely from their own resources. That renewed confidence resulted in their next important action in the development of policy.

International Validation
Unwin and Geddes

By 1914, the city had become accustomed to Mr Raymond Unwin and Professor Patrick Geddes and their fervour for the concept of town planning. Seeking advice from them, though, seems to have been a tricky matter. There were sensitivities within the Council. The Citizens' Housing League offered, on 6 July 1914, a consultation between them, Mr Unwin and Professor Geddes with a view to improving the schemes under review by the LGB. This was rebuffed by the Housing Committee who took the view that the time had passed for such an intervention. However, the City Council passed a resolution on 10 August 1914 which asked Mr Raymond Unwin and Professor Geddes to comment on the developments proposed for Beresford Street, Church Street, Ormond Market and Trinity Ward Schemes. The vote was far from unanimous, Sinn Féin members opposed the suggestion. The Lord Mayor then suggested that there would be a consultation with Unwin and Geddes that would involve representatives from the Citizens' Housing League as well as officials and members of the Council. This was also summarily rejected by the Housing Committee who instructed its officers to prepare notes and plans for Unwin and Geddes only (Report 229/1914). The impatience of some members with the idea of involving Unwin and Geddes is seen in a motion proposed by Councillor Cosgrave on 5 October 1914 but which was ruled out of order. In essence, since the consultants had not yet delivered their report, this asked to Council to forget about it and proceed with the schemes as previously agreed (Minutes, 5 October 1914).

After all of that, the consultants got on with the job of reviewing the Corporation's schemes and their views were contained in Report 78/1915 which was noted by the Council at its meeting on 2 November, 1914 and referred to the Housing Committee. It was a very comprehensive report, particularly for one completed in such a short time and it went beyond the brief suggested by looking at other proposed developments and making general observations about the nature of the housing problem and the solutions required. This generated interesting responses from both Corporation officials and members of the Council, making the report required reading for anyone interested in the development of housing policy in Dublin. It is fair to say that the members of the Housing Committee were not overawed by the reputations of their international consultants but some of their advice seems to have been absorbed.

Unwin and Geddes went on a field excursion and looked at the various sites which were under active consideration at the time. They passed through Crabbe Lane, near St Stephen's Green and Redmond's Hill Cottages near the Meath Hospital where they noted the advantage of having good front gardens, which were four feet deep and mostly well cultivated. They seem to have been shocked by Ash Street and Spitalfields and saw it as 'evidently a very bad quarter', which needed more extensive improvement than present plans showed. It was so bad that they suggested that bringing families of more respectable character into the area would lead to their degeneration. Living in such a neighbourhood could not be favourable to anyone seeking steady employment. They wondered if would not be possible to devise a scheme that would link up the DADC developments and the Guinness Trust. New Row, and other improved buildings on the Meath Estate was approved of. The houses had small garden fronts, evidently cared for and appreciated but though Brabazon Playgrounds were both excellent, they were still quite insufficient for so large a population.

Their short comments on other sites were as follows:

- Fairbrothers' Fields – Despite inconvenient accesses this is an excellent site. We think the existing plan admits of improvement in road communications, &c.; and submit a sketch plan and memorandum thereon. [Plan No. 2, I. and ll.].

- McCaffrey's Fields, South Dublin Union site (about 10 acres, but 4 acres reserved by Guardians), an excellent situation and exposure, though the slope of the ground interferes with conventional planning.

- Inchicore, Great Southern Railway – Large cottages for railway workers, with the garden plots generally well cared for. Planned so far with only traditional bye-law streets; but these could be diminished with economy and advantage.

- Cook Street Area – This site has the disadvantage of extreme sunlessness, and of consequent permanent low hygiene, despite substantial endeavours of the City Architect, who has done what was possible under difficult circumstances.

The remaining ground might more profitably be reserved as an open space, in fact as a playground, with trees enough to give the effect of a small park. The importance of this central situation for Town Planning improvements should also be kept in view.

- Great Western Railway, an excellent situation, the accesses to which might be readily improved. This whole neighbourhood seems well adapted to City Extension.

- Jervis Street Lots – Small, difficult, and troublesome to superintend. Suitable neighbourhood for Rent Collecting by methods of Octavia Hill, &c.

- Beresford Street, Church Street, and Ormond Market – We considered these sites with their whole neighbourhood in peculiar detail, and append a separate report, see Part II.

General Comments on the Housing Issues

Unwin and Geddes felt that the housing problem in Dublin had many unique features with housing and poverty two separate but entwined issues. Rather than there being a shortage of houses of a particular type, there was a general lack of good houses. Building new bad houses just to address the accommodation problem on a temporary basis was not a real solution. They had a clear view as to what constituted a 'good house', drawing attention to the then new standards for accommodation for rural labourers in England (Cd. 6708, 1913) and pointing out that these people were similar in income to those in the Dublin slums. Their view was that health improved with lower densities and that open space, fresh air and sunlight were potent factors in promoting health. The most efficient way to provide this space was to give bigger gardens because, they assumed, the extra produce which was grown would significantly contribute to the rent of the house. They developed the argument that the return from building at high density was over stated and that high densities can actually be more expensive per unit (see Unwin, *Nothing Gained by Overcrowding*, 1912). Moreover in Dublin, much of the land available for building had no commercial value except for housing. The expectation that building in inner city areas would be at high density served to push the price of land up. However in the outskirts, the land was cheap and people could have a good house with a garden, which could help them pay the rent. Since they would be healthier then they would be more efficient. If those who could best manage it financially were the first to move to the suburbs, this would free better accommodation in the centre, reducing pressure on rents.

They disagreed with the approach of buying up small, irregular plots of bad property in central areas and rebuilding a large number of houses there. It was too expensive for the small return received because the site required too much work and not enough houses could be built. They give the example of the Beresford Street area where the cost of land and development of a three-roomed dwelling was £81 versus £18 on Fairbrothers' Fields.

They understood that money would remain tight for Dublin Corporation so they suggested that the rateable value of the city could be improved by concentrating development on the main streets, removing dereliction on these streets and from those behind them. Essentially, they suggested that economic benefits would result from a sprucing up of the city but they did not explain from whom this additional money would be extracted.

In terms of overall strategy, they accepted that because of the very low wages of many, it would be necessary to house them in the city centre at low rental but what they outlined above offered the best opportunity and would facilitate the trickling down of better houses in the centre to the poorer classes by removing the better off to the suburbs. In the meantime, they asked that the Corporation be given stronger powers to deal with derelict sites and that, as a palliative measure, some money be put into refurbishing some of the better tenements. This was a short term measure only while the process they outlined above was taking place.

Comments on specific proposals

Trinity Ward

Trinity Ward, an area east of O'Connell Street and along South Brunswick Street (Pearse Street) continued to be difficult from the Corporation's point of view. Unwin and Geddes liked the opportunity these sites provided to renew the street frontage and so give a better overall appearance to the area. They liked the proposals for Luke Street, a small rather narrow street immediately to the east of Tara Street railway station. The narrowness of the street was probably in their minds when they suggested that the two buildings be moved back about 2m (5ft) from the street line. All they had to say about Moss Street and South Gloucester Street was that better access to the midday sun could be provided for the northern facing living rooms. In Townsend Street and Magennis Place, they felt that the scheme needed to be reduced from twenty eight to twenty four dwellings, otherwise there would be not be enough amelioration of congestion. They also suggested a revised plot arrangement which would give more air and light to the buildings.

> We think that the congestion of the buildings at the back of the street line is not sufficiently relieved. This might be mitigated on the West side by omitting the two end houses; but a simpler and more economical arrangement, as well as one giving more air and light about the buildings, with only the sacrifice of two additional houses is indicated herewith, (Plan 8). Its twenty-four instead of twenty-eight houses are certainly the maximum number of dwellings which should be put upon this site.

Ormond Market

They did not like the plan for Ormond Market. Since the site was immediately adjacent to the Four Courts, they saw grander possibilities for it. They could, they reckoned, achieve what was being proposed with a more economic layout but they chose not to put forward any proposal. The site was unsuitable for artisan housing, not because of any defect of the ground but because it would waste an opportunity to do something special around a building with the 'monumental dignity' of the Four Courts. Unwin and Geddes were town planners and they had an urban view which saw the city capitalising on the opportunities and advantages which it had. In their view, there were opportunities arising from the necessity of clearing this area – opportunities which would not otherwise be available – and it would be a mistake to close them off by hasty redevelopment. The town planning competition was underway and they must have known what was being suggested. A cathedral had long been an ambition of the Catholic Archdiocese and the town plan was going to make a firm proposal.

> We therefore strongly urge the postponement of this building scheme, at least until the Dublin Town Planning Competition now in progress, and its resultant exhibition of comprehensive Town Planning Schemes, have afforded the Corporation the materials for a more thorough consideration of this important site in its wider bearings. We would suggest for the present that it be cleared and levelled as an Open Space, retaining only such buildings as may be useful as shelters, &c.

As will be discussed below, they were not only ones who had an interest in keeping the site for other purposes.

The Beresford Street / Church Street Area

The Beresford Street / Church Street scheme was generally liked but here too the possibilities for grander urban design weighed heavily with them. This block was also likely to be required for the environs of the new cathedral. They wrote of a *Via Sacra* which would provide the access to the cathedral and which would be 'unparalleled among cities of the world.' The planning scheme would also need a *Via Practica*, which would require the improvement of Church Street and Bridge Street, Lower and Upper. These routes did not require the abandonment of this scheme but rather the avoidance of anything that would limit the possibilities of the town plans. They were clearly thinking of what Abercrombie had suggested.

So, they felt that there was scope to reduce the number of houses on this site but that the value of the development could be improved by extending it to North King Street and including the derelict area on the south of May Lane. They did not see the need for additional new roads and felt this cost saving would go a long way to meeting the revenue loss from reducing the number of houses. The Corporation's response was quite interesting, if not terse.

The Report (78/1915) approves of the Church Street site for a Housing Scheme, but proposed an entirely new lay-out which would have involved a large extension of the building area, principally on the east side, the construction of a new route passing from south to north, and a reduction in the number of cottages from about thirty-nine, as proposed by the Housing Committee, to twenty-four per acre. It is pointed out that the number of through roads shown on the Committee's scheme is unnecessary, with a different and somewhat extravagant layout, by reducing the number of cottages from 156 to 95 – or a loss of 61 cottages. The cottages are laid out in blocks of from two to eight of irregular and costly plan, and having front gardens with extensive open garden spaces at rear, as well as a central playground. The proposed arrangement is typical example of English Garden Suburb Planning, and in our opinion thoroughly impracticable within the congested area of a large city. Such methods of housing have achieved success elsewhere under totally different conditions, but not, so far as we are aware, at the expense of the ratepayers. The variety of cottage planning necessary to the artistic success of a scheme such as proposed by Messrs. Geddes and Unwin, would involve a corresponding variety of accommodation and individual cost, creating difficulties with regard to uniform rental and imposing on the tenants in every case a burden in connection with natural fences and garden maintenance.

Fairbrothers' Fields

They suggested some detailed improvements in the circulation system with new roads and new connections with existing roads but their most significant suggestion was to reduce dramatically the scale of the development. If no more than 450 houses were built it could reduce the amount of required road space by half while providing a large playground in the centre and all houses with a considerable amount of garden space. The houses should be good cottages. They presented figures which showed that the cost of providing a house with a plot size of 170 sq. yards, would be £59 compared to the £42 for a plot of 66 sq. yards in the Corporation's own draft scheme. Costing this on a weekly basis meant that for a modest increase in rent, the tenant would get nearly three times the space.

Marino

Even though Marino not under active consideration, Unwin and Geddes felt the need to comment on the proposals. The Corporation had considered a garden-suburb type development at Marino as early as 1910 but the property was not yet in their hands and the advent of the First World War had removed the possibility of getting the necessary funding from the Local Government Board. The knowledge that the land would revert to Dublin Corporation in the relatively near future also caused them to pause. Even so, Unwin and Geddes reported in considerable detail. They produced not only a sketch map of the site but also looked at how the existing farm land might be acquired, how the needs of the Christian Brothers might be accommodated and how the site might be improved by the acquisition of adjacent lands.

Taking Stock – 1915

Having had the opportunity to reflect on all that had happened over the past two years, the Corporation thought it useful to set out its agenda for the immediate future at the beginning of 1915 in Report 15/1915 (dated 8 January 1915). The list of current projects was as follows with a short commentary being provided on each.

- Lisburn Street and Lurgan Street (see 207/1913)
- Blackhall Place and St Paul Street
- Oblate Site (completion) (see 208/1913 and above)
- Trinity Ward (Luke Street, Moss Street, Magennis Place)
- Beresford Street and Church Street
- Ormond Market
- McCaffrey Estate (see 58/1915)
- Fairbrothers' Fields (see 16/1914)
- Spitalfields and Ash(e) Street (see 17/1914)
- Glorney's Buildings
- Crabbe Lane
- Boyne Street
- Mary's Lane (Southern Side) (See 18/1915)
- Cook Street (extension scheme)
- Nerney's Court
- North Cumberland Street
- Loftus Lane and Bolton Parade
- Little Ship Street and Werburgh Street
- Dolphin's Barn
- Marshalsea Barracks
- Coady's Cottages (West Road) and St James' Walk Rialto. (See 27/1915 and 75/1915)

It was reported that 38 three-roomed two-storey dwellings in **Lisburn Street and Lurgan Street** were almost complete and the tenants had been selected. Similarly the buildings for the extension to the existing scheme in Blackhall Place and St Paul Street would shortly be ready for occupation. The building for the final phase of 113 three-room two-storey cottages on the Oblate site were in the hands of the contractor.

Trinity Ward

Development was continuing here and this report noted that an LGB inquiry took place on 4 and 6 July into a proposed scheme of 16 two-roomed tenements in Luke Street, 32 two-roomed tenements in Moss Street and 28 three-roomed cottages in Magennis Place. Approval had been received on 20 October and tenders were being considered at the time of the report. The suggested rents were 3*s*. 6*d*. for tenement flats and 5*s*. for cottages.

Beresford Street and Church Street

The plans had been in development for some time and had been the subject of comment from Geddes and Unwin. The LGB inquiry took place on 3, 4 and 6 July and the Corporation accepted the Board's suggestion to widen Church Street to 50 feet and to provide front gardens to the cottages. Amended plans had been sent to the Board and tenders had been sought in anticipation of acceptance. The Scheme envisaged 146 dwellings with rents of 6*s*. for four room cottages, 4*s*. 6*d*. for three room cottages and 2*s*. 6*d*. for two room dwellings.

Ormond Market

Following the LGB Inquiry which took place on the same days as Beresford Street, sanction was given to acquire and clear the site and that was underway. The Board had made suggestions about layout and they were being considered. However in a surprising development a resolution was adopted by the Council agreeing to hand over the site to his Grace, the Most Reverend Dr Walsh, Archbishop of Dublin, for the purpose of erecting thereon a Roman Catholic Cathedral. Just as the suggestion came out of nowhere so the idea evaporated once the Archbishop really understood the implications.

McCaffrey Estate (Mount Brown)

Mr Cowan held the inquiry on 1 July and made the necessary order in August, confirmed by Board in November. The Arbitration hearing was held in 21 December 1914. However, the Corporation report noted that it was found desirable to reconsider the scheme and this was not yet completed.

Fairbrothers' Fields

The Inquiry was held into the making of the Provisional Order on 1 July and the order was made on 31 August. An objection delayed confirmation by the Board until 26 November. At the date of the report, the Law Agent had made application for the appointment of an Arbitrator but no appointment had been made. The report noted the intention to build 800 dwellings comprising four-room and three-roomed cottages and two-room flats at rents of 7s., 6s. 6d., and 4s. 6d. respectively. At this point it seems that the Corporation had NOT decided to take the advice of Geddes and Unwin.

Spitalfields

The inquiry into the Provisional Order held during 26–28 July and the Corporation was strongly opposed. The provisional order was made in August and confirmed on 19 November but only for the clearance (see below). The intention was for 62 three-room cottages at 5s. 6d. and 36 two-room flats at 3s. 6d.

Glorney's Buildings

The Provisional Order was refused as the LGB Inspector was of the view that the Corporation was not justified in excluding certain property, which he considered insanitary, from the petition. The Corporation since agreed to deal with an enlarged area extending to Marlborough Street, Summerhill, Buckingham Street, Gardiner Street, Gloucester Street, North Cumberland Street.

Crabbe Lane

The scheme provided for 126 two-room flats, and 36 three-room flats to be let at 3s. and 4s. per week. The application for the Provisional Order was pending and would shortly be heard.

54. Nerney (Nerney's)
Court. Ordnance Survey
plan, 5-foot, Sheet 18 (37),
1909 edition.

Boyne Street

The Council had approved an application for a provisional order and loans (Report 232/1914) and the advertisements had been published. The scheme provided for 42 three-roomed cottages and 46 two-room cottages at rents of 6*s*. 6*d*. and 4*s*. 6*d*. respectively.

Mary's Lane and St James' Walk

Improvement schemes were now before the Council.

Nerney's Court

The Housing Committee decided to recommend that the derelict portion be converted to a playground.

Cook Street

Plans were at a preliminary stage for further development.

Little Ship Street and Werburgh Street, Dolphin's Barn

On the advice of the engineer it was decided to abandon these areas as they both appeared to be unsuitable for housing purposes.

The First World War

One of the major impacts of the First World War on the housing plans of Dublin Corporation was that loans from the Local Government Board were suspended, except in exceptional circumstances. Since this would have the effect of significantly increasing the costs of any housing scheme, this caused much distress within the Corporation. The alternative of raising the capital on the open market was not an attractive option because credit had shrunk there too and costs had increased. Some time could be bought by using current income but that could not be sustained. This change was first experienced with the Ormond Market scheme but it really came to a head with Spitalfields. Dublin Corporation later set out its arguments for special treatment in Report 35/1916.

The bad news was communicated formally by the LGB to the Corporation in a letter dated 8 January 1915. The exceptional circumstances in which money could be advanced were expected to be truly exceptional. This required that underemployment in the building trade be 'exceptional in amount, urgent and insistent'. Where it was agreed that such circumstances existed then money would be advanced partly as a grant but mostly as a loan. The grant would not exceed one tenth of the capital sum and the loan was to be repaid within the normal period allowed for works of the character proposed with interest of 4¼ percent per annum (Report 103/1915).

Though this was bad news, the Corporation felt that it provided sufficient wriggle room for them to operate. Unemployment in the building trades was high and was getting worse. However, they were to find that HM Treasury were not so easily persuaded.

Church Street

The first involvement of Dublin Corporation with housing the working classes was, via the DADC, in the Liberties. However, once they began direct provision, their focus was on the area west of Capel Street because of its ruinous condition. It was never a particularly fashionable area, despite the location of the Blue Coat School there and though there was good housing in the area it had seen less of the systematic planning that gave spatial coherence to the Gardiner and Pembroke estates. The number of Corporation developments offered the opportunity for an overall plan and design concept but that seems not to have been considered and development was piecemeal and tended to maintain the existing street pattern.

The initial planning of the Ormond Market Scheme pre-dates the Church Street scheme but it stalled and both schemes were developed in parallel with changes in one scheme prompting changes in the other.

Dr Charles Cameron had, in 1911, made the required declaration under the Act that the Church Street area was unsanitary. A visit by member of the Corporation confirmed that assessment. 'The Sub-Committee, accompanied by the responsible officers, made a most exhaustive examination of the site on 12th October [1911] last and found that the conditions of human existence in all the courts and passages comprised in the area are most deplorable. Apart from the insanitary condition of the houses on the boundary streets of the area, the place is honey-combed with narrow lanes and courts, occupied by several families. These lanes and courtways are close and narrow, thereby shutting out the necessary amount of light and air required for healthy conditions of human existence. The houses situate in these places have no backyards, and in some instances there is only one convenience for several families. A very large proportion of cases of smallpox during the epidemic of 1902 was taken from the houses on this site and its immediate surroundings. This fact in itself would tend to prove that the unhealthy housing conditions in this district must have greatly assisted the spread of the epidemic' (Report 5/1912).

The crowded and incoherent nature of the area is clearly shown on the Ordnance Survey 5-foot plan. It shows a warren of narrow alleys and internal courts with very poor access to natural light and fresh air in many locations.

The proposal was to build 90 three-room two-storey cottages at £130 per cottage and 156 three-room two-storey cottages at £120 per cottage on the cleared site. Rents were proposed at 5s. for 66 bigger cottages with the remaining 156 cottages at 4s. 6d. At that time 308 families (1,540 people) lived in 121 houses with 61 unoccupied rooms at rents that varied from 2s. to 3s. for one room and 3s. 6d. to 4s. 6d. for two room tenements with one room cottages at 3s. and two room cottages at 3s. 6d. The total cost per family rehoused at £185 bore favourable comparison with Cook Street (£185 per family house), Lurgan Street (£170) and Liverpool (Hornsby Street area, £280).

The development would have five new roads, each 40 feet in width and some existing roads would be widened. Stirrup Lane would change from an average of 18 feet to an average of 33 feet 6 inches; Church Street from an average of 34 feet to an average of 46 feet; Beresford Street from an average of 21 feet to an average of 36 feet 6 inches.; Mary's Lane from an average of 23 feet to an a average of 46 feet 6 inches. This version of the design is very simple with the houses arranged in rectangular blocks along the new roads, running at right angles to Church Street and linking it with Beresford Street.

The retention of shops was felt to be important. There were 31 shops within the designated area and the report suggested that 24 new shops could be distributed across the area at a rent of 10s. per week. If it was found that demand for them was

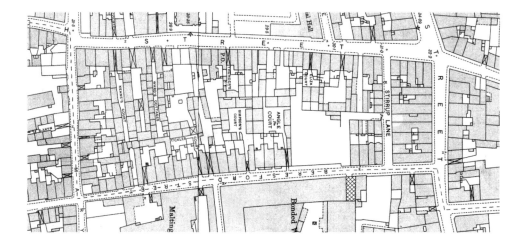

55. Church Street and Beresford Street environs. Ordnance Survey plans, 5-foot, Sheets 18 (46 & 56), 1908/9 editions. The plan has been oriented east-west to match the Corporation's plans.

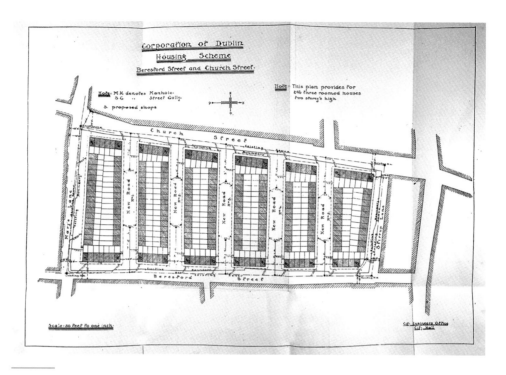

56. Church Street and Beresford Street scheme, 1912 design. Report 5/1912, Volume 1, p.64.

not sufficient, they could be turned to housing, the cost of building was not much greater. Not only would they provide important local services but the higher rents reduced the annual deficit considerably to £35 16s. Another interesting element was a measure of pedestrianisation. 'It is proposed that pillars about 2.5 feet high shall be erected at the entrances to the new roads in order to prevent vehicular traffic passing through, and the streets will thereby answer the purpose of playgrounds for the children. The shutting out of vehicular traffic will also have the effect of lessening the cost of maintenance. It has been suggested by the City Architect that a row of trees in the Centre of each of these new roads, with seats interspersed between them, would considerably improve the general aspect and amenities of the scheme. We may also mention that the total open space area which the new roads will provide, will amount to over an acre' (Report 5/1912). Not quite what might be understood by a 'playground' perhaps but at least a recognition of the importance of the concept.

The site, comprising 3.75 acres and having the advantage of being almost rectangular, was described as being:

most suitable and convenient one for the working classes – being in close proximity to such large centres of employment as Jameson's Distillery, Jameson and Pim's Brewery, Midland Great Western Railway Co., Crean's Soap Works, Corporation Workshop in Stanley Street, the City Markets etc., besides many other minor industries in the locality. As we have already pointed out in previous reports relating to housing reform, the City Treasurer has advised us that the block system of dwellings has proved most objectionable; they are unpopular with the working classes, and from the ratepayers standpoint they are uneconomic. The cottage system therefore at once commends itself as the preferable one and accordingly we recommend self-contained cottages for adoption.

The larger (A Class) house comprised a living room with dimensions of 19 feet x 11 feet 3 inches, with the room height at the common 8 feet 6 inches while the B Class was 17 feet in length. Both houses had two bedrooms with those in the larger one having a cubic capacity of 910 and 646 respectively while the smaller house had bedrooms with 776 and 614 cubic feet. This was to become a problem. A majority on the Council took the view that no bedroom should have less than 1,000 cubic feet. To that was added a view that rents should be lower, so that a significant gap opened up between rent levels recommended by the officials and those supported by the Council.

Obtaining Council approval proved difficult. Report 5/1912 was considered at a meeting on 26 January when it was decided to refer it to a Committee of the Whole House which took place on 2 February 1912 (Report 32/1912). This recommended the formation of a special Housing Committee but it also recommended that the Improvements Committee look at the scheme again to produce dwellings with bedrooms of not less than 1,000 cubic feet each and rents of 1s. per room per week. This report was considered on the Council meeting of 4 March when it was adopted and the amended scheme was considered in Report 99/1912 of the Improvements Committee (dated 2 April 1912). The Report provided for 181 cottages, at a cost of £165 each and all with much the same area as previously and bedrooms of the required size.

This report was adopted at the meeting of 6 May but with an amendment that the Improvement Committee consider the question of erecting some two-roomed cottages at 2s. per week. The amendments were made and the improvement scheme was formally adopted at the Council Meeting on 10 June 1912. The redesigned scheme was set out in Report 149/1912 (dated 11 June 1912) and adopted on 12 August 1912.

The decision of the Council to limit rents to 1s. per room per week now meant than a subsidy of £1,569 was required – much on the same scale as the Ormond Market below. This was greatly in excess of what would have been considered even a few years previously and it propelled the city towards larger and larger rates. The Improvements Committee urged the Council not to go down the road of subsidizing rents to the extent intended (Report 99/1912).

> We could not possibly see our way to recommend the alternative plan, involving it does a loss of close on £1,600 a year to the ratepayers. Therefore, we again strongly recommend the Council to adopt the scheme outlined in Report No. 5/1912, and if there are any details connected with it which in the opinion of the Council should be modified, either as regards the number of shops or the rents proposed to be charged, the matter can be dealt with by an amending resolution in connection with the adoption of the Report (No. 5/1912), and such modifications can be given effect to at the Local Government Inquiry. We may mention that the dimensions of the rooms proposed by us are similar in every respect to those contained in the dwellings erected at Inchicore, and also to the dwellings which are about to be erected on the Cook Street Area. These schemes have been approved by the Municipal Council and the Local Government Board.

The revised proposal provided for 147 three-room houses two storeys high costing £165 to build, and 34 two-room houses one storey high at a building cost of £120. As ordered, each bedroom had a cubic capacity of not less than 1,000 cubic feet. Once again, the Committee pleaded with the Council to be more reasonable in terms of rent.

> If the resolution above is to be taken as indicating a definite line of policy on the part of the Municipal Council in dealing with the housing problem,

there is no doubt that the clearance of slum areas, and the erection of large and cheaply rented dwellings will entail a considerable charge upon the rates. The Ormond Market area, which is also being dealt with by the Committee on the basis set forth in the resolution of the Council will, we have no doubt, shew a similar deficit.

....

We would, however, suggest the desirability of reconsidering the question of the rents to be charged. The accommodation provided is in excess of the requirement of the Local Government Board, and the rent charged are exceptionally low. By an all-round increase of 6d. per week per tenement, and, in addition, the provision of, say, a dozen shops on the site at 8s. per week, a considerable reduction in the annual loss would be brought about. There will, undoubtedly, be a demand for shop accommodation on such a large area.

The City Treasurer also expressed his concern.

It is proposed to provide for 3s. per week cottage dwellings for which 5s. would be readily obtained. The grounds on which the Improvements Committee are prepared to justify the lower rent are the necessity for providing sanitary dwellings for that section of the poorer population which cannot afford to pay a rent higher than the lesser figure. The difficulty which you will, under the circumstances, have to face is that at present you are receiving at Inchicore for cottages costing £140, 4s. per week; whilst in this scheme you propose to build larger cottages of a similar type at £165 each to let them at 3s. per week. It may be difficult to convince the occupiers at Inchicore as to the grounds on which they are expected to pay more than the more favoured citizens in the Inns Quay Ward for somewhat lesser accommodation. I am not oblivious of the Committee's difficulty, but I think it would have been better to design something of lesser accommodation to justify a lesser rent, as otherwise you will produce an all-around agitation for a reduction in the existing rents of three-room dwellings, which will not be disposed of by the arguments that you are endeavouring, in this particular scheme, to proportion the rent to the capacity of the particular class you intend to admit.

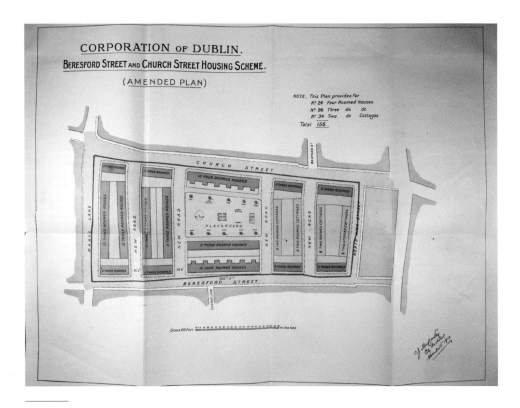

57. Church Street and Beresford Street scheme, 1913 design. Report 15/1914, Volume 1, p.66.

As with Ormond Market, the plan was again reconsidered in 1914. The revision (Report 15/1914) provided for 24 four-roomed houses and a playground, in addition to 98 three-roomed houses and 34 two-roomed cottages; a total of 156 instead of 181 dwellings. The economic rents for these houses would have been 7s. per week for four-room cottages; 6s. 6d. for three-room cottages; and 4s. 6d. for two-room cottage, showing very clearly the impact of the Council's policy of 1s. per room per week. The scheme shows the playground as a central feature with four new roads linking Church Street with Beresford Street. The streets were not now intended to be pedestrianised. While many of the houses face onto these quieter streets, there was still a substantial number facing Church Street, without front gardens.

There was a further small change before the request for tenders was published on 31 December 1914. Taking a suggestion by Mr Cowan, they decided to give small front gardens to the cottages. 'The existence of front gardens will prevent

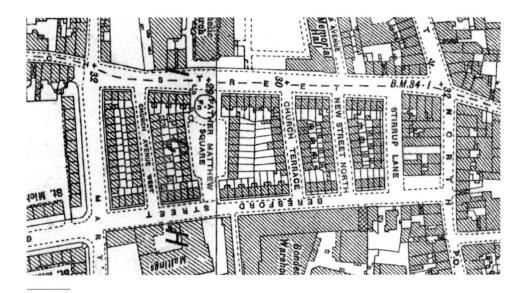

58. Church Street and Beresford Street environs. Ordnance Survey plans, 1:2,500, Sheets 18 (7 & 12), 1939 edition. The plan has been oriented east-west.

idlers squatting on the window sills – a practice which destroys the appearance of the buildings, increases wear and tear, and is most annoying to the occupants' (Report 14/1915). This was at the cost of 10 houses. Tenders were considered at the Council meeting of 3 May 1915 and the winning bid from the seven valid tenders went to Messrs Fraser and Co., who were based in Bray.

As the Ordnance Survey map for 1939 shows, the final layout contains the elements of the scheme as outlined above but with significant change to the size and orientation of the playground. This particular change arose from a request from the Capuchin Fathers who asked that the street linking Beresford Street and Church Street (later named Father Matthew Square) line up with the church of St Mary of the Angels across the road (Report 103/1915). Though it took a long time to complete, the development has stood the test of time. The development retains its character although the cross-routes have been largely closed to vehicular traffic.

59. Present-day housing Church Terrace: Church Street scheme.

60. Present-day housing along Beresford Street: Church Street scheme.

Ormond Market

The Corporation had made a limited attempt at providing housing in the Ormond Market area in 1904. This would have created two new streets – one a continuation of St Michan Street opening onto Ormond Quay, and the other running at right angles to it and opening into East Arran Street. The Local Government Board did not give approval at the time so it was 1912 when the issue was revisited, this time with a view to a more extensive clearance. Conditions were so bad that the report to the Corporation stated that: 'the present condition of the Ormond Market Area is so well known to the Members of the Council that your Committee do not deem it necessary to give any detailed description of it. Several houses have been completely demolished on a large portion of the area, some of them are still in ruins, and others either partly or entirely inhabited'.

The Ordnance Survey map for 1909 shows the original plan of the market clearly and the names of the streets testify to the activities of the area: Beef Row, Egg

61. Ormond Market and Environs. Ordnance Survey plan, 5-foot plan, Sheets 18 (56 & 57), 1907/8 revision, 1909 edition.

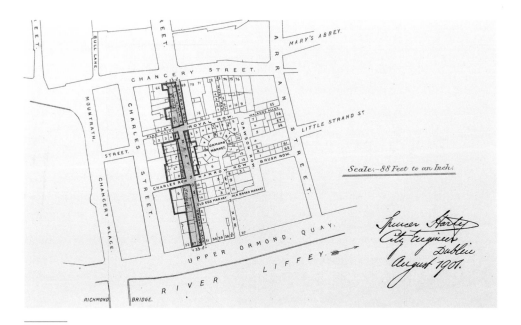

62. The Ormond Market as proposed in Report 114/1901, Volume II, p. 210.

Market, Bread Market. There were 222 families living in tenements, a total of 796 people. Most families (189) were in one room units with 31 families having two rooms and nine families with three rooms. A further 90 people lived in private houses. In total there were 76 standing houses, of which 41 were tenements with a further four unoccupied and sixteen derelict. There was some debate within the Council as to whether the site (A on the plans) on which the later Simms-designed flat block was built should be developed. The entire site could accommodate 128 houses but there was concern that such houses would detract from the dignity of the Four Courts building and the Corporation's officials were of the view that the block should be left for some other public use. This view was later endorsed by Unwin and Geddes who did not think the site suitable at all for housing. The Improvements Committee agreed and that reduced the planned build to 100 houses, displacing some 587 people. As they noted: 'The dwellings proposed will be similar in every respect with those designed for the Church Street and Beresford Street Area, and agreeably with the policy adopted by the Municipal Council the cubic contents of each bedroom are not less than 1,000 cubic feet, and the rents have been fixed at 3/- per week. We have not provided for any two-room dwellings' (Report 186/1912).

The perennial issue of rent also arose here. The committee was prepared to recommend a rent of 3*s*. per week but they noted that this was not an economic rent and would result in an annual cost to the city of £1,362 10*s*. They also noted that the cost of the tenants' current accommodation ranged from 1*s*. 6*d*. to 3*s*. 6*d*. for one-roomed tenements, 3*s*. to 7*s*. 6*d*. for two rooms and 5*s*. to 8*s*. 6*d*. for three rooms. Additionally, they pointed out that the size of these dwellings had been increased as a result of a recent policy decision by the Council to a point which was never before suggested and which was in excess of the requirements of the Local Government Board. They argued that if the development proceeded on the lines of what had been built in Inchicore, they could fit 165 houses on the FULL site and if they charged rents of 5*s*. per week, then the annual cost would be reduced to £576. 'It will thus be seen that suitable dwelling of modern sanitary design and complying with the maximum requirement of the Local Government Board could be built on the Ormond Market Area at rents which, compared 'with those paid by the people at present living on the area, cannot be considered unreasonable'.

The 1912 plan was for a very basic grid layout of houses fronting directly onto streets with no front gardens. A playground was provided but along Chancery Street and not at all integrated into the scheme. This scheme did not get built either and the matter was again considered in 1914 (Report 83/1914). At this point the Housing Committee had decided to build a mix of housing types, using the entire site. The plan was now for 155 dwellings comprising 36 four-roomed and 53 three-roomed cottages and 66 two-roomed flats. Still hedging their bets, the report also provided for NOT building on the Chancery Lane plot.

It was the latter plan they ultimately agreed to submit to the LGB and this was approved with some minor changes to the layout. The final plan provided for 104 dwellings with 49 three-roomed cottages and 56 two-roomed flats, each bedroom having an area larger than 1,000 cubic feet. The central area was laid out as a playground some 50 x 30 feet in dimensions. It was felt that it would be a pity to lose the central granite paved area of the old market and it was suggested that it might be enhanced by a fountain with a suitable marker (Report 103/1915). Provision was made for a future linking road to Ormond Quay by ensuring that no demolition would be necessary to achieve it.

The scheme came close to not happening at all. For a brief period, it looked as if

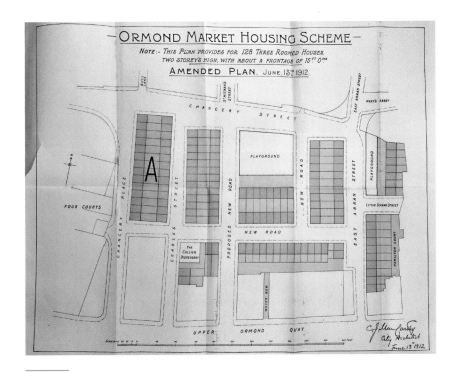

63. Ormond Market Housing Scheme, 1912 version. Report 182/1912, Volume II, p. 709.

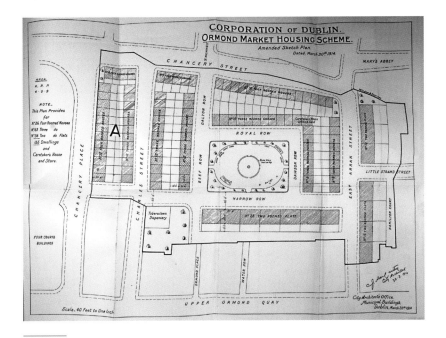

64. Ormond Market Housing Scheme, 1914 version, Report 83/1914, Volume 1, p. 825.

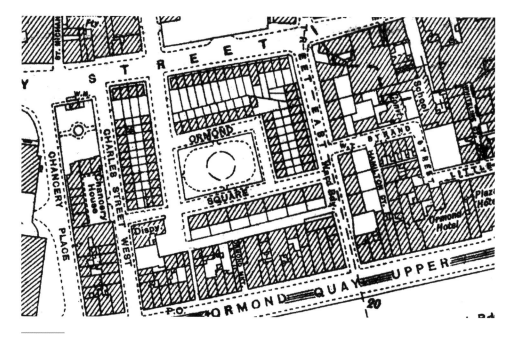

65. Ormond Market and Environs. Ordnance Survey plan, 1:2,500 plan, Sheet 18 (7), 1939 edition. Note that the route connecting with Ormond Quay was never completed.

66. Ormond Market prior to renovation in 2005.

67. Ormond Market present-day housing.

the site would be where the new Catholic Cathedral, a project given new energy by the Town Planning Competition, would be built. It seems that the Lord Mayor gave the Archbishop to understand that the site could be made available and the Archbishop wrote taking the Lord Mayor up on the offer. However, the Housing Committee was less than enthusiastic. Naturally they were never going to refuse the Archbishop but they set out all the reasons why it was not a good idea in the order that they made on 11 December 1914 which concluded 'The Housing Committee, however, desire to inform His Grace, the Archbishop that, having detailed the various matters hereinbefore described, should his Grace still desire to obtain this site, the Corporation would acquiesce in any reasonable demands of His Grace which concern the Archdiocese'. This order did not please the Council and at the meeting on 16 December 1914, they rescinded the order and instructed the Housing Committee 'to take all necessary steps to carry out the intention of this resolution, and make arrangements with His Grace the Archbishop as to terms, etc.:'. The proposal/offer had been leaked to the newspapers and had created quite a flurry, especially when it was reported that the Housing Committee had rejected the proposal (see *Belfast Newsletter*, 14 December 1914, p.7). Following the Council Meeting, there was a lengthy report in the *Freeman's Journal* which set out the various steps and correspondence (17 December 1914, p. 6). The matter was formally reported in Report 15/1915 and it was clear that the Housing Committee was content to do nothing and see how it worked out. Thus they were able to say 'On receipt of the Council's resolution, we learned that His Grace was negotiating for the purchase of premises situating on the Quay Boundary of the Site. We, therefore deferred taking any action in the way of arranging terms with His Grace pending an intimation from him that his negotiations with these other interests were likely to prove successful. At our meeting of the 19th February, the following letter, addressed by His Grace to the Right Honorable the Lord Mayor, was laid before us. It will be seen that His Grace has found it impracticable, having regard to the prices demanded, to proceed further with the project'. The Archbishop found that assembling the site was going to be a lot more complicated than he had been led to be believe. There were many owners and such was the degree of civic piety that the price of property shot up once it seemed that it might be needed for the cathedral. All of which led the Archbishop to decide that it was not worth the effort. There was little upset within the Housing Committee at this news and the ease and speed with the scheme was resumed was another indication of less than unanimous enthusiasm.

By March 1915 the clearance of the site was underway, the Board having sanctioned a loan of £12,103 for acquisition and clearing of the area. The wartime squeeze on credit was first felt in 1915 when the LGB told the Corporation that the Treasury would not fund any schemes beyond those underway in Church Street and Trinity Ward. The City Treasurer was asked to see if the necessary funding could be found on the open market but he reported that the rates available made it impossible. The Corporation were disappointed and felt that since the loan for acquiring and clearing the site had been given that the necessary funds for housing would follow in due course. The amount required was £24,400 which, in the scheme of things, was not prohibitive especially since if they could not build, they would be left with an unproductive site which had cost them £12,100 which would be a continuing cost. Their solution was to seek £8,000 from the rates income to allow them to build on at least part of the site and the Council voted to approve this on 4 October 1915 (Report 211/1915).

Intensive lobbying and negotiation took place, especially as a letter from the LGB indicated that it was not they who had stopped the loan and that the issue lay with HM Treasury (Minutes 3 May 1915, See Report 35/1916 for a detailed case for funding written from the Housing Committee). This ultimately led to the approval of the loan for £24,400 for Ormond Market, leaving the Council with £8,000 already voted but they now had the problem of Spitalfields to deal with. The date for receipt of completed tenders was 13 January 1916 and sixteen were received, more than usual and probably reflective of the straitened times. The bidders were asked to price the job based on four combinations of granite versus limestone for the cut stone and Killaloe versus Welsh slates. The winner was H. & J. Martin for £20,037 and for limestone and Killaloe slates. Six additional three-roomed houses were built on Chancery Street in 1922 (Report 186/1921).

The 1939 Ordnance Survey plan shows the completed scheme complete with the playground. Herbert Simms' completed small flat complex on the reserved plot (A) is also evident. The connection from Ormond Square to Ormond Quay was never completed, ensuring that the scheme remains today a quiet oasis in a very busy area. The landscape is substantially as it was constructed but there was a major renovation project in 2000. This resulted in the amalgamation of two flats into one on Ormond Square, Little Strand Street and the block at the corner of Arran Street East and Little Strand Street together with the building of a bedroom extension to rear of the remaining units on Arran Street East. This still left them as one-roomed flats but with a greater area. This reduced the number of these units to 38.

Mary's Lane

Mary's Lane was nearby and an earlier proposal had not proceeded which would incidentally have provided some new housing. Report 18/1915 reminded the Council that they had dealt with a proposal at the beginning of the century to widen Mary's Lane. This followed the opening of the Fruit and Vegetable Market building in 1892 and better access was badly needed. The Markets Committee were not prepared to take on the proposal. Nor were they interested in a later development proposal from the potato factors in the area. The streets were crowded and it was difficult for transport to operate and the suggestion from the factors was that more market accommodation would be appropriate. The idea was never developed because the Corporation could not get a guarantee from the factors that they would support any redevelopment. The Improvements Committee now decided that the time had come for a comprehensive housing scheme, as conditions had not improved in the interim. The need to improve access could also be met by including the plot between Greek Street and Bull Lane.

> A glance at the map will show an improvement which has been agitated for some years past, namely, the widening of Mary's Lane, is partially effected in connection with the present proposal. The frontage of the south side of the street will be set back a distance of 22 feet, making a total width when the north side is also set back under the Beresford Street and Church Street scheme of 57 feet. A continuation of the widening of Church Street which is contemplated in connection with the Beresford Street and Church Street Area adjoining, is also provided for – the existing width in this case being 26 ft and the proposed width 60 ft.

Cameron made the necessary declaration on 20 August 1913 for an area comprising 2 acres, 1 rood and 6 perches and which housed 71 families in very insanitary conditions. The proposal would house 74 families at a density of 32 dwellings per acre.

The plan comprised 60 three-roomed cottages with a build-cost of £200 and 14 two-roomed cottages at £144. With other costs, the total came to £14,500 excluding the cost of making roads, sewers and the laying of water and gas mains.

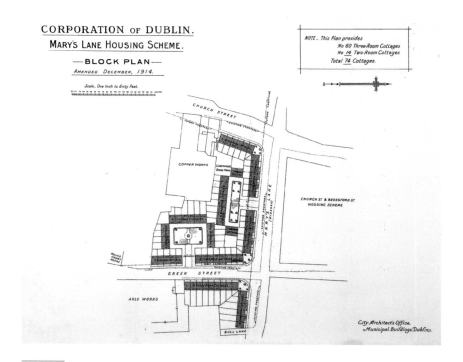

68. The revised scheme for Mary's Lane, 1915, Report 18/1915.

The suggested rents were 6*s*. 6*d*. for the three-roomed cottages and 4*s*. 6*d*. for the two-roomed cottages, significantly higher than what most current residents were paying, as the comparison data demonstrated. This showed that the families lived in 15 tenement houses and five privates houses, with 253 people (66 families) in the tenements. There were 47 families in one-room tenements for which they paid rent of between 1*s*. 6*d*. and 2*s*. 6*d* per week, 17 in two-room tenements paying between 2*s*. 6*d* and 4*s*. 6*d*. and between 4*s*. 6*d*. and 6*s*. per week for those in tenements of 3 or more rooms.

The Housing Committee's report was approved by the Council on 8 February 1915 but nothing happened until 1919 when in the improved post-war funding environment the LGB was once again able to consider projects. The LGB made some critical comments about the layout (Report 110/1920) but the Corporation was prepared to accommodate these and Mr Cowan held the necessary inquiry on 12 June 1919. He granted the Provisional Order, which was later confirmed but the Corporation did not proceed with arbitration until they had clarity in relation to funding. Building did not take place until the 1930s and to a very different design (Report 190/1928).

Glorney's Buildings

This was another awkward site. It comprised a rather disjointed series of lanes and alleys for which 'Glorney's Buildings' was the useful label between Gloucester Place Upper to the north and Lower Gardiner Street and Rutland Place to the west and east respectively. This included Murphy's Cottages and Willet's Place and the Ordnance Survey plan for 1909 shows a complex landscape, though with quite an amount of open space, compared to other insanitary locations. Though very close to the Montgomery / Purdon street scheme, it was quite separate. What was contemplated was quite a big development, with 20 four-roomed houses at a rent of 7s., 60 three-roomed houses at 6s. 6d. and 100 two-roomed flats at 4s. 6d. It was

69. Glorney's Buildings and environs. Ordnance Survey plan, 5-foot, Sheets 18 (38 & 48), 1907 edition.

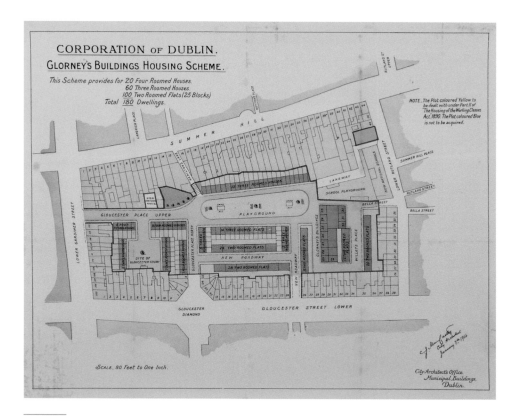

70. Plans for Glorney's Buildings and environs. Report 17/1914.

expected that 589 would be dispossessed but that 1,067 would be housed. The block plan, prepared by Charles MacCarthy and dated 7 January 1914 shows that good use was made of the open space to provide a large oblong playground complete with sandpit and away from the main roads. The accommodation was set out in a series of rectangular blocks of conventional layout. The houses and some of the flat blocks were provided with gardens to the rear but perhaps the most interesting element was the almost enclosed courtyard design on the site of Gloucester Court. A new entrance to Gloucester Street was provided by the demolition of no 25, while another access route which avoided the Monto completely was provided to Gardiner Street via Gloucester Place upper.

Perhaps surprisingly, while Cameron agreed that the area as a whole was insanitary, he identified a small number of buildings which were in sufficiently good shape to be left alone. These, marked blue on the block plan (and ironically which were

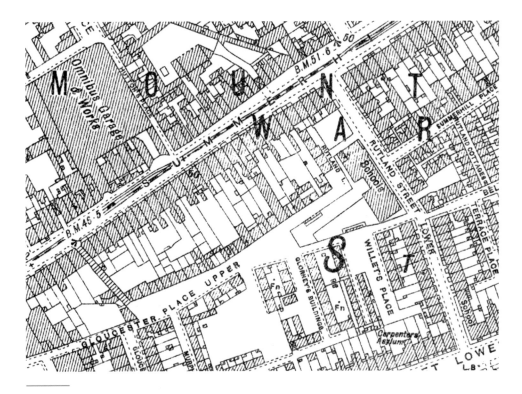

71. Glorney's Buildings and environs. Ordnance Survey plan, 1:2,500, Sheet 18 (VII), 1939 edition.

the eponymous Glorney's Buildings) were excluded from the application for a Provisional Order and this proved to be the undoing of the proposal. The Inspector did not agree to the order because the exclusion of these buildings impacted upon the coherence of the site and the Corporation dropped the matter. The Corporation revisited the proposal in 1932 (*Irish Times*, 11 October 1932, p.4) but the site is still visible on the OS 1:2,500 plan 18(VII) for 1939.

Spitalfields

The Corporation, via the DADC, had begun its involvement with housing in the Liberties in the 1870s but had undertaken very little additional building there since. The area was badly in need of renewal. By the end of the eighteenth century, this part of Dublin had slipped into decay and there was a marked contrast between the quality of life in the west of the city compared to that in the bright, shiny and modern Georgian capital city to the east. This reality was graphically described by the Revd Whitelaw in his census of the city undertaken during what seems to have been a very hot summer in 1798. Not only do we get a good picture of the social composition of the city, his essay on conditions in this area described stomach-churning scenes. So, it was no surprise when those indefatigable travellers, the Halls, visited here in the 1840s that they found similar scenes of decay.

> The present state of this once flourishing region forms a strong contrast
> to its former; but it still retains many evidences of what it has been.

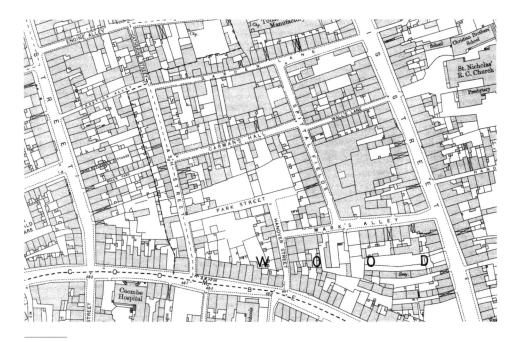

72. Spitalfields and Carman's Hall environs. Ordnance Survey plan, 5-foot, Sheet 18 (66),
1907 revision, 1909 edition.

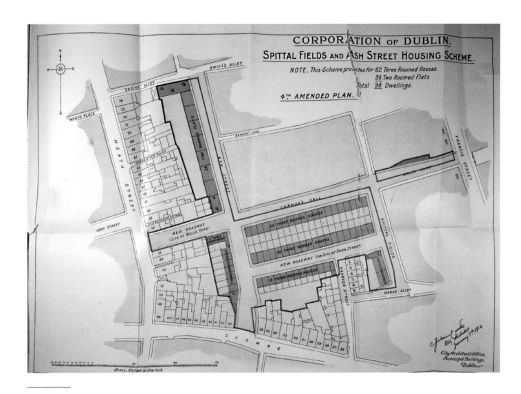

73. Plans for Spitalfields and Carman's Hall, 1914. Report 17/1914, Volume I, p.100.

74. Blue line shows the completed Spitalfields and Carman's Hall scheme.
Note the central park/playground.

In passing along its desolate streets, large houses of costly structure everywhere present themselves. Lofty façades adorned with architraves, and mouldings to windows, and door-cases of sculptured stone or marble; grand staircases with carved and gilded balustrades; panelled doors opening into spacious suits of corniced and stuccoed apartments all attest the opulence of its former inhabitants. They are now the abode only of the most miserable. As they were deserted by the rich, they were filled by the poor; and as they decayed, they became the resort of the more abject, who could find no other shelter (Hall, 1842, II, p.326).

Spitalfields had long been an important marketplace for ham and bacon and regular reports of the trade appeared in the newspapers but otherwise it tended not be newsworthy until the Corporation decided on a renewal scheme. Dubliners would have heard more about Spitalfields in London given the notoriety of the 'ripper' murders.

The scheme was initiated in 1914 and was for 180 dwellings on the south side of Carman's Hall and bounded by Spitalfields, the rear of the houses on the Coombe and the left side of Ash Street. It was an awkward site and that is reflected in the design with Ash Street standing quite removed from the remainder. As was required, the area was declared an unhealthy area by Charles Cameron on 3 June 1913 who followed the required formula and declared that 'I hereby certify that within the above area many houses, courts and laneways are unfit for human habitation and that the narrowness, closeness and bad arrangement and bad condition of the streets and houses, and the want of light, air and ventilation and proper conveniences, and the general sanitary defects are dangerous and injurious to the health of the inhabitants of the buildings of the said area'. The Ordnance Survey plan for 1909 does not convey that impression of density, in fact the area immediately to the west between Ash Street and the Meath Street looks considerably worse. The area did have the advantage, though, of having a relatively large amount of open space which could be absorbed more cheaply into the scheme.

It took four iterations but on 7 January 1914 Charles MacCarthy, City Architect presented the fourth amended plan for the area. It comprised 62 three-roomed houses and 36 two-roomed flats. The continuing sensitivity as to how to present costs was reflected in the following paragraph.

It has been contended that the costs of acquiring and clearing an insanitary area should not be debited against a housing scheme when the calculations of profit and loss are being made. They are held to be charges beyond and apart from the mere site value, which should be regarded as the true basis for the fixing of an economic rent. This principle has been adopted in arriving at the rents which are proposed for these two schemes [Spitalfields and Glorney's Buildings]. The larger losses, however, as shown in the two tables marked 'A' will become charges on the rates until liquidated by the annual deductions indicated in each case. The annual cost on the 'B' basis would be £1,504 of which rents would contribute £1,469 (6s. 6d. for the 62 cottages and 4s. 6d. for the flats) while 'A' would cost £1,844 leaving an annual loss of £390 (p. 93).

The scheme also pointed up the limitations under which the Corporation had to work. The site was difficult. Indeed, it was such that the City Valuer was of the view that no private builder would take it on, raising the issue of whether it was realistic to speak of 'an economic rent'. Unwin and Geddes had endorsed the view that the site was unsuitable in their review of current schemes (Report 78/1915). It was not

75. Spitalfields and Carman's Hall, July 2018.

that the Corporation was of a fundamentally different view. It would have chosen to build on a site with a better configuration but the properties they would have had to acquire were in better condition and beyond the budget of the city authorities.

The LGB inspector in this case was once again Mr Cowan. The inquiry began in June 1914, considering both Spitalfields and Glorney's Buildings at the same time, and the preliminaries show that though the idea of 'town planning' was widely known, not everyone in the Corporation was convinced about its value or indeed of the skills of Professor Geddes. Doubtless responding to the argument that the city needed a unified planning scheme, Mr Clancy, counsel for the Corporation, said that he did not know what 'town planning' meant in the context of Dublin. He seemed of the view that town planning required redevelopment on a grand scale and that was not appropriate for these small 'plague-spots'. He felt that the Wide Streets Commissioners had done all that needed to be done on the wider scale. The inquiry also provided the opportunity for the various shades of opinion to restate their views on how to deal with the housing issue. Alderman Kelly stated that he had been on a deputation to Glasgow and Edinburgh and had seen nothing of Professor Geddes' work that would warrant them following him in Dublin. He also seemed not to hold the Town Planning Association in much esteem. However, the Inspector was more positively disposed and said that the Professor was a most important advocate for more sunshine and air for the children of the workers and his opinions should not be disregarded. Dr Cameron took the opportunity to state his opposition to suburban schemes since there was plenty of 'waste land' in Dublin though he agreed that there were many who would like to live in the suburbs. The Trades' Council favoured suburban schemes because they did not want to see slum property being made more valuable by virtue of being used for housing while the Chairman of the Citizens' Housing League, said that business supported better housing for the workers not only to 'lift them out of their ugly surroundings' but to develop the industrial potential of the city. They supported the Corporation's efforts but not when they sought to house people at 200–300 persons per acre. The representative of the Citizens' Association said that with rates as high as they were, the Corporation should be careful in what they undertook. His view was that this scheme was unsuitable and should be bypassed in favour of Fairbrothers' Fields.

There was nothing new in these views but it demonstrated that the Housing Inquiry had not ended debate. With that range of views, it is no wonder that the Corporation often felt under siege. The Inspector gave only partial approval for Spitalfields in that he approved the acquisition and clearance of the site (*Irish Independent*, 2 July 1914, p. 6). He did not approve any building, however, because he believed that the site was unsuitable for a housing scheme.

The arbitration hearings on compensation for property owners in Spitalfields took place during 1915 and once again showed how difficult it was for the Corporation. There were accusations of grossly inflated claims with houses which were described by the owners as being in good condition being described as 'rotten' by the Corporation. Mrs Annie Cummins had a claim for property that reached from Engine Alley to the Coombe. Mr Clancy, once again the legal advocate for the Corporation, described it as the most extortionate claim that had even been put before a court. He noted that the arbitrator would visit the property and he expressed the hope that he would come back safely (*Irish Times*, 12 March 1915, p.3).

The Arbitrator produced the required report and the process was over by 6 May 1915. The Corporation believed that this would produce the necessary approval to build. They had got the necessary loan to complete Ormond Market so this left them with some leeway for Spitalfields, or so they thought.

The Council by resolution decided to use the £8,000 which had been budgeted for Ormond Market to build on a portion of the Spitalfields site and set about getting permission to do this. They had the additional problem that the LGB did not wish them to build on the site, regardless of the availability of funds but the Corporation developed the view that the completion of the arbitration process had created a financial liability on the Corporation which could not be ignored. Awards had been made and they must be paid. Whatever the standing of that argument, the LGB was not for moving. Following a resolution by the Council on 14 March, the town clerk, Henry Campbell, wrote to the LGB on 15 March 1916 seeking permission to proceed with some building. They were responded to on 22 March and told that they should NOT.

> The Board do not consider that the area to be acquired is of a suitable size or shape for the erection of new houses for the working classes in an advantageous way.

> The Confirming Order was made in this case on the strict grounds of Part I of the Act of 1890, and not because the area would serve as a site for new buildings, and before the latter should be erected a considerable amount of bad adjacent property should be acquired. If this is done, a scheme providing for open spaces as well as houses would be favourably considered by the Board.

This provided some wriggle room and while the Corporation reply of 5 July was cranky, it wriggled and noted that it was willing to work on modified plans that would meet 'most, if not all of the objections raised to the scheme as originally presented'. They received a reply on 12 July 1916 saying that the matter was under consideration.

Other weighty matters had occurred in the meantime and the 1916 Rising had an effect on the views of the Chief Secretary. There had also been considerable public protest about the LGB's failure to sanction the scheme and intensive lobbing. Typical was the lobbying of the Chief Secretary by William Field MP who published the response in the *Freeman's Journal* (8 April 1916, p.7). The Chief Secretary restated the LGB's position that the site was a bad one and that the Corporation would be building in the midst of slums. It was appropriate, though, that they would clear the site as a first step. Moreover the straitened times meant that the £8,000 allocated in the Corporation's budget would have to be met out of current revenue and the LGB did not feel that was something with which the ratepayers should be burdened. Much of the protest was more strident. There was a public meeting on 2 April 1916 where the same William Field, together with councillors such as Alderman Kelly expressed dissatisfaction with the LGB for their indifference to the people and with those elements within the council who where not prepared to stand up for the needs of the workers.

Alderman Kelly captured the spirit of the times when he said that: 'the Local Government Board apparently meant to try and sour the citizens of Dublin but if the wishes of the people were not met they were prepared from now to back up their claims with their blood' (*Freeman's Journal*, 3 April 1916, p.5).

Not everyone was as convinced that the Corporation was acting from altruistic motives. A lengthy article, perhaps more properly described as a rant, which occupied almost two columns appeared in 1917 and accused the Corporation of proceeding with the scheme because of the self-interest of at least three councillors who lived on the site and sundry others, unnamed but described, who would benefit personally from the clearance (*Evening Herald*, 10 April 1917, p.10).

The Corporation revised the plan based on an expanded site (which they did not yet own) which provided for open space as well as housing, something they felt that the LGB would support. The Fifth Amended Plan was presented on 30 November 1916 (Report 24/1917) and it provided for development in three phases. In the first section would be 75 three-roomed houses and a playground (costing £800). The second phase would have 15 three-roomed houses, 31 four-roomed houses and 5 two-roomed cottages. Electricity would be provided in the houses. The third phase, which was submitted for the sake of completeness only and its building was seen as some time off [indeed they did not have the ground] would involve 15 two-roomed cottages, 5 three-roomed houses and 17 4-roomed houses. This new mix reflected the development of the Corporation's thinking as seen in the Church Street and Beresford Street developments.

While Dublin Corporation seemed prepared to proceed by means of a direct cost on the rates, the funding position had improved by Spring of 1917. The Chief Secretary found himself able to 'intimate' to Dublin Corporation in April that £10,000 would be made available at once for Spitalfields, even though there was no change of view about its unsuitability, with a further £10,000 to be made available in July. Furthermore a sum of £80,000 would be made available for Fairbrothers' Fields, St James' Walk and Crabbe Lane (*Irish Times*, 23 April 1917, p.4). The Government certainly was appealing to 'hearts and minds', though at the formal announcement the Chief Secretary felt it necessary to note that the Spitalfields project was the only one which had raised objections from many of the citizens and that it would help greatly if the question of ownership of property was cleared up publicly'.

The LGB Inquiry began on 4 May 1917, again with Mr Cowan in the Chair. It was explained by the City Architect that the three-roomed houses would be similar to those in Ormond Market and Church Street with rents set at 5*s*. 6*d*. Questioning revealed that the cost-recovery rent would be 13*s*. 6*d*. Once again the various arguments were stated with the addition that the Housing Reform Committee, an entity of the Chamber of Commerce, suggested that the three phase plan was an ingenious ploy and that it was never intended that the second two phases would be completed (*Irish Times*, 5 May 1917, p.3). The Housing Reform Committee did not confine its objections to the Inquiry and they, together with the Dublin Citizens' Association and the Dublin Tenants' Association, sent a Memorial to the Lords of the Treasury restating the scheme was ill-conceived and would be a serious burden on the ratepayers. By then, though, they had conceded that the scheme could not be stopped. so they asked that the city be asked to repay the principal only as a special concession (*Irish Times*, 27 June 1917, p.5). In fact, permission to proceed had come quickly, though the Inspector's report seems not to have been made public. By June 1917, the Housing Committee was able to report that 12 tenders had been received for the first phase of development, the lowest and that accepted being from J.M. Clarke at £22,918, with plans for the second phase well advanced (*Irish Times*, 12 June 1917). Section 1 was complete by 1919 but consideration of Section 2 had to wait for the funding environment to improve. This was considered at the end of 1919 and the plans were approved by the LGB with changes to the street layout to integrate the scheme better. The amended plan, approved by the LGB on 2 March 1920, provided for 14 two bedroomed houses plus six with parlours, 24 three-bedroomed houses plus six with parlours and 4 four-bedroomed houses with parlours at a total cost of £46,000. The houses have a distinctive design, section 1 with a date plaque of 1918, with coloured brick courses and variation in the roof line adding interest. The final design incorporated a large park or playground in a central rectangle, which conveniently retained the prior name of Park Street.

Mount Brown / Ceannt Fort

Originally referred to as McCaffrey Estate, this was a site of 9.75 acres close to the South Dublin Union and on the high ground which overlooks James' Street / Old Kilmainham. A portion of the site (3.25 acres) would be given to the Board of Guardians of the Union for a crèche.

The Corporation's original conception was for 240 houses, comprising 78 four-room and 162 three-room houses. The block plan, dated 6 November 1913 shows a very conventional block design on a grid with a playground placed in a corner (and awkward part) of the site. The required inquiry took place on 26 June 1914 and the Inspector, P.C. Cowan, said that, there being no objections to the scheme, he would make the required order (*Irish Times*, 27 June 1914, p. 7). During this time, the Corporation decided to redesign. There had been criticism that the Corporation was sticking to rigid, monotonous, high density designs even when land availability was not an issue – see for example, the letter to the *Irish Times* from E.A. Aston, the indefatigable secretary of the Citizens' Housing League (10 February, 1914, p.9). The revised plan was still somewhat rigid, but the houses were now given front gardens and setbacks were employed to give a more varied streetline and there was a more interesting geometric layout at the front of the site. What the plan cannot show is the variation which was provided to the roofline of each terrace and the use of a warm multicoloured brick. The internal roads are narrow and on a pedestrian scale, making it challenging for contemporary car owners. The outcome, as modified by later changes, is much more appealing than the plan might suggest. There would be 205 four-room houses at a density of 31 dwellings per acre. Each house would contain a living room, two bedrooms, and a parlour or third bedroom, with scullery and w.c. and a ten-foot garden in front. Two house types were envisaged but with basically the same area, one with a frontage of 15 feet and the other with 24 feet. It was intended that the 42 houses in the centre would have rear gardens of 45 feet with the remainder having 15 feet. The intention was to have this difference reflected in the rents but it is not clear that this ever happened. Irregular plots not suitable for housing were given over to playgrounds or for planting. Charles MacCarthy estimated that the scheme would cost about £55,000. The houses would cost about

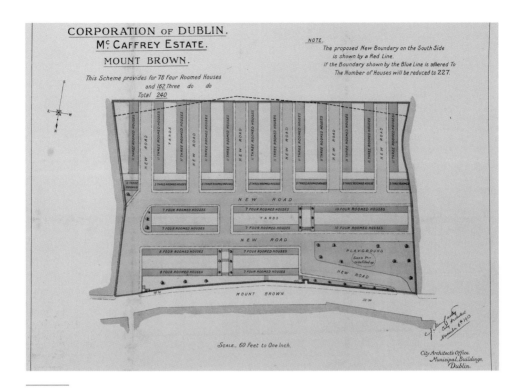

76. Mount Brown Housing scheme, 1914 version, Report 16/1914, Volume 1, p 80.

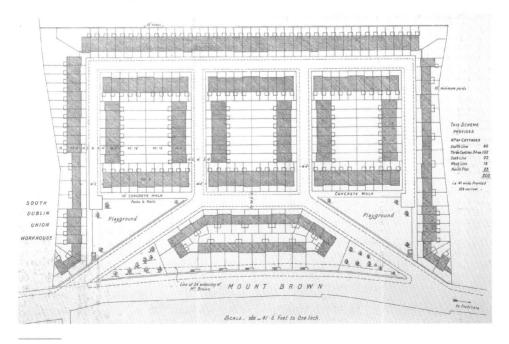

77. Mount Brown Housing scheme as approved. Report 58/1915.

78. Housing on McDowell Avenue at Ceannt Fort.

£220 to build but that would rise to £273 6s. 3d. when development costs were factored in (Report 58/1915). Rents of 7s. per week (quite high for the time period), were suggested because the houses were large and in close proximity to large business concerns, which provided constant employment and good wages.

This scheme too fell foul of the restriction on credit in 1915 and the LGB refused to sanction the required loan. Dublin Corporation could do no more than acquire the site and wait for less restrictive times. By then prices had risen and the Corporation's loan application in 1917 was for a total sum about 30 per cent greater than previously. Buildings costs had risen by an even greater amount and the submission to the LGB noted that a four-roomed cottage which cost £220 in 1915 would now cost £387 while a three-roomed cottage had increased in cost from £200 to £355. Approval was given on 30 August but on condition that the plans were modified. The LGB asked that the four-roomed houses follow the designs then being used in Fairbrothers' Fields and they felt that railings and hedges could be used to better advantage rather than concrete walls in dividing the properties. The latter point could be settled during construction. These changes were agreed by the Corporation in October and tenders were sought in early December. Only three were submitted and the winner was Louis Monks of Monkstown who agreed to build 202 cottages for just over £78,000 in 60 weeks or less (Report 10/1918).

St James' Walk / Colbert's Fort (Rialto)

Two reports are of interest for this very small site. The first was 27/1915 and dated 15 January 1915. The second was Report 75/1915, dated 19 February 1915. Report 27/1915 was never considered by the Corporation, a vote having been taken on to defer consideration of it for a month. By the time of consideration, it had been superseded by Report 75/1915 which was adopted by the meeting of 12 April 1915.

The block plan shows a small triangular site in Rialto bounded by the Grand Canal and the Poddle River and it is somewhat surprising that it was chosen for development.

The required inquiry took place on 12 June 1915 at the same time as that for Mount Brown with Mr Cowan as the inspector. There was little to say about the application because the Corporation owned the ground and there was general agreement that the housing would be useful. Mr Cowan, wondered though if it was wise to continue with the proposal given the funding position. The Corporation replied that they would make representations that the circumstances were extraordinary and funding was therefore possible. It was at this point that Mr Cowan made an intervention that was very interesting, especially given the later souring of relationships. He said that 'the Corporation had more sympathetic friends they knew of in their efforts to solve this dreadful difficulty' (*Irish Times*, 13 July 1915, p. 6).

The money was not forthcoming until the more general relaxation in the wake of the 1916 Rising. Consideration of this scheme was resumed at the same time as the Mount Brown development and tenders were sought in December 1917. The winning bid was from Mr Alexander Hull for just under £21,000 and the building was to be completed within nine months.

Delays to both projects

Things did not go well for either Mr Monks or Mr Hull and both found themselves unable to complete the contracts on time, much to the dissatisfaction of the Corporation. In the case of Mount Brown there was an issue about widening the

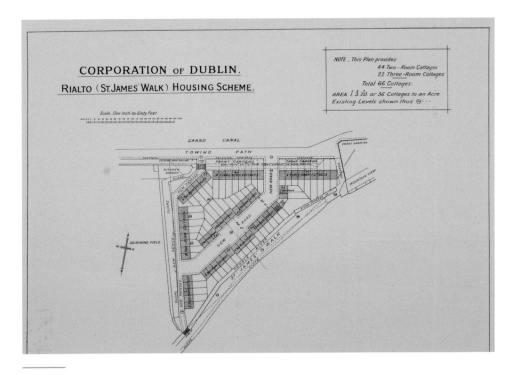

79. St James' Walk Rialto. Report 75/1915.

approach road which delayed matters but the general problem was both a shortage of men and material and to make matters worse, there was a strike by craftsmen. Once this was settled, the Housing Committee set a completion date of 1 May 1920. They were even less satisfied with Mr Hull and considered legal action against him but were persuaded by the Law Agent to give him a little more time also. The quarterly Breviate for 30 September 1920 (Report 56/1921) explained:

> It had not been practicable to obtain workmen at all times, and in the proportion desirable, many of the workers seeking more permanent or attractive employment and higher wages elsewhere. On the question of securing materials, the Contractor had on his instruction placed orders for slates, brick, drain-pipes, sanitary goods, eaves, gutters, grates and ranges, ironmongery, etc., at very early dates in his contract, most of which, except ironmongery, had been secured. Timber had also been procured in large quantities, and reasonably well in advance of requirements. It had not been possible to obtain large quantities of

cement, the Contractor's allowance in this regard being at one period limited to four tons per month.

It was now expected that the houses would be ready before Christmas 1920. The Corporation was sufficiently satisfied to agree to the insuring of housing in both developments and to the naming of the streets in July 1920. This was a time for recognition of those who had fought for Irish freedom during 1916 and who had been associated with the area. Mount Brown was formally renamed Ceannt Fort with the streets commemorating Burke, Traynor, Owens, Quinn, McDowell, O'Reilly and Donelan (Donnellan) while St James' Walk became Colbert's Fort with the streets remembering Malin (Mallin), Clarke and MacCarthy (McCarthy) (Report 160/1920). In the event though, the Colbert's Fort houses were not handed over to the Corporation until 21 March 1921 (Report 21/1922). The Colbert's Fort houses have weathered reasonably well and the alternating two storey houses with one storey cottages adds a degree of interest to the landscape.

Crabbe Lane

This scheme demonstrated that the Corporation's commitment to particular policies could sometimes take second place to pragmatic considerations. This site was on the edge of the city centre, a stone's throw from St Stephen's Green and the very fashionable shopping district of Grafton Street and its environs. It involved Cuffe Street, Cuffe Lane, Upper Mercer Street and all the houses between Digges Street and Aungier Place but did not involve the wonderfully named Cheater's Lane. It was going to be an expensive project, costing £39,350. The Ordnance Survey 5-foot plan of 1909 shows a regular urban landscape with none of the obvious signs of dereliction that could be seen, for example, off Church Street.

Dr Cameron made the necessary declaration on 16 February 1914 and the Housing Committee developed its plans. They decided that they had to build tenement blocks, notwithstanding all that had been said about Cook Street and other schemes and that there would be 36 three-roomed and 126 two-roomed tenements. The configuration involved three blocks of three storeys with 27 individual buildings: Block A would house 84 families, Block B would provide for 42 families and Block C would house 36 families. All external walls would be faced with red brick to provide a pleasing aspect. The gap between rents and costs were greater than in other schemes. Costed on the basis of what a speculative builder would be prepared to give for it, the scheme involved a loss of £1,300 2s. per year but costed on the basis of the housing scheme only the loss was reduced to £1,188 (Report 84/1914).

The Housing Committee felt the need to explain why they were building tenements and they included a most interesting justification as well as creating a new concept – 'non migratory' residents. The Committee seemed to have a very narrow view of what constituted 'migration' and wanted to house people exactly on the location from which they were displaced.

> The policy pursued by the Corporation in recent years is to provide self-contained dwellings, of one or two storeys for the working classes. We propose, with the approval of the Municipal Council to treat this area in a different way from most of the areas which have been dealt with. We

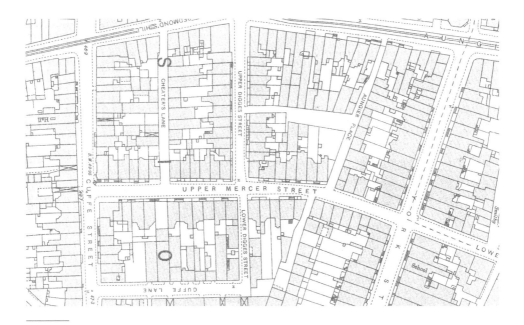

80. Crabbe Lane and Digges Street environs. Ordnance Survey plan, 5-foot, Sheet 18 (67), 1908 revision, 1909 edition.

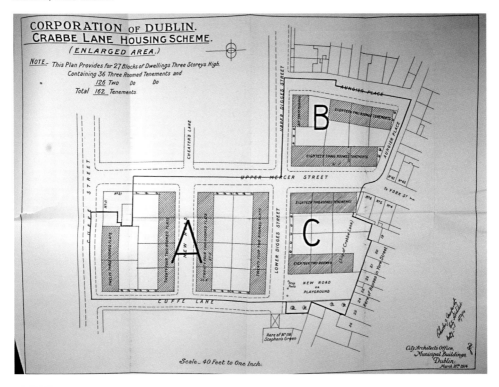

81. The Crabbe Lane Housing Scheme, 1914. Report 84/1914, Volume 1, p. 835.

are informed that the population of the area is a non-migratory one, and hence a difficulty arises in the carrying out of an improvements scheme on the self-contained cottage principle, which would meet to any appreciable extent the requirements of the district. The present population of the area is, of course, greatly congested, and it might be argued that the substitution of new block tenements for the present dilapidated and insanitary four-storey dwellings will not reduce that congestion. We are, however, convinced for the reason already stated with regard to the local prejudices of the inhabitants against removing from their present environment, that it will be necessary to provide accommodation for as many as possible of the dispossessed families, having regard to the preservation of general healthy surroundings. We therefore propose to provide for 162 families at rents of 3*s*. and 4*s*. These rents closely approximate what is being paid at present for miserable and unhealthy accommodation, namely, from 1*s*. 6*d*. to 3*s*. 6*d*. per week per room.

The Inquiry into the Provisional Order took place in early July 1915 with Mr Cowan in the Chair. On this occasion, the objections of the Dublin Citizens' Association were offered in a 'friendly' way, suggesting that building flat blocks in the centre was not the way to go and that it ran counter to the advice of Unwin and Geddes. They suggested that the designation of areas as clearance areas simply pushed the price of land to levels that used up too much of the Corporation's budget, a point made by them and others previously and taken up by the 1913 Housing Inquiry. It would be better to wait, build on virgin land and allow the price of slum land to fall. The Corporation took the view that people wanted to be housed close to their place of work and they could not simply allow people to live in their current conditions. There was now an imperative on the Corporation to build now that the area had been declared 'insanitary' (*Irish Times*, 9 July 1916, p.6). This was a legal ploy which they had tried with Spitalfields and it implied that Sir Charles Cameron acted independently of the Corporation. Certainly, he had a legal obligation to declare areas 'insanitary' if that is what they were. However, the 1913 Housing Inquiry had demonstrated a pragmatism in Cameron's actions. He would have made the designation only because the Housing Committee was prepared to build on the site.

Mr Cowan could see the sense of getting approval to acquire and clear the area but he was not convinced that building flat blocks was appropriate. He expressed the view that the Corporation should be building houses not boxes, especially when it was at the ratepayers' expense. He described the idea of blocks as 'warehousing' rather than housing. He saw the plan as a backward step and pleaded with the Housing Committee to reconsider. He was also interested in what was meant by a 'non migratory people' and he noted that the concept had not been explained to him.

The Inquiry concluded with the funding question unanswered. There was by now a moratorium on new loans by the Treasury but as with Spitalfields, the Corporation thought that exceptions were possible. Little was gleaned as to why the Corporation should have taken such a fixed view on housing the greater proportion of the existing population on exactly the same site; a solution necessitating flat blocks. They had other sites nearby and they had built extra capacity into some of them. Indeed even with the flat blocks some of the 'non migratory' people were going to have to migrate. It was a retrograde shift in policy and it is a pity that the opportunity was not taken at the Inquiry to expand upon it.

The money to build was not immediately forthcoming but the site was duly acquired, though the Corporation had difficulty in getting some of the tenants to surrender possession. By the time it was feasible to consider the building project, the LGB had become much firmer in its opposition to the original plans. In July 1919, the Corporation received a letter which noted that:

> The most serious objection in this case is the proposed use of three storied blocks of flats. Such buildings are in many ways most unsatisfactory, and are more costly and less convenient than self-contained houses, or even two-storied blocks of flats; and the Housing Committee of the Board will be glad if the plan is reconsidered and provision made for two-storied buildings only.

The Corporation duly complied, and the revised plans provided for only 46 dwellings, two-roomed houses and 14 three-roomed houses. There was no further mention of the needs of the population displaced or their 'non migratory' condition (Report 110/1920). The plans were approved on 20 March 1920 but the development did not proceed.

Trinity Ward

Trinity Ward was never far down the Corporation's agenda but, as already discussed, though poverty was widespread, the worst manifestations were dispersed. The problem that this posed was stated once more in a 1912 report of the Improvements Committee when they reported on a delegation that they had received from the Trinity Ward Improvements Association.

> The principal members of that Association, who are thoroughly conversant with local needs in this respect, have been deputed on various occasions to confer with the Improvements Committee, and several conferences have taken place. Both the Association and your Committee were strongly impressed with the difficulties of obtaining suitable sites. All the areas suggested were very small, and consequently the Improvements Committee were precluded from formulating anything in the shape of a satisfactory housing scheme for any one of the suggested areas.

On this occasion, the Improvements Committee decided that the time had come to have these various enclaves declared insanitary and at least cleared and this was recommended to the Council, which approved the Report (51/1912) on 4 March 1912. The area included parcels on Magennis Place, Moss Street and Rath Row, Moss Street and Bracken's Lane, Luke Street and Townsend Street, Boyne Street, other parts of Townsend Street near Spring Garden Lane.

Despite the geographical spread of the designated areas, the proposal was quite modest. The Committee suggested that 44 three-room cottages and 48 two-room tenements could be built in the area with a temporary garden on Townsend Street.

	Dwellings	Rent
Magennis Place	28	5s.
Boyne Street	16	5s.
Luke Street	16	3s. 6d.
Moss Street and Bracken's Lane	32	3s. 6d.

There would be two four-storey blocks on Luke Street, while Moss Street would

82. Flat blocks on Moss Street in 1987 before the view was obscured by the George's Quay development.

83. Close-up view of flat block on Moss Street in 1997, demolished 2019.

get four such blocks. The intention was to build 28 three-roomed self-contained houses on Magennis Place

The tenements were to be similar in style to those already built on Townsend Street while the cottages were to be of the same style as provided in Cook Street and Inchicore. Once again the reluctance of the Council to build tenements instead of self-contained cottages emerged. The Committee made it clear that it was only the representations of the Trinity Ward Improvements Association that convinced them the class of people who needed to be housed in the area could not afford the rents suggested for cottages. They strongly recommended that the 'flat tenements should not be let to any person earning greater wages than 25s. per week. These tenements should be entirely reserved for wage-earners of this class'.

While the average cost of housing a family at £250 was not hugely out of line with other schemes, keeping the rents low required a considerable annual subsidy. It was estimated that the annual loss on Moss Street would be £384 and £246 on Luke Street while it would amount to £475 on Magennis Street (Report 82/1914). This scheme was considered by the LGB at the same time as those in Church Street and Ormond Market. The LGB criticised the variation in rents across the schemes and

84. Magennis Place in 2019.

asked for consistency. However, the Corporation was of the view that there were sound reasons for the differences and held to its position (Report 31/1915).

The Townsend Street site was chosen by Patrick Abercrombie to provide an example of inner city housing in *Dublin of the Future*, his 1914 town plan published in 1922. He suggested combining cottages with flats, the flats in the form of a three-storey building with a classical façade. The scheme was laid out in series of geometric figures with a circular park providing the main focus and the entrance onto South Brunswick Street. The Park or promenade space was complemented by children's playgrounds and a great deal of planting. It bears more than a passing resemblance to the Corporation's own plans for North Lotts and Newfoundland (see below). The caption in Abercrombie's report makes the point that 'it may be questioned whether these tenements may be required if new houses and adequate transit facilities were to keep pace with slum clearance schemes (Abercrombie, 1922, fp.24).

A request for tenders was published on 31 December and these were considered at the Council Meeting of 3 May 1915. There were five tenders submitted and that from Messrs Alex Fraser and Co. for £15,352 was accepted (Report 14/1915). While Magennis Place remains a quiet enclave most of the flat blocks have been demolished.

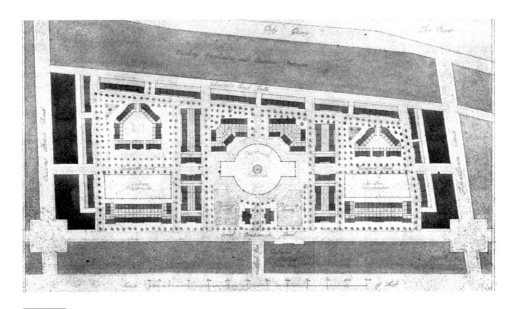

85. Abercrombie's plan (1914) for a mixed development of cottages and flats in Townsend Street. Abercrombie, 1922.

Boyne Street

This was originally part of the Trinity Ward improvement scheme but Mr Cowan suggested during his Inquiry into the proposed clearance that the site was too small to be useful and that it should be extended up to South Cumberland Street, otherwise he could not see his way to making an order for the 88 perches as originally conceived. This was accepted and the Housing Committee's report to the Council (Report 232/1914) which was discussed and approved on 2 November 1914, dealt with an enlarged site. Cameron duly made the required declaration on 30 April 1914 for an area which was now about 2 acres with some vacant plots due to the demolition of old and dangerous houses. A total of 110 families with 391 persons lived in 25 tenement buildings while there were 21 private houses. The majority (95) of the dwellings were one-room tenements with 11 two-room and 4 three-room tenements.

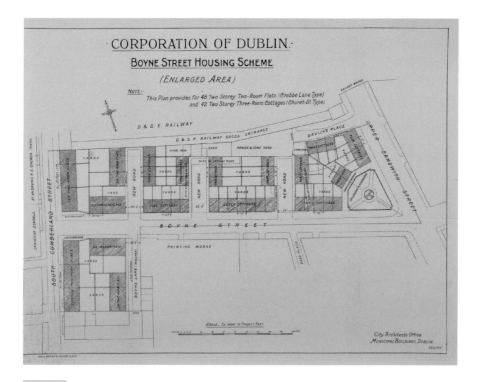

86. Boyne Street scheme as planned. Report 232/1914, Volume 3, p.370.

The scheme was for 42 three-roomed houses, two storeys high, similar to Church Street and 46 two-roomed flats, two storeys high, giving a total of 88 dwellings at a density of 44 dwellings per acre. The three-roomed house comprised a living room and two-bedrooms and the two roomed flat comprised a living room and bedroom. Each dwelling would have with a separate w.c., scullery and water supply. The building costs of the houses were estimated at £190 each and the flats at £175 each. The total cost was estimated at £22,075, of which £16,500 was building costs, the rest involving acquisition, clearance, road and sewers and misc. expenses. The deficit would be £437 3s. 6d. As previously, they found themselves justifying the use of flats rather than houses, even though these were not going to be higher than two storeys.

> Turning again to the evidence given at the Local Government Board Inquiry in December, 1912, we find that the question of erecting flat tenements was well considered, This evidence would go to show that there would be a great demand by the workers of the district for two-room tenements. In addition, the restricted extent of the areas throughout the Ward makes it desirable to utilize the space to the best advantage while avoiding anything that might tend to create over-crowding. In this case, we propose to erect 46 two-roomed, two-storey flats, which, from our experience of similar dwellings in Bow Lane and St Paul Street, appear to be a popular type of houses with the working classes. The remainder of the site will afford space for 42 three-roomed cottages and a children's playground. It has already been proved that housing accommodation is urgently required in this part of the city, where extensive industrial concerns – affording means of livelihood to a large proposition of the workers – are carried on (Report 232/1914, p. 366).

The suggested rent was 6s. 6d. for the three roomed house and 4s. 6d. for the two-roomed flats and was in line with Bride's Alley and Townsend Street.

Clearance was very slow in Boyne Street and had only been partially completed by 1920. The condition of the houses in the area was bad and by 1921 some houses were in need of urgent repairs. This made little sense since they would be soon demolished so the decision was made to undertake a partial building programme on the portion of the site at the junction of South Cumberland Street and Boyne Street (Report 192/1921). The LGB had not liked the original set of plans; they did not

87. Boyne Street scheme facing onto the street.

88. Rear view of Boyne Street scheme. This is probably the first instance of maisonettes in Dublin.

89. Boyne Street as completed. Note that the layout is much simpler than envisaged.
Ordnance Survey plan, 1:2,500, Sheet 18 (XI & XII), 1939 edition.

like how the corners were treated or the layout of the houses and they suggested that
a simple design be followed making more use of the street frontage. After 1919, the
Corporation had taken to outsourcing some of its design work and G.L. O'Connor
had been chosen as the architect for the scheme (see Report 110/1920, p.398). They
now decided to bypass him and came up with their own design, which would cost
about £12,000 to build. He was naturally displeased but once he had been assured of
his fee, though he did not like the design, he declared himself willing to get involved
in the design and building process. This was simpler than usual because the land
had already been acquired and the building was going to be paid for out of the rates.

There were eighteen dwellings in this partial scheme. While the street layout is
conventional, the houses are three storey, the top two storeys being maisonettes
which are accessed from the rear of the buildings. This, the report claimed, was the
first usage of maisonettes in Dublin and it is a pity that the Housing Committee did
not feel it necessary to explain whence the idea developed.

> The erection of six blocks, three storeys high, each block comprising one
> four-room flat, and two four-room cottages, having a frontage of 23 feet
> 5 inches. The flat to occupy the ground-floor, with the entrance from the
> front. The cottages to be approached from the rear, with an external iron

staircase to first floor and internal stairs to two bedrooms on second floor. The external walls to be built of 14-inch brickwork, faced with red facing bricks from ground to second floor, and the remaining storey to be 9-inch brickwork, finished externally with rough cast. The planning is different from anything erected in Dublin of a similar character heretofore.

Tenders were sought on 13 March 1922 for the dwellings, the cottages to have living room, two bedrooms and a kitchen and the usual sanitary facilities. Reflecting the times, it generated a lot of interest and nineteen tenders were received, of which five were deemed to be reasonable by the architect. The final choice went to Fitzgerald and Leonard for just under £11,000 (Report 96/1922).

The construction process was complicated by the fact that people had to be moved somewhat like Chinese tiles as houses were demolished, people temporarily housed and then moved into the new units as they were completed. A second phase followed quickly and was completed by mid-1923, increasing the number of dwellings to 36; four of the blocks fronted Cumberland Street and two faced Boyne Street (*Irish Times*, 23 August 1923). The third and final phase was approved in November 1923 and was for 42 dwellings with the same basic design though the frontage was slightly wider, giving increased area to the rooms. H.& J. Martin underbid Fitzgerald and Leonard to obtain the contract (Report 354/1923). The houses retain their distinctive character today with red brick on the lower two storeys with a nicely emphasised door case and impressive lintel. The entrance to the maisonettes at the rear has been redesigned in recent years and, as shown in the photograph, was originally a simple iron staircase.

Newfoundland and North Lotts

The docklands of Dublin had both considerable tracts of underused land as well as one of the larger concentrations of the working classes, so they commended themselves to Dublin Corporation as a location for new housing. Two projects were developed and because good sites could be obtained, they permitted the City Architect to spend more time looking at overall design, rather than trying to work out how to fit the maximum number of units on a very limited site. The plans show how the model village and garden suburb ideas had influenced thought with geometric designs, culs-de-sac and a great deal of green space both in the individual houses and in the schemes generally, though still at quite a high density.

Newfoundland

The Newfoundland area was not a particularly old part of the city, developed between the latter decades of the eighteenth century and the middle of the nineteenth century but had fallen into decay by the early years of the twentieth

90. The Newfoundland area. Ordnance Survey plan, 5-foot, Sheet 18 (48), 1909 edition.

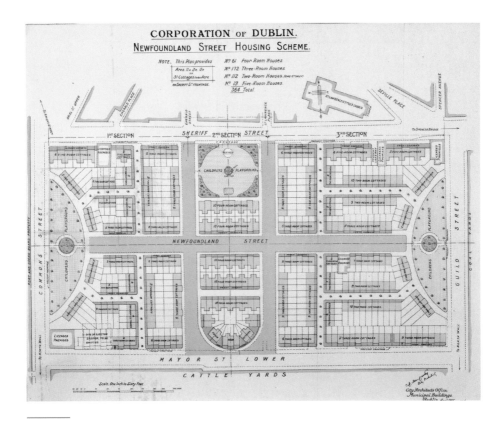

91. The Newfoundland Street housing scheme, 1916. Report 34/1916.

century. There was a total of 378 houses in the area, of which 89 were tenements and most of the rest were small cottages. They housed a total of 521 families or 2,082 persons. Report 34/1916 explained that:

> All the cottages in the district are very old and a large number have very little or no yard space. In fact, several of them have scarcely any reres or proper sanitary arrangements, and the whole area is very congested and gradually drifting into a derelict condition. The existing cottages, besides being old and decayed are very low and consequently the very limited cubic capacity of the rooms produces unhealthy conditions. This is a matter of vital importance both to the employers of labour and the workers themselves as inadequate air space naturally tend to weaken physical stamina and produce inefficiency resulting in loss of earning power. The continuance of such conditions must ultimately react injuriously on the City's general prosperity.

An examination of the Ordnance Survey plan from 1909 confirms the description. The area was bounded on the north by Sheriff Street, on the east by Guild Street, on the south by Lower Mayor Street, and on the west by Common Street, a more or less rectangular area of approximately 11¼ acres. Cameron made the necessary declaration under Part I of the Act in January 1915. The plan provided for five-room, four-room, three-room and two-room cottages with the better houses on Sherriff Street at a quite high density of 32 per acre. These new houses would be lit by electricity. The scheme also gave the City Architect the opportunity to experiment with a new five-roomed design, though there would only be 19 of them. He proposed undertaking the development of the 364 dwellings in three stages.

The First (Western) Section was of 8 five-roomed houses, 73 three-roomed houses and 44 two-roomed. The three-roomed houses and the two-roomed cottages were similar to those in course of construction on the Church Street area. The Second (Central) Section would contain sixty-one four-roomed houses while the final (Eastern) Section would contain 11 five-roomed houses, 99 three-roomed houses and 68 two-roomed cottages. The different types would cost £280, £220, £195 and £145 respectively.

The 1916 plan took the form of a H with its short axis extended to end in a semi-circular feature, a children's playground, at its western and eastern sides. Houses were arranged around these features in a manner reminiscent of the circuses of more genteel developments. This axis formed the main street of the scheme, Newfoundland Street, with housing on both sides. The north-south central axis also focused on a children's playground, a circular feature, at its northern edge. At its southern edge on Mayor Street, interest was maintained by arranging the houses in a hemi-cycle. A feature was the separation of pedestrian and vehicular routes throughout and the provision of trees along the former. It will also be noticed that the plot sizes were quite generous, despite the high density. As indicated above, the better houses were on the Sherriff Street frontage.

As with the North Lotts scheme, described below, rents would not be sufficient to cover costs and there would be a significant annual charge on the rates. However, the argument made in exactly the same words in both reports was that it was important to remember that the debt would gradually decrease and be eventually paid off at which time the property would come into the absolute ownership of the city. In addition, there were the less tangible but just as important benefits to public health.

That noted, the City Treasurer still felt that rents needed to be in some alignment with costs and reflective of the cost of money, so he suggest rents of 10*s.*, 8*s.*, 6*s.* and 4*s.* respectively, which, he explained, were in line with what was being paid for the present insanitary accommodation.

Reports 33/1916 and 34/1916 (for North Lotts, see below) were considered at Council Meeting 14 March 1916. The meeting read a letter from Revd James Brady PP, Seville Place in which he noted that: 'According to your report, it contains 378 houses with 2,182 dwellers. Most of these houses have only a ground floor, and the tradition is that they were run up in a hurry soon after the reclamation of land about the middle of the nineteenth century... The conditions of life here at present for such a deserving class can only be realized by one who lives on the spot and comes in daily contact with them. Indeed I can hardly describe them as decent, and I venture to think that but for the healthy and cleanly habits of the majority of the population the area would have been long since closed as unfit for human habitation'. Both reports were approved but the events of Easter 1916 delayed any further consideration.

The Inquiry into Provisional Order took place in June 1919, part of the same process that looked at North Lotts and Mary's Lane. Mr Cowan declined to make the order for Newfoundland on the grounds that the plans were not well founded, economical or expedient. He was not convinced that clearance was absolutely necessary but rather that Part II of the Act might be used. This placed the responsibility for action and the resulting costs onto the owners of the property. As usual, the various lobby groups attended but the session on 16 June was more lively. What the *Irish Times* described as a 'scene' took place. Mr W.J. Larkin, President of the Tenants' Association was having a heated exchange with W.T. Cosgrave when Mr Cosgrave took hold of Mr Larkin and shoved him towards the door and he 'was almost borne from his feet'. It took some time before order was restored with both men remaining at the inquiry (*Irish Times*, 17 June 1919, p.6).

Following their experience with Fairbrothers' Fields (see below), the Corporation were less accommodating than they might have been previously. They felt that Mr Cowan had exceeded his authority and instructed the Law Agent to initiate legal proceedings, despite his advice that such were unlikely to succeed. Advices were obtained from two senior Counsel and each agreed that it was more than

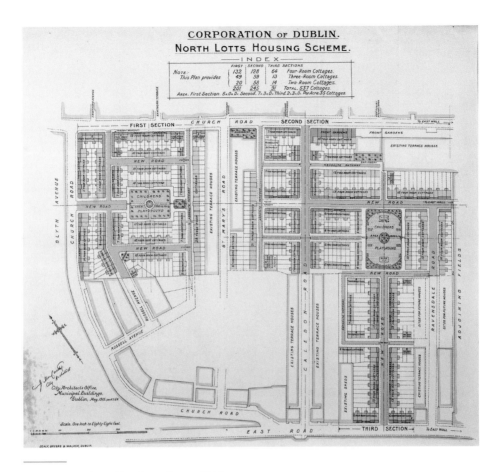

92. The North Lotts Housing scheme, 1916.

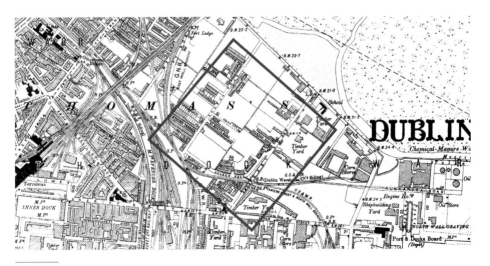

93. North Lotts. Ordnance Survey plan, 1:10,560. Sheet 18, 1912 edition.

likely that the Court would side with Mr Cowan as the Corporation would have to prove that no reasonable man could have come to the decision to which Mr Cowan had arrived. The case was dropped but Newfoundland fell off the Corporation's agenda until the 1940s.

North Lotts

The area described as the North Lotts, bounded by East Wall, East Road and Church Road, was an easier proposition. It contained about 15¼ acres of practically vacant land, though because it was low lying it needed significant filling in. The vacant nature of the land allowed the Corporation to proceed under Part III of the Housing of the Working Classes Act, 1890 which allowed them to use vacant land to house people displaced by other clearances or similar activities.

The plan developed by the City Architect was for a big scheme of 537 dwellings, at a slightly higher density of 35 to the acre, and he proposed also undertaking it in three sections. The First Section would contain 134 four-roomed houses, 49 three-roomed houses, and 20 two-roomed cottages, similar to those being built at the time in Church Street. The Second Section would contain 128 four-roomed houses, 59 three-roomed houses, and 58 two-roomed cottages. The final section would comprise 64 four-roomed houses, 13 three-roomed house, and 14 two-roomed cottages. As in Newfoundland, the cost of the houses was estimated at £220, £195 and £145 respectively. The Committee sought the approval of the Corporation to seek a loan of just under £139,000 from the LGB (Report 33/1916).

Unlike Newfoundland, the North Lotts site did not lend itself to the same symmetry and there was no attempt to produce separate circulation spaces. There were symmetrical elements in the various sections but no sense of an overall design. The scheme is quite rectilinear but with generous provision of playgrounds while internal circulation of vehicular traffic was controlled by the use of culs-de-sac.

As with Newfoundland and a number of other proposals, discussed above, formal consideration of a housing scheme resumed in Spring of 1919 but with an entirely new layout, prepared by the Corporation's chosen architects, O'Callaghan and Webb. Initial submission to the LGB, in advance of the formal Inquiry, indicated problems with the design. The LGB took the view that though the area was quite large it was difficult to create a good plan because of the incoherent nature of the existing streets and the impact of the existing railway lines.

However, the plan now submitted 'appears to have a somewhat excessive area of roads, and it is questionable whether a part of the area shown as "greens" would not be better disposed behind the houses for allotments or recreation grounds. It is unlikely that the greens could be kept in a way making the outlook on them from the front of many houses desirable, except at excessive cost. This difficult case probably warrants a moderate departure from the general rule now decided on with respect to the density of building allowable in schemes for which State aid will be given.

They probably would have preferred what they referred to as 'the very clever layout prepared by the City Architect in 1915. Revised plans were submitted on 29 October 1919 which provided for 279 houses at eighteen per acre, of which 28 had parlours and four bedrooms. The architects seemed to believe that this is what the LGB required so when the LGB queried the need for some many large houses, the architects immediately indicated their willingness to reduce the number of these houses to fourteen. The revised plan which was submitted for formal consideration had the following configuration.

	Number
Two bedroomed houses	50
Two bedroomed houses with parlour	48
Three bedroomed houses	85
Three bedroomed houses with parlour	82
Four bedroomed houses with parlour	14

This was accepted by the LGB because the layout was capable of being adapted to smaller houses, if that proved necessary and the Corporation was asked to be mindful of this (Report 110/1920). Mr Cowan made the provisional order on 30 June 1919 but the Corporation did not move to the arbitration phase until they were assured about money.

The Housing Committee's breviate for the quarter ending 30 June 1923 noted that the North Lotts scheme had been abandoned because the site would need expensive filling in (Report 64/1924).

Position as of 1921

Artisan Dwellings, Return for Quarter ended 30 June 1921

Development	Dwellings
Benburb Street	142
Bow Lane	85
Blackhall Place	109
St Joseph's Place	80
Elizabeth Street	14
Bride's Alley / Patrick Street	172
Clontarf	57
Donnycarney	8
Lurgan Street / Linenhall	48
Inchicore (Oblate)	331
Foley Street	456
Cook Street	45
Trinity Ward	76
Townsend Street	20
Church Street	144
Ormond Market	105
Spitalfields	74
Colbert's Fort	60
Ceannt Fort	163
Chancery Street	4
Total	**2,193**

It is clear from the above data that the Corporation's schemes, though small, were spread across the city. From time to time, they were invited by residents, owners or both to consider making schemes in other areas. One such case in 1909 related to the North City Ward, which had not had any schemes to date. The City Surveyor, Spencer Harty, was asked to report on buildings in Stafford Street, Jervis Street, Liffey Street Upper and Abbey Street Upper and Middle. Although the owners or lessees were willing to sell their interests the Corporation, the Surveyor advised that none of the sites would be suitable for workingmen's dwellings (Report 142/1909).

The schemes they had in prospect in 1921 were a mixture of old and new (Report 110/1920).

Boyne Street Housing Scheme
Crabbe Lane Housing Scheme
Fairbrothers' Fields Housing Scheme (already in progress)
Friends' Fields Housing Scheme
Mary's Lane Housing Scheme
Marino Housing Scheme (under active consideration)
Millbourne Avenue Housing Scheme
Newfoundland Street Housing Scheme (effectively abandoned)
North Lotts Housing Scheme (effectively abandoned)
Spitalfields Housing Scheme (in progress)

The Millbourne scheme ultimately became the Drumcondra scheme. Friends' Fields was a site of just over 5 acres in Ballybough on which it was proposed to build 81 dwellings. However, such was the nature of the site works necessary that it was deemed unsuitable and the proposal was dropped. It was reconsidered in 1932 and plans developed for 145 houses (Report 64/1932).

Fairbrothers' Fields

Weavers Square / The Tenters

By the end of the nineteenth century, the circumstances described earlier in relation to Spitalfields ensured that streets such as Chamber Street and Weavers Square in the Liberties were derelict and they were placed on the Corporation's list for renewal.

The instruction to the Improvements Committee to look at the Weavers Square area dated from a motion approved on 13 March 1911 that officials be directed to examine the acquisition of the premises known as Weavers Square Mill (including 31 to 36 Chamber Street and 3 Weavers Square) and the plot of ground known as the Tenter's Field. It was to be acquired if this could be done without putting any undue burden on the rates. This was done and an outline plan was approved for the area in 1913 (Report 203/1912).

On 9 December 1912, the council adopted a resolution instructing the Improvements Committee to initiate the process of acquiring land in the area

94. Weavers Square in the early years of the twentieth century.

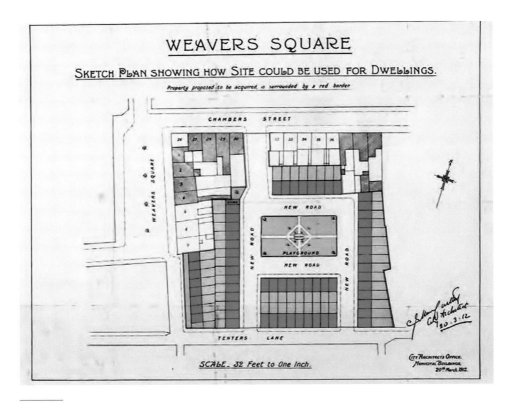

95. The original plans for Weavers Square.

known as Fairbrothers' Field, extending from Tenter's Lane to the South Circular Road. The LGB's inspector had issues with the proposals and P.C. Cowan refused to sanction the Weavers Square scheme because he felt it would be advantageous to put this together with the Fairbrothers' Field site. The combined site was 22 acres (9ha) and could be expected to accommodate about 700 dwellings. This was a big step up for Dublin Corporation and would mark their entry into the world of largescale building. The Corporation agreed to Mr Cowan's proposal in 1914 (Report 16/1914) and felt that they had acquired a good site.

> The clearance of several of the slum areas in the decaying parts of the City, and the substitution of self-contained dwellings will provide for a lesser number of families than are displaced. This surplus population must be provided for elsewhere, and it, therefore becomes necessary to acquire suitable vacant sites within the City Boundary, such as is the subject of the present proposal. In addition, the site is located in close

96. Fairbrothers' Fields and environs. Ordnance Survey plan, 5-foot, Sheet 18 (76), 1909 edition.

> proximity to some of the largest centres of employment in the City, and
> the provision of dwellings there will be a great convenience to the workers
> employed in those concerns (p. 68).

They also saw the opportunity to build a road that had been in contemplation for
some time – from the South Circular to James' Street and Thomas Street. The roads
in the scheme would connect with Weavers Square, Chamber Street and Ardee Street
with a street of 55 feet in width from Weavers Square to Greenville Terrace.

This led to an amended plan in 7 January 1914 for 108 four-roomed houses, 480
three-roomed houses and 212 two-roomed flats in 25 blocks, two storeys high. A
large playground was also planned. Despite the presence of a large playground
in the centre it is a very regimented angular design with the houses arranged in a
conventional grid. As with the Spitalfields scheme, there was debate as to the cost

basis with the report providing costings on the basis of the total cost of the scheme and the Housing Committee's view that only the actual value of the site when acquired and cleared should be entered into the equation.

The required inquiry began on 6 June with P.C. Cowan as the inspector. As had become usual, the Dublin Citizens' Association and the Citizens' Housing League were professionally represented in making their objections. However, at the conclusion, Mr Cowan intimated that he would make the requested order under Part III of the Act. This was duly noted by the Corporation (Report 183/1914). The provisional order was approved but the Corporation found that it needed to use compulsory purchase to obtain the lands; it had not proved possible to get agreement from the

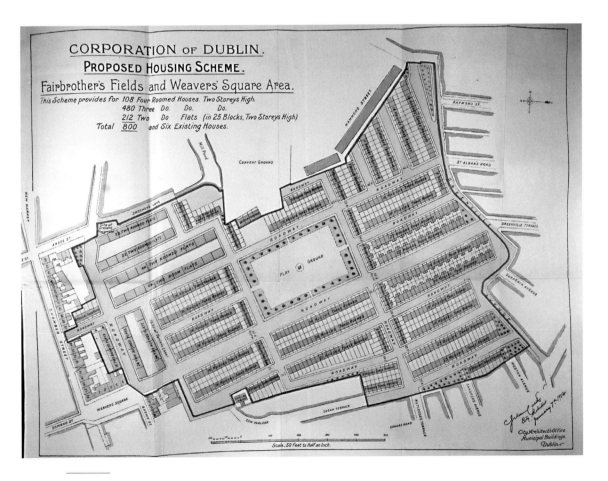

97. Fairbrothers' Fields Proposed Housing Scheme for 1914. Report 16/1914, Volume 1, p.80. The plan (and the 1918 revision) is incorrectly titled Fairbrother's Fields.

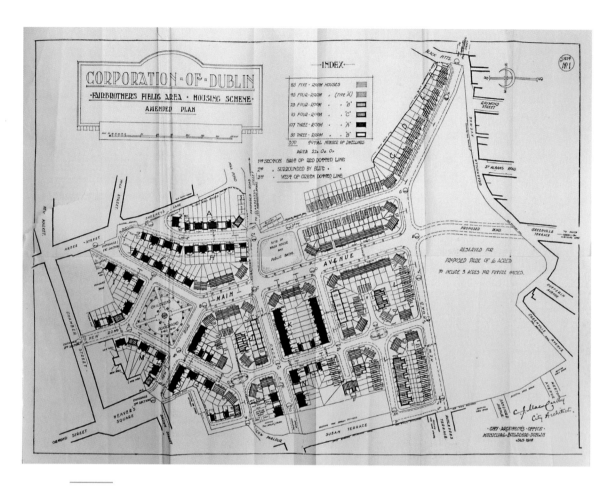

98. Fairbrothers' Fields Proposed Housing Scheme for 1918. Report 22/1918, Volume 3, p.444.

99. Fairbrothers' Fields as seen by Google Earth. Map Data: ©Google Earth Pro.

owners. It took until 26 November 1914 before they had the necessary authority. The arbitration process began on 3 March 1915 but by May the scheme had fallen foul of the restrictions on credit. As with the other schemes similarly caught, the Corporation pleaded its case for exceptional treatment. By December 1915, the Corporation felt that they had approval for funding for site acquisition, if not for building. This proved to be incorrect and it took until December 1916 before the necessary funds of acquisition were put in place. In April 1917, with the special funding scheme put in place by the incoming Chief Secretary, Mr Duke, that the project, together with others mentioned above, began again.

Given that such a long time had elapsed, it was necessary to draw up revised estimates for the plan, which were submitted to the LGB. A new inquiry was deemed necessary and it took place over two days from 11 September 1917 with Mr Cowan once more acting as the LGB Inspector. The design of the scheme had changed, reflecting the evolution of the Corporation's thinking. The City Architect explained to the inquiry that the scheme was now for 568 houses comprising 100 five-roomed, 215 four-roomed and 253 three-roomed cottages. Not all would have bathrooms and when queried, the Architect commented that they were very expensive to install. The rationale for the Corporation's new position was explained in the later report 109/1917.

The idea of building on virgin land in the suburbs had been developing momentum for some time. Fairbrothers' Fields provided the opportunity to adopt a somewhat suburban scheme. As the Architect put it: 'Although the site is within the city boundary it may be regarded as a semi-suburban one and I have taken advantage of this fact to reduce the number of houses from 800 to 568 and to adopt a layout more nearly approaching the treatment recommended by the advocates of garden suburbs'. Unwin and Geddes (discussed above) had argued for such an approach.

> (14). We would recommend that a good type of cottage be built upon this land, and would point out that comparatively little reduction in the cost of building a house is secured by cutting down the size of the rooms. All the expensive items, fireplaces, doors, windows, fittings, &c., for each room have to be provided for the small room as well as for the larger one; and it will be found that the smaller the rooms, the higher will be the cube price of the buildings. It is therefore in a real sense economical to build rooms of adequate size. Seeing also that the repayment of loans is now spread over a

100. Fairbrothers' Fields - Example of housing.

> period of sixty years, it is important that cottages should be built of such a type that they will be likely to satisfy the standard of accommodation which the people will require over the whole of that period (Report 78/1915).

The revised scheme would be at 36 to the acre and this did not please the Dublin Tenants' Association who saw the scheme as an attempt to avoid having to build on suburban sites at lower densities.

Mr Cowan had a number of suggestions to make regarding the scheme and it took some time for these to be worked out. The interactions between the LGB and the Corporation were unusually tetchy. In the Corporation's view, the LGB felt that their 'suggestions' were in fact 'directions' and the Corporation was not going to put up with that. The Corporation agreed to take note of the suggestions and, in fact, they adopted most of them. Relations, though, seem to have been irrevocably damaged. Sanction for the loan of £233,593 was obtained on 2 December 1918 but the scheme had now been reduced to 370 houses.

Even though the scheme had been approved, the LGB urged the Corporation to proceed only with putting in the sewers and roads until the terms of post-war loans became known. This was agreed but a point was reached in August 1919 where

101. Fairbrothers' Fields - Example of housing.

it became necessary to demolish certain houses on the site in order to complete these works. The people displaced would need to be housed and so funding was sought to begin building. Matters went downhill very quickly with the LGB finding itself caught between an increasingly exasperated Council and an inflexible HM Treasury. By this time, the 1919 Housing (Ireland) Act was a reality and one of its provisions was a subsidy to assist local authorities in their housing programme. The price was that larger Corporations such as Dublin would not be entitled a loan from the Local Loans Fund; they would have to raise their money elsewhere. There was a number of interactions between Corporation, LGB and LGB and Treasury with the latter agreeing that Dublin Corporation could proceed under the special loan arrangements put in place in 1917 OR they could operate under the 1919 Act: They could not do BOTH. The LGB tried to keep out of the argument by taking the view that they were merely facilitating the exchange of positions. However, when they asked the Corporation to choose between the approaches, it provoked a response, dated 27 November 1919, from the Housing Committee which put it up to the LGB.

> In reply, we are instructed to state that the Housing Committee of the Corporation of Dublin expected that the Local Government Board – being in full possession of all the facts in connection with this scheme

– would themselves have dealt with the latest incubus introduced by the Commissioners of Public Works, who, it is presumed, are acting as the mouthpiece of the Treasury. Your Board must surely recognise the impossible position which is now attempted to be set up by the proposition contained in the letter from the Board of Works, and which is so fatuous, in face of existing conditions, that our Committee are, indeed, driven to the conclusion that the Government Authorities are merely trifling with this tragic question.

The letter went on to say that:

The attitude of the Corporation in all their dealings with the Local Government Board has been to comply cheerfully and unreservedly with every suggestion made by the Board, but we feel bound to say that they are growing weary and disheartened of meeting difficulty after difficulty raised by the Board and other Government Departments in this matter, without effecting any practical progress towards the alleviation of the sufferings of the thousands of families who are crying out to the Corporation for relief, and whose condition is now on the border line of despair and desperation.

...

Surely, therefore, this is not a time for obstructing progress on the pretext of shallow technicalities. We have demonstrated that the money for building cannot be borrowed from the banks or otherwise in the open market. In these circumstances, are the Government still determined to refuse facilities necessary to have the new accommodation provided, seeing that the immediate issue concerns itself with the welfare of thousands of human lives?

It was still stalemate in December 1919 as a headline in the *Freeman's Journal* asked 'How Fairbrothers' Fields is being held up' (22 December 1919, p.4). The solution was found following an appeal to patriotism and an aspect of the new housing legislation which permitting the raising of bonds for housing purposes. Dublin Corporation decided to issue 3¼% Redeemable Stock, redeemable in 1944, for the entire amount required. This was supported by the decision of Bank of Ireland to purchase £100,000 worth (*Freeman's Journal*, 17 September 1920, p.6).

The scheme was approved by the Council at their meeting on 8 November 1918 (Report 221/1918) and the costs were estimated as follows.

Average Cost per house	£659 0s. 0d.
Average Proposed Rent	£24 14s. 8d.
Rates (paid by Corporation)	£6 16s. 4d.
Annual deficit per cottage	£33 10s. 10d.
Cost of collection/rents/repairs	£3 18s. 6d.

As building commenced, the costs continued to rise and the gap between these and the rents proposed continued to widen. The concern within the Corporation led to consideration of economic rents and ultimately to the hugely important decision to move to tenant purchase. This is discussed below.

The adopted plan was quite different from the original suggested in 1914. It provided for 370 two-storey houses with front and rear gardens occupying about two-thirds of the site (16 acres), the remainder being kept for a park and further houses. Space was also left for a bath and wash house and a playground. The accommodation included 85 five-roomed cottages, 128 four-roomed cottages in three variants (A, B, C) and 157 three-roomed cottages in two variants (A, B). The five-roomed cottage included a parlour, kitchen and three bedrooms, with an upstairs bathroom. The four-roomed cottages included either a kitchen and three bedrooms or a kitchen, parlour and two bedrooms. The three-roomed cottage offered a living room with two bedrooms. Each cottage had a w.c. and a scullery with the usual water supply and space for a bath.

The scheme had lost its strict geometry, the edges of the blocks were now curved and the cul-de-sac had been introduced. A diamond-shaped part at the apex of the scheme recalled Weaver's Square but also provided a focus. The design was signed off by Charles MacCarthy but H.T. O'Rourke was now deputising for the City Architect, who was indisposed. The garden suburb and model village influence is clear in these plans here and the provision of different house types and their distribution throughout the scheme to produce variety would be a feature of the Marino scheme which O'Rourke would present to the Corporation in 1919.

The first phase was for eighty houses but at the Council meeting of 25 January 1922 it was felt that it was feasible to build another 198 houses and to that end they authorised the laying of foundations. It was subsequently decided that these should all be five-roomed and of a larger size than the earlier five-roomed houses provided (Report 53/1922).

It was at this time that the Council decided that they would not build any more three or four-roomed houses but concentrate on five-roomed houses. Though they did not state it, this was an inevitable move to tenant purchase because these houses would be available only to the better-off working classes or the Council would have to pay massive subsidies. They explained their reasoning.

> We are of opinion that at present the number of four-roomed, three-roomed, and smaller dwellings now in existence ought not to be increased, and that the Council should turn its attention to the provision of a better class of dwelling. Experience has shown that the average householder regards a parlour as an essential adjunct to the house, so that the family may enjoy the ordinary comforts of home life. The provision on the ground floor of a room other than the kitchen or living room leaves the latter at the complete disposal of the domestic manager, enabling her to do her work with comfort and satisfaction. It is obvious also that for the average family three bedrooms are essential. These considerations lead us to the conclusion that a five-roomed house ought to be the minimum standard, and we are strongly of opinion that this standard should be adopted for the houses now proposed to be erected on the Fairbrothers' Fields Site (Report 68/1922).

They made this a formal policy a little later in the year so as to be ready for the Million Pound Grant (discussed below). They recognised that this might exclude people with lower incomes but they suggested that there would be a trickle-down effect in that many of those who would take up the new houses would be current tenants and they would release smaller but good housing. They added these housing schemes were to be undertaken on virgin sites (Report 309/1922).

However, in 1926, they DID accede to a request from the Minister for Local

Government for some four-roomed houses. A scheme of 59 houses was fitted onto some vacant land at Greenville Avenue, at an average building cost of £444 per house (Report 37/1926).

Building was sufficiently advanced by 1924 to permit the naming of streets. It seems that people had already named Merton Gardens, Sandford Park and Sandford Gardens and no attempt was made to alter them. The Commissioners liked the idea of commemorating poets and patriots and so the following was decided (Report 265/1924).

Main Avenue	St Thomas Road
Road from Ardee St to Blackpitts (partially completed)	Clarence Mangan Road
Road A	O'Donovan Road
Road B	Madden Road
Road C	Geoffrey Keating Road
Road D	O'Carolan Road
Road F	O'Curry Road
Road fronting vacant site at Greenville A venue	Petrie Road
Children's Playground	Oscar Square

How to build

This scheme also allowed the Corporation to develop its approach to building. As far back as the Oblate scheme, there had been support for Dublin Corporation doing its own building by direct labour. Then the Dublin Building Guild arrived on the scene; a form of co-operative building organisation, while the standard building contractors formed the third strand. The Council decided that it would put each method to the test by apportioning the building of 198 houses for which foundations had been approved in January 1922. The houses were allocated as follows.

(a) 80 houses to be built by a private contractor;

(b) 58 to be erected by the Dublin Building Guild;

(c) 60 to be erected by the Municipal Workshops Department.

Report 154/1922 approved the laying of foundations for a further 134 houses to be given to the Dublin Building Guild and a later report (186/1922) recommended for scheduling and other reasons that 70 of these houses should be built by the Guild with the balance being built by the Council directly. All this was subject to ministerial approval and while he did not specifically object to the allocation, he suggested that some of the houses should be given to a private contractor. Ever alert to a ministerial suggestion, the Corporation decided on a reallocation (Report 48/1923) which saw 46 go to the Dublin Building Guild, 34 to the Municipal Workshops and the remaining 54 to a private contractor. This was not to be the last time that a ministerial suggestion that more private enterprise be involved was acted upon.

The experiment showed to each approach worked but no one approach was clearly superior to the others. The Minister favoured contracts to private builders and the Corporation, while happy to use both direct labour or the Dublin Building Guild from time to time, tended to follow any ministerial suggestion.

The *Irish Times* reported in 1923 that construction was proceeding well. A total of 139 houses had been completed and occupied and it was expected that the entire scheme would be completed within nine months. They reported that only four of the houses had baths because of the expense involved but that all houses had provision for one, 'if thought necessary' (*Irish Times*, 28 June 1923, p.5). Costs were going down and the final phase was costing approximately £690 per house compared to the first phase of 25 houses which had cost of the order of £900.

Tenant Purchase

As has been explored above, there had long been a lively debate in the Corporation about rent levels. Any rent set below the economic rent (the rent that could be obtained in the private market) resulted in a long-term charge on the rates. Subsidies of this kind had become part of the normal provision of housing schemes but this remained a matter of debate and discussion. It became accepted by even the most subsidy-inclined members of the Corporation that bigger developments in the suburbs could not operate on that basis. The reasoning was never made explicit but it must have been because the increased scale of development would have required a very large charge on the rates. So, from early on, it was assumed that suburban developments were going to be for the better-off 'artisans'; those who could afford the full rent.

When the Corporation decided to proceed with the Marino scheme, in consequence of the comprehensive report presented on 19 September 1919 (Report 210/1919), they envisaged the tenants paying rents of 10*s*., 8*s*. and 6*s*. for the five-, four- and three roomed houses respectively. These were pre-war rent levels and should have been much higher at a time of rising building costs. It was reckoned that it was all that could be afforded, though there was hope that costs would fall in the future and rents would come more in line with costs. Even with the State providing a considerable subsidy it was clear to the Corporation that 'a heavy burden will fall on the ratepayers' (p. 56).

At the public inquiry into the loan for Marino in January 1919, P.C. Cowan made the point that the suggested rents would require a very significant subsidy. He suggested rents of 2*s*. 6*d*. per room per week or 25% more than the City Treasurer was suggesting. This would be enough to ensure that there would be practically no loss on the scheme. This was necessary, he argued because: 'The system of people paying other people's rents could not last long. If the Corporation was to attempt to let these houses on what might be called charity rents they would certainly fail to solve the housing problem in Dublin' (*Irish Times,* 5 January 1920, p.3).

It was a relatively small step from charging rents at that level to move to the sale of Corporation-built houses. The moment came when a motion was put to and carried by the Corporation on 13 September 1920 (Minutes, p. 462).

> It was moved by Councillor Forrestal; and seconded by Councillor Doyle: That the Housing Schemes of the Council place an ever-increasing strain on the general body of ratepayers, who have this year to provide a sum of £52,000, equivalent to a rate of 1*s*. 2*d*. in the £, for the repayment of loans, interest, supervision, and upkeep; and further as the tenants in occupation at present ought not, and do not, desire to be a burden on the ratepayers, most of whom are struggling workers themselves, this Council requests the Estates and Finance Committee to report on the feasibility of disposing of the property to the occupying tenants and submit a scheme for the consideration of Council.

The subsequent report of the Estates and Finance Committee was favourable to the idea (Report 240/1921). It was submitted to the Council on 6 February 1922.

A last ditch amendment would have put consideration off for some time but once this was (narrowly) defeated, the report was accepted. There were attempts to rescind the decision over the next couple of years but these came to nothing.

The rationale for tenant purchase was given as follows.

> We have had under consideration a scheme drafted by the Town Clerk, under which the existing tenants of self-contained cottages, erected by the Corporation under the Housing Acts, will be given facilities for purchasing the premises in their occupation. His view is, and we agree with him, that the responsibility of ownership will naturally induce tenants to take a greater interest in the care of their dwellings, and obviate to a large extent the expenditure in repairs, which the present conditions of tenancy involve. It will further add some thousands to the number of direct ratepayers in the city, and consequently inspire amongst them a greater civic spirit.

The report set out a payment schedule for each of 1,172 cottages which had been built by Dublin Corporation since 1893. The repayment period ranged from 39 years to 60 years and the price was, in most cases, to be an annuity equal to twice the Poor Law Valuation of the cottage, plus ground rent at a rate of 25 per cent of the Poor Law. These tenants had a choice, they did not have to give up their rental tenancy. New tenants would not have that option and would have to become purchasers.

This scheme was not popular. It was reported in 1924 that only one application had been received and it was decided to abandon the scheme. In hindsight, this was probably to be expected. Many of the current tenants were on low incomes, which was reflected in the design and type of the schemes in which they lived and the rents they paid. While the offer was a good one, it was never clear from where these people would get the necessary money. It did not cause any immediate rethink of the general principle since future tenants would have a different income profile.

Despite this experience, 'tenant purchase', whereby the 'rental' paid by each tenant was in fact a mortgage repayment which led ultimately to the transfer of the property to the tenant at the expiry of the term was implemented in the Fairbrothers' Fields development which was nearing completion. Houses were offered in a range between £327 to £429 for the four different house types or 10s. 9d. to 15s. 9d. per week (Report 162/1922). Building continued during 1926 and terms were fixed for 59 houses in May 1927 with prices at £350, £340 and £330 for types A, B and C respectively (Report 97/1927).

Fairbrothers' Fields Purchaser's Annual Payments

Type	Sale Price	Purchase Annuity	Ground Rent	Rates	Total Annual	Weekly Cost
Living room, scullery, three bedrooms	£327	£19 0s. 0d.	£2 0s. 0d.	£6 9s. 8d.	£27 18s. 8d.	10s. 9d.
Parlour, living room, scullery, two bedrooms	£361	£21 0s. 0d.	£2 5s. 0d.	£9 3s. 0d.	£32 18s. 6d.	12s. 8d.
Parlour, living room, scullery, two bedrooms	£378	£22 0s. 0d.	£2 10s. 0d.	£10 3s. 4d.	£35 3s. 10d.	13s. 7d.
Parlour, living room, scullery, two bedrooms bathroom (H&C)	£429	£25 0s. 0d.	£3 0s. 0d.	£12 4s. 0d.	£40 16s. 0d.	15s. 9d.

Note: Expenses of collection and bookkeeping payable by purchaser, as under:-
1¼ per cent., or three pence in the £, in the case of half-yearly payments of annuity and ground rent.
2½ per cent., or six pence in the £, in the case of quarterly payments of annuity and ground rent.
5 per cent., or one shilling in the £, in the case of monthly payments of annuity and ground rent.
10 per cent., or two shillings in the £, in the case of weekly payments of annuity and ground rent.

Housing Allocation

Another issue arose in 1922 that produced an important policy approach. A councillor alleged that the allocation of the first tranche of 25 houses in Fairbrothers' Fields was not open and transparent (Report 93/1922) and that friends and clients of the members of the Housing Committee were given unfair access to the houses. This resulted in a sworn inquiry held by the Minister for Local Government on 6 June 1922 which did not find any evidence of the practices complained of but did identify serious issues with the procedures used in the allocation of houses (Report 161/1922). Discussion of the report of the sworn inquiry was delayed until 5 March 1923 when, following an angry meeting during which insults were widely traded, the newspapers described the meeting as 'warm', Report 308/1923 was adopted by a significant majority. This was NOT the report of the sworn inquiry, an attempt to have it endorsed failed by a large majority, but rather a commentary on the report of sworn inquiry together with a process for the allocation of houses in the future.

Report 308 improved transparency in that it removed selection from the Housing Committee, but it did not expand on the specifics of how the selection process would work. The Council returned to the issue in the context of deciding to build only five-roomed houses. Report 162/1923 set out four considerations; the number of persons in the household (a minimum of five for the five-roomed houses), the maximum average weekly household income, their housing conditions and the rent that they were paying. The Superintendent of Dwellings was asked to assess each applicant in terms of suitability and to classify them on the basis of the type of dwelling to which they were suited. There would then be a ballot among those within each class for the available dwellings. Those who were not successful would be eligible for future ballots. However, the Council was not prepared to set specific levels for each of the criteria, feeling that some discretion was necessary.

The 'Million Pound Grant'

The new government of the Free State knew that it needed to act quickly on the housing crisis but it was wary of taking on long term financial commitments so early in the life of the State. It hit upon the device of raising the sum of £1m (the 'Million Pound Grant') for new construction. The details of the scheme appeared in the newspapers on 17 March 1922. The grant would be made available to local authorities, operating under the existing housing legislation. The authorities were asked to strike a special housing rate of at least 1s. in the £ for one year and to raise short term loans of three times the amount raised by the rate. The State would then make a grant in the proportion 2 to 1 to the total amount raised locally. Under this scheme Dublin, including the townships of Pembroke and Rathmines received £561,910.

Donnelly's Orchard

This was a small scheme which Dublin Corporation undertook because it could be done just in time to qualify for the Million Pound Grant. Their attention was drawn to a 12 acre plot on the banks of the river Tolka which was part of the Holy Cross College estate but peripheral to it. It had been used for allotments but that had ceased and the Trustees seemed happy that it should be used for housing. The Corporation liked the site. It was bounded on three sides by main roads and was close to the Ballybough tram terminus. The site was good except for a small portion that was liable to flooding by the River Tolka, the fourth boundary of the site. The Church, however, did not let the site go cheaply. The Trustees asked for £2,400 and it took the intervention of the Archbishop, Most Rev. Dr Byrne, to get the site at £1,800, what the Corporation's valuer judged to be its market value.

The Corporation's own housing department was too busy to undertake the project but they already had contracted a Dublin firm of architects to prepare a plan for the nearby Millbourne Avenue area. That scheme was sometime off, so the Corporation agreed to ask Messrs McDonnell and Dixon to undertake the work (Report 148/1922). Tenders were sought on 6 March 1923 for 84 cottages and H.&J. Martin were the successful bidders. The houses contained a parlour, living room, three bedrooms, a scullery and indoor sanitary facilities, a configuration which was becoming the standard, though not every one on the Council agreed. At the meeting of 31 April 1923, Alderman Hubbard Clark commented that he would like to see smaller houses being built so that the people who were the special care of the Corporation could afford the rents (*Freeman's Journal*, 1 May 1923, p.7). The Housing Committee's report to the Council seeking final approval for the scheme (Report 111/1923) also noted that when the full costs of the scheme were factored in, the average cost per house came to £31 more than the £750 limit set by the Minister for funding. This was due to the underbuilding on the site in that only 5 acres of the 11.25 acres were being used for housing at that time. A paring exercise which involved replacing slates with 'Poilite' asbestos tiles was undertaken and this and other savings managed to reduce the 'all-in' cost to £743. They had originally made provision for a school site at the junction with Distillery Road. However the

102. Donnelly's Orchard on the banks of the Tolka River. Ordnance Survey plan, 5-foot, Sheet 18 (28), 1888 edition.

103. Donnelly's Orchard, the later completed scheme. Ordnance Survey plan, 1:2,500, Sheet 18 (4 & 8), 1938 edition.

local parish priest Canon Walsh, had decided not to proceed with the project. The houses were featured in the Building and Reconstruction section of the *Irish Times* for 18 October 1923 which included a photograph of houses nearing completion. The report noted that while the bathrooms had been built, the installation of the baths and the hot water system had been delayed. This was in line with a similarly bad decision made in Fairbrothers' Fields and in Marino.

Matters were sufficiently advanced to permit a public lottery to take place on 26 March 1924 for 71 of the houses, the remainder being allocated to transfer applicants. There were 1,283 applicants who claimed to meet the criterion of having a household of at least 5 persons, three of whom were children.

The Housing Committee hit upon what the Lord Mayor described as a 'novel idea' by holding the drawing in public in the Mansion House. This allowed the Lord Mayor to extol the virtues of the Corporation while giving a degree of assurance as to the probity of the draw, at least. This was further assured by having the draw made by two blind persons from the National League of the Blind. It captured the public imagination and got good newspaper coverage but it is probable that the large crowd comprised mostly those who had deep interest in the proceedings (*Freeman's Journal*, 27 March 1924, p.7).

The Housing Committee seems to have felt keenly its loss of influence because there was an attempt at the Council meeting on 14 April 1924 to set aside the results of the lottery and put selection back into its hands. An amendment was passed which instead suggested that nothing be done for two months to allow members to find out how the ballot worked out. No more was heard about the matter, presumably because the Law Agent indicated the difficulties in overturning a ballot which had been undertaken with such publicity. The development was extended to its current size in 1933 by the building of 10 four-roomed and 138 three-roomed cottages. At the same time, the baths and hot water systems were installed in the original 84 houses (*Irish Times*, 8 December 1932, p.3). The 1938 Ordnance Survey plan shows the completed scheme with the same design elements present as in Drumcondra – culs de sac, short terraces with ample gardens front and rear (See below for a fuller discussion of these elements).

Kehoe (Keogh) Square / Emmet Road
Formerly Richmond Barracks

In the early years of the Free State there had been political interest in the idea of turning former imperial barracks around the country to other uses, including housing. In response to a Dáil question from Peadar Doyle T.D., President W.T. Cosgrave announced on 17 June 1924 that the Richmond Barracks would be made available for housing on a 90-year lease from the Office of Public Works. Thereafter the project moved quite quickly and the City Commissioners decided in September 1925 to convert the barracks into flats while building houses on the adjoining property. In all, the site comprised about 13 acres, to which an additional 36-acre plot was added in 1926, with a further 27 acres acquired in the following year. This development, which was undertaken at about the same time as the suburban Marino and Drumcondra schemes, does not seem to have generated the same level of interest, despite its large scale. It has a number of parallels with the two more celebrated schemes. The decision to build mostly five-roomed houses in the first phase at Keogh Square, but a mix of sizes in the second, chimes very well

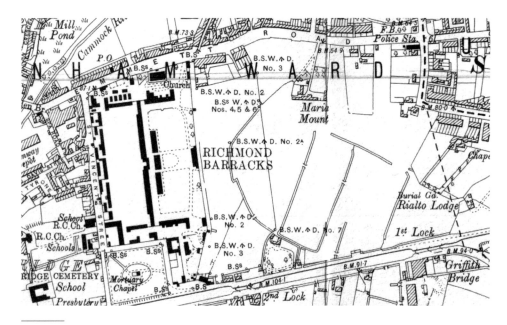

104. Richmond Barracks and environs. Ordnance Survey plan, 1:10,560, Sheet 18, 1912 edition.

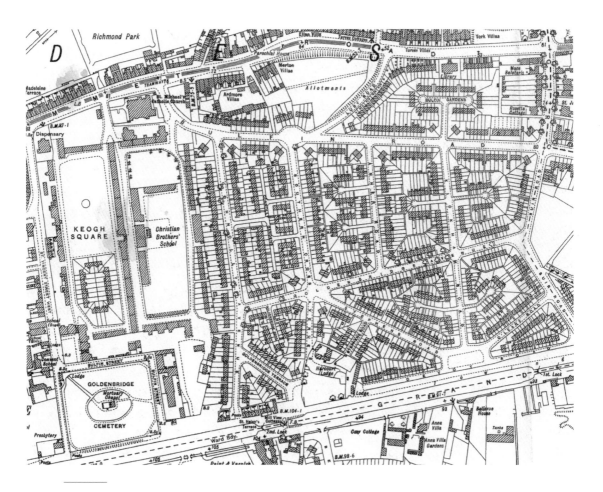

105. Keogh Square / Emmet Road, the completed scheme. Ordnance Survey plan, 1:2,500, Sheet 18 (10), 1943 edition.

with changes in approach between Marino and Drumcondra. The layout of the later phases (Kehoe Square Extension and Emmet Road Extension) is also similar in character to the Drumcondra Scheme.

The Commissioners for Public Works handled the flat conversion in the barracks directly (see *Irish Times,* 15 January 1925, p. 5), while the City Commissioners invited tenders for the construction of houses on the adjoining property. John Kenny of Harcourt Street won the tender in September 1925 (Report 196/1925). The plan involved the conversion of the barracks into 202 self-contained flats varying from two to five rooms, with a further six self-contained two-roomed flats to be housed in converted buildings on the St Vincent Street frontage. Kenny would build 218 five-roomed houses on the vacant land, but there would be 45 three-roomed cottages, of which 21 would be on St Vincent Street. Given that the scheme would add almost 2,000 people to the area's population, it was decided to make the former 'recreation buildings' available for a school.

The development was extended for the first time when the Commissioners acquired a 36 acre parcel of land to the east of the scheme in September 1926. The plot, previously used for market gardening, had the potential for 570 houses: 114 five-roomed houses costing £505, 200 four-roomed houses costing £430, and 256 three-roomed houses costing £245. As part of this Kehoe Square Extension, a new road would be created from the South Circular Road to the first lock on the Grand Canal, linking up with Crumlin Road (Report 169/1926). A second extension became possible when a further 37-acre parcel was acquired in 1927, so that the entire scheme now reached from Emmet Road to the Grand Canal. This second 'Emmet Road Extension' comprised 480 houses, the majority of which were four-roomed, with just 60 five-roomed houses included. In the interest of getting the houses completed within a year, the Commissioners offered two contracts, to H. & J. Martin (251 houses) and Kenny (229 houses) (Report 178/1928). An 'experimental method' using poured (monolithic) concrete rather than bricks was used, the virtues of which were extolled in a full feature in the *Irish Times* (2 September 1928, p. 7).

All in all, this scheme had turned into a major development, almost as big as Marino, which if not quite suburban was at the limits of the city. The *Irish Times* in commenting on the Emmet Road Extension (the third phase), did not appear to like the development, but did not like Marino, Fairbrothers' Fields or Donnelly's Orchard either as being too congested. According to the writer, this scheme at a density of 14 to the acre was better than most but had the Commissioners gone a mile or so further out, the development could have been in a rural area where space would not be so confined. The writer pointed out that this development was only 2.5 miles from the centre but that in these days of good motor transport a journey of five miles to work would not cause any great problem for artisans. Clearly, the writer had a different view to many and felt that: 'The new housing scheme ought to be extended over at least four times the area proposed and by opening up the rural areas between the three and four mile radii from the city this could be done without excessive expense (*Irish Times*, 20 July 1927, p.6). As with the other schemes, the houses on the city's land were made available for tenant purchase. The closing date for applications for the Kehoe Square extension scheme was 3 December 1926 (20 November 1926, p.1) with the final tranche being made available in June 1929 (Report 130/1929). In both cases applicants were required to be resident within the city and to have at least four children. The prices for the second tranche were as follows.

5 Roomed Houses	16 Semi detached	£440
	14 End of Terrace	£420
	34 Intermediate	£400
4 Roomed Houses	12 Semi-detached	£340
	134 End of Terrace	£320
	274 Intermediate	£300

Rents in the flats in the former barracks at 1*s*. 9*d*. per week were low and, while the conversion met an urgent need, this element of the accommodation quickly developed a reputation as being sub-standard. People balanced this against the low rents and many tenants were long term but Dublin Corporation also used the development as a place of last resort for tenants who were difficult or who were in arrears. By 1959, it was felt that the time had come to redevelop the site and replace the barracks with the new standard five-storey flat block. With the development came a new name – St Michael's Estate.

Marino

In many ways, the scheme at Marino was the culmination of Dublin Corporation's early housing efforts. It was an idealistic interpretation of the garden suburb, intended to be a model both for future public and private housing developments. From the start, the site was associated with the emerging ideas of modern town planning. In 1910 the City Council considered a suggestion that a 50 acre (20 ha) plot of land in Marino, a part of the city estate which had been sub-let by the Christian Brothers to James Walker, a well-known and successful businessman of Sealy, Byers and Walker, might be developed 'on garden city lines'.

Mr Walker had been anxious to develop this property for some time but he needed the co-operation of Dublin Corporation because of the terms of his lease. He had made overtures to the Corporation but these had not obtained the desired result. The idea was revived at a meeting of the Clontarf Ratepayers' Association (essentially a survival of the township) at which it was proposed that Mr Walker be asked to restate his offer to the Corporation and that body be respectfully asked 'to afford Mr Walker facilities for undertaking this commendable project, whereby a large number of artisans and labourers will be afforded employment and the city as a whole benefit from the increased rating resources resulting from the erection of the buildings' (*Freeman's Journal*, 20 October 1910, p.9). The presence of a number of aldermen and councillors on the platform, including Councillor Briscoe (see below), ensured that the Corporation was receptive to the proposal.

Mr Walker duly wrote to Dublin Corporation and his letter was considered at the council's monthly meeting on 14 November 1910. The speed with which the letter was written and found its way onto the agenda of the Corporation in the form of a fully developed proposal suggested that the matter had been under active consideration by both proposer and supporters. Nonetheless Mr Walker claimed that he had been approached by a group of Clontarf residents, following a public meeting, and asked to reconsider developing his property as a 'miniature garden city.' He said that he was pleased to do so and he asked for a meeting with the authorities to further the plan (*Irish Times*, 19 November 1910, p. 11). He felt that he was offering a good deal to the Corporation in that they would see good houses

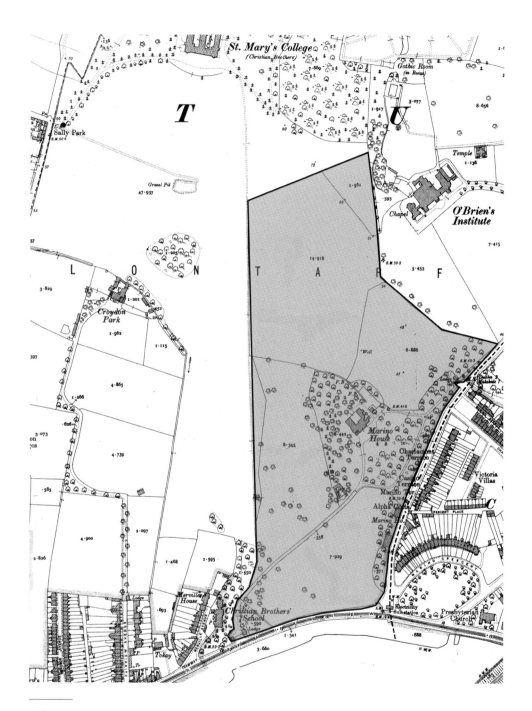

106. The 50-acre site in Marino. Ordnance Survey plan, 1:2,500, Sheet 18 (IV), 1911 edition.

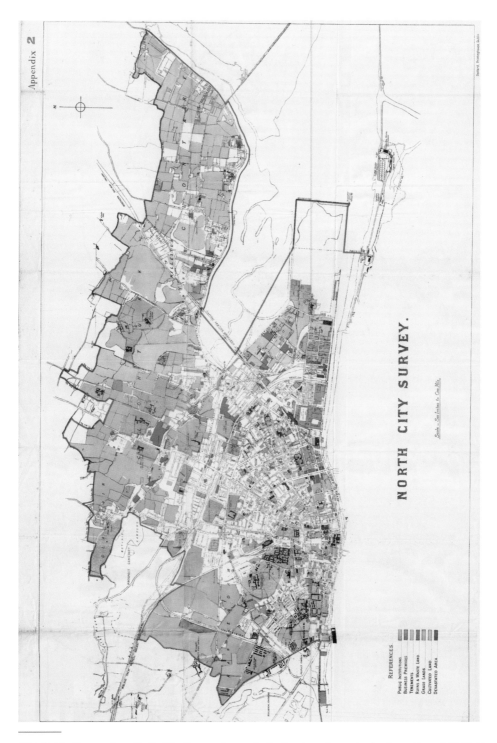

107. Dublin Corporation, North City Survey, Appendix 2, showing city centre landuse. Report 38/1918.

108. Dublin Corporation, North City Survey, Appendix 1, showing proposed major projects. Report 38/1918.

built, resulting in an increase in their rate book. The property would be further enhanced by his willingness to permit the installation of electricity.

The cost to the city in developing the land was estimated at £50,000 and a motion in the name of Councillor Briscoe asked the Estates and Finance Committee to examine the proposal. Mr Briscoe was an enthusiastic supporter of the garden city idea and he noted that he had recently visited the UK and he was convinced that this was the way to build houses. Not everyone agreed and the motion that was eventually passed replaced the reference to a 'garden city' with the more generic 'houses'.

It was not until 1911 that the matter was considered in detail (Report 270/1911) and the initial reaction was not entirely enthusiastic. The report from the Estates and Finance Committee pointed out that Walker's property was only part of a larger lease of 228 acres which would lapse in 1921. It might also be suggested that Mr Walker's proposal was not entirely altruistic. In asking for a reversionary lease from Dublin Corporation, the ultimate owners of the property, he would ensure his continued ownership and ground rent income. He also wanted to control the development. His intention was that the Corporation would build '£30 per annum' houses on the 'backwards part of the site' with the implication that more expensive housing would be built on the better sites. This was not in keeping with the principle that the houses would be for the better class of artisan.

There was also a cooling of enthusiasm from the Corporation's own officials.

> It is quite true that the Corporation have from time to time advocated the building of artisan dwellings in the open country adjoining the city but in doing so we always felt that the erection of dwellings should be contiguous to large centres of industry and employment – for example, Kilmainham, close to the Inchicore Railway Works; Bride Street, contiguous to Guinness' and the other large employment centres, Townsend Street, for the workers on the quays – whereas this site, being removed from the centres of employment, will not, in our opinion, be a suitable position for the erection of working-class dwellings (p. 881).

They were reflecting on their experience in building at Conquer Hill, Clontarf (See earlier discussion and McManus, 2002), which had not been entirely satisfactory as tenants complained about being too far from their employment. The report to the Council was without recommendation and Mr Walker's specific proposal proceeded no further and, indeed, he died in 1915. This was not the end of the matter for the site. Some preliminary planning of the Marino site was done in 1911 with one option being a development on the lines of what was being built in London's Hampstead Garden Suburb (Report 270/1911).

This never developed into a formal proposal and the recommendation agreed at the Council meeting on 7 October 1912 was that nothing be considered for five years. Yet, despite this moratorium, during 1914 there was a number of attempts (see Minutes, 10 August) to come to a definite view on the Marino scheme. Although it was never explicitly stated, the report of the 1913 Housing Inquiry, which was published with remarkable speed in February 1914, must have been the catalyst. The Corporation finally decided (7 December 1914) to take all necessary steps to secure Mr Walker's interest in the plot of 50 acres, 2 roods and 9 perches (20.4ha) and to prepare a scheme for erecting houses for 'artisans at economic rents'. There was now no suggestion that Mr Walker would have any involvement in the development. The phrase 'at economic rents' is important because it indicated that this development was to be treated differently to the ones discussed above. Notices appeared in the newspapers in 1915 announcing the intention of the Corporation to seek a provisional order for an improvement scheme for Marino and to acquire compulsorily the 50 acre site (*Irish Times*, 11 January 1915, p.6). The project stalled at this point as funding dried up because of the war and the Corporation came to the view that it was pointless getting land on which they could not afford to build. The land at Marino eventually fell into their hands via the war-time government requirement that idle land be pressed into food production and control passed to the Land Cultivation Committee who put it to allotments. As the First World War ended, the land could be diverted from food production and this meant that as of 9 December 1918, it was again available for housing.

Marino was never going to be a garden city as conceived by Ebenezer Howard (1898, 1902), despite the description of the site in 1910 as being suitable for 'a miniature garden city'. There was never any suggestion that it was going to be a self-sustaining city with industry and employment, and, in any event, it was too close to the city centre. Nonetheless, the first UK attempt at the concept,

Letchworth (1903), was well known and the later design for Welwyn Garden City (begun 1919) was also studied with interest as Marino's development came closer. Hampstead Garden Suburb provided important inspiration too. In their report to the Corporation in 1911 (Report 270/1911) John G. O'Sullivan, City Engineer and Surveyor and C.J. MacCarthy, City Architect, offered a number of suggestions for development, the plans having been prepared in O'Sullivan's office by W. Cranwell Wilson. In one plan, the design was for 588 two-storey cottages. Each had a frontage of 14 feet (4m), with an average depth of 150 feet (46m), the large depth being justified by the likelihood that tenants would have had an agricultural background and so interested in growing vegetables etc. This report was notable for a brief comment in that 'provision for 30 houses having a frontage of 20 feet (6m) is shown facing Fairview Strand, where a slightly better class of house could with advantage be erected, and a better appearance presented for the main public road'. This will be explored a little later.

Perhaps of most interest was plan no 3 where 'I have endeavoured to adapt as much of the Hampstead design as would work in with local custom'. It envisaged a broad avenue, 71 feet (21m) wide, having a centre line of trees. Marino House was in a central position and accessed from both the new avenue and Malahide Road. Five large plots for detached houses of the best class would adjoin it. Houses of a variety of sizes were envisaged with 'a broad belt of plantation' being provided at the rear of second class houses so as to screen them from the front of houses on the lower road, while at the same time giving a pleasing outlook (Report 270/1911).

Marino remained in the Council's thoughts and, as discussed above, Unwin and Geddes spent considerable effort in exploring the site and suggesting how it might be developed. It figured in the Corporation's survey of the north side of the city in 1917. The Council, in Report No. 69/1917, considered and adopted a 'proposal (vide Minutes of 11th June, 1917, item no. 397) made by us for the preparation of a Survey of the North side of the City, with a view to ascertaining the evolution of the tenement system and the social and economic conditions and requirements of the working classes in that district. The information obtained on these lines is, we consider, essential in the drawing up of a programme to meet the insistent demand for healthy housing accommodation for the enormous section of the population in need of relief in this respect' (Report 13/1918).

Although it was a report of the Housing Committee to the Corporation, it was issued separately, doubtless to fulfil its propaganda role, as well as appearing in the printed volumes of Corporation reports. That said, it was an excellent report, containing two fascinating and important maps. The landuse map provided a detailed picture of the usage and condition of the entire north city. The development map set out the main building agenda and included schemes for Marino, Cabra, docklands and a fascinating idea which would have seen Upper Sackville (O'Connell) Street and its environs redeveloped for housing. In all cases, the geometric nature of the plans is evident but the Marino development was still confined to the original 50 acres.

Development came closer to becoming a reality when a detailed plan was presented to the Corporation in September 1919 by the City Architect (Report 210/1919). The developing interest in town planning and garden cities has already been mentioned. This was given greater focus when the report of the Tudor Walters committee became available. Promises had been made to those going to fight in the trenches during World War I that they would return to 'homes fit for heroes'. A first step to meeting that promise in the United Kingdom was the establishment of a Committee by the President of the Local Government Board and the Secretary of State for Scotland to consider 'questions of building construction in connection with the provision of dwellings for the working classes in England and Wales, and Scotland and report upon methods of securing economy and dispatch in the provision of such dwellings'. The chairman was Sir John Tudor Walters and Unwin was a member and it is hardly surprising that garden city ideas influenced many of the recommendations. It was a hugely influential report and had a profound impact on working class housing provision certainly up to the Second World War, if not beyond. Though it did not specifically apply to Ireland, its influence was felt. The Tudor Walters report had been available only for a short time but even by 1919 it was already 'a work of reference on housing questions' (p.51).

The UK published its first Housing Manual in 1919 and by 1919 the Corporation had available a guide published by the LGB which offered a series of plans for typical sites and various types of houses. This arose on foot of a competition held by the Royal Institute of Architects of Ireland and sponsored by the LGB which invited entries for 'suitable and economical types of houses grouped in the most advantageous manner on typical sites' (HM Stationery Office, 1919).

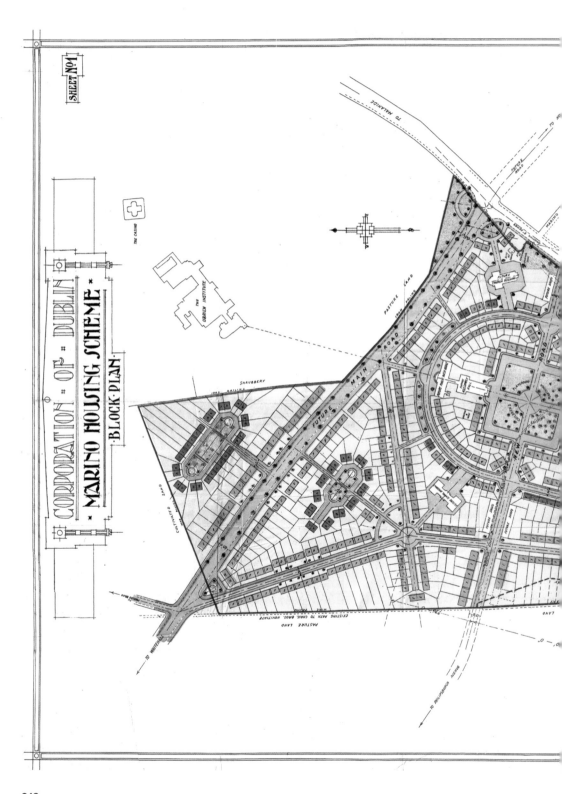

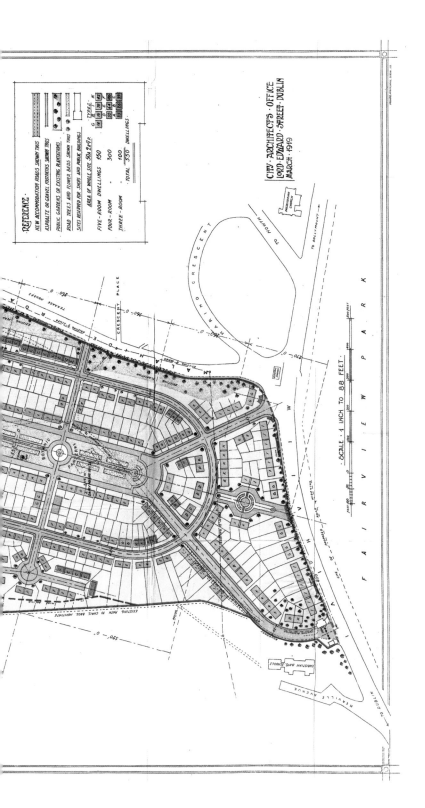

109. Layout Plan for
Marino, 1919. Report
201/1919.

These developments confirmed the City Architect in his view that they needed to build bigger dwellings than before and the majority of dwellings had three bedrooms, living room, scullery, coal store, larder and WC. His plan allowed for 100 three-roomed houses, 350 four-roomed and 150 five-roomed; all to have baths with hot and cold water. Smaller families would be accommodated in two-bedroomed houses while larger five-roomed houses would be available for those who could afford it. All this became possible once the Corporation decided that these houses would be for tenant purchase only.

Accompanying the report was an impressive outline plan, drawn at a scale of 88 feet to 1 inch (1:1,056). While Hampstead Garden Suburb was an inspiration, this plan owed much to model towns such as Port Sunlight (Hubbard, 1988) and to Letchworth. The main feature was an extended oval, running approximately north-south, with two rings of houses. The outer ring faced onto the surrounding roads while the inner ring faced onto a monumental linear park, surmounted by a formal square. In this park a library and an assembly hall were placed. Marino House, which by now seems to have become ruinous, would be demolished. To the north-west smaller geometric patterns of houses were suggested with roads intersecting to provide an overall focus for the development. Marino was very green though the reader will note that trees were relatively absent. A look at the plan provides the explanation. The area was mostly under cultivation and there were few trees on the site. Those that were there are carefully noted on H.T. O'Rourke's (Assistant City Architect) plan. Perhaps surprisingly, the Corporation did not plant many additional trees, preferring grass, except along its signature roadway, Griffith Avenue, which is notable for its double line of trees on either side of the road. It is only in very recent years that Marino has begun to take on a 'tree-lined' appearance and only to a limited extent. By the time of the plan, the Tudor Walters standard of no more than 12 houses to the acre (30/ha) had been enshrined in the 1919 Housing Act but here the density was somewhat lower at 11 to the acre (27/ha).

The scheme was bounded by the existing main roads of Fairview Strand and Malahide Road to the south and east respectively while a new main road, linking Whitehall and extending on the Howth Road would provide the northern boundary. The western boundary was less marked because it comprised cultivated land and, even at this point, there must have been some suggestion that the scheme could be extended.

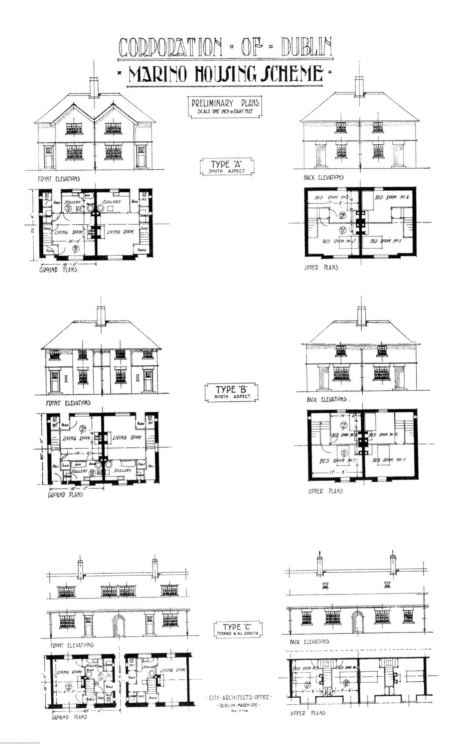

110. Proposed housing types at Marino, Report 210/1919.

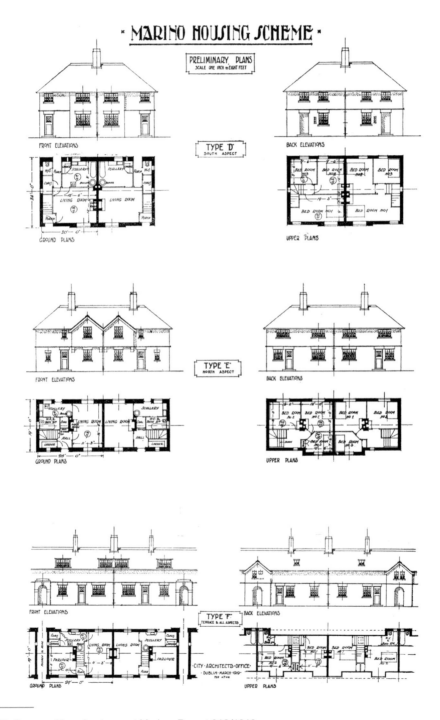

111. Proposed housing types at Marino, Report 210/1919.

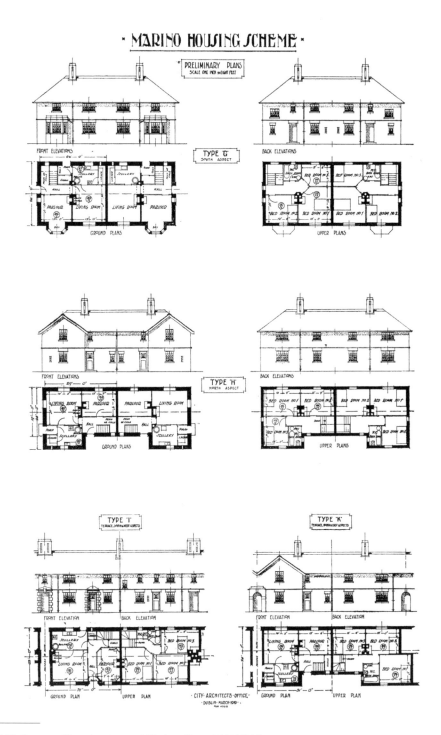

112. Proposed housing types at Marino, Report 210/1919.

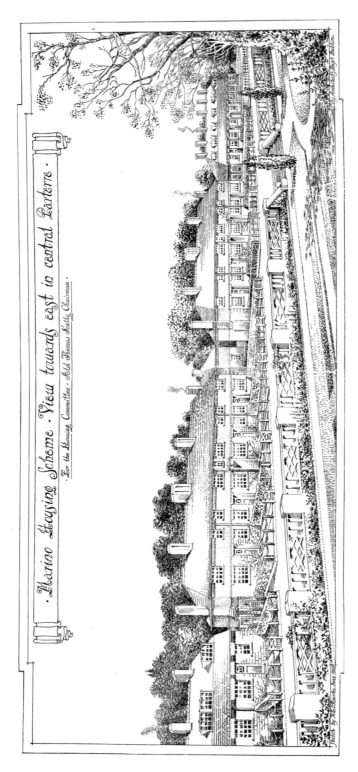

Sheet No. 5.

Marino Housing Scheme. View towards east in central Parterre.

For the Housing Committee. Ald. Thomas Kelly, Chairman.

113. Sketch for houses on the parterre by H.T. O'Rourke. Report 201/1919.

The 1919 plan was notable for the variety of housing types, not quite as many as provided in Port Sunlight but certainly more than might be expected in a typical local authority housing scheme. There would be ten different house types, four for the five-roomed houses and three each for the four-roomed and three-roomed houses. The larger houses were concentrated along the Fairview edge and the northern edge and especially around the main square. Here an interesting effect was obtained by having a particular design for each side of the square. Elsewhere variety was ensured by breaking up the sight lines by using setbacks and by limiting the runs of individual designs. This was true also of the smaller house types.

The design-values for the different house types were very high and the image here shows a number of these. The house types varied in roof line, window design and door placement as well as in internal configurations. In contrast to the semi-detached larger houses, the smaller units were terraced but had a covered passageway to allow access to the rear and the large gardens without having to use the house. A line drawing of one design by H.T. O'Rourke shows an impressive attention to detail. Looking at the model designs in the early editions of the Housing Manual produced in the UK to give practical effect to the Tudor Walters ideas, it seems likely that these designs were also well known in Dublin even then.

But the Corporation's concern with cost got the better of them. The estimated cost at £542,500 was a very significant sum but of greater worry was the continuing annual cost on the rates which would amount to around £20,000 after the third year. Additionally, at the time, material prices were fluctuating dramatically and the estimated building cost for one design of five-roomed houses rose from £784 to £1,176 between June and September 1919 (Report 210/1919, pp 67–70). As a result, they suggested that three house types would be enough – one for each of the sizes, choosing the one which provided the best value. This would cut the cost to £505,345 and leave the rates to carry under £18,000. In overall terms this was not a huge saving but it was a recurring one and the Housing Committee was prepared to sacrifice one of the novel aspects of the scheme. It was clear that the City Architect's Office was not happy and H.T. O'Rourke wrote that the 'scheme as submitted has received long and most careful consideration by the City Architect and fulfils all modern requirements in housing. In the City Architect's absence, through illness, I feel it my duty to the Housing Committee to point out that if the scheme is altered in the manner now proposed, there would be very little chance of its being approved by the Local Government Board' (Report 210/1919, p. 66). Further consideration reduced the cost to £503,673 for 550 houses and that amount was sought as a loan.

The inquiry into the loan was scheduled for 2 January 1920 and it had the additional element of theatre in that the Chairman of the Housing Committee, Alderman Tom Kelly, was being held in Wormwood Scrubs prison without any charges against him. The Corporation asked the Chief Secretary to make him available to the inquiry since his evidence would be invaluable, but the Chief Secretary was unable to accommodate them. Following some further debate on the first day of the inquiry, it proceeded and lasted two days. The decision, communicated on 12 February, was generally favourable (see the section on Fairbrothers' Fields for the discussion on costs) but the Board wished some changes to both the houses and the layout of the scheme to make it as economical as possible.

The Corporation was open to discuss the matter and the Breviate for the quarter ended 30 September 1920 (Report 56/1921) noted that following discussion between Dr Cowan, the Borough Surveyor and the City Architect, it had been decided to reduce the number of houses from 550 to 468. However a sub-committee of the Housing Committee, including Councillor Cosgrave, recommended that the number be increased to 530. Since this required building on land which was not in the ownership of the Corporation, it was decided that further consultation was needed.

Matters came to a halt until the new government of Saorstát Éireann was installed. With a new Minister in place, discussions resumed and an iterative process between the Minister and the Corporation resulted in approval in 1922 for 681 houses on the 50-acre site to the design of F.G. Hicks. However, for reasons which are examined below, the proposal which was adopted by the Council on 22 January 1923 was for 468 houses (Report 14/1923).

This was now going to be only phase 1 of a much more ambitious scheme. Notice of this had been given at the Council Meeting on 31 July 1922 when Mr MacCaoilte in moving the report of the Housing Committee said that while all of the energies of the committee were focused on Fairbrothers' Fields, they were making plans for Marino. They hoped to obtain additional land and, combined with the existing site, they hoped to build up to 1,500 houses (*Irish Independent*, 1 August 1922, p.6). The site in question comprised 76 acres (31 ha) to the west, extending to Philipsburgh Avenue, generally known as the Croydon Park extension (see McManus, 2002).

So as not to delay or hinder the opportunity to avail of the 'million pound' grant then available, it was agreed to proceed with a scheme for the initial 50 acres but in such a way as to join up with the second tranche of land. For both it was agreed to build at 12 to the acre with a new main thoroughfare to the north (Report 162/1922).

The final layout was still quite geometric, with a variety of house types, the use of setbacks and the north-south axis was retained. Large gardens were provided and the communal areas were transformed into much larger spaces, especially the two circular parks, keeping the density low.

Some principles

During the iterative process with the Minister a number of important decisions were made. Firstly, while the Corporation was keen on direct labour, it found that there was less support for the idea in the Department of Local Government, who kept a tight rein on all projects. Secondly, they began to develop their reserved area idea (discussed in detail below) whereby the boundaries of a housing scheme were given special treatment to improve the overall appearance of the development. As approved in report 14/1923, they withdrew the boundaries from the development to form 'reserved areas'. The 428 houses agreed to would be of the parlour type with living room, parlour, three bedrooms, scullery, larder, bathroom and w.c. plus a coal cellar. They were to be built in blocks of eight, six, five, three and in pairs with a variety of materials and construction methods to avoid monotony. There was a commitment to use Irish materials when this could be done at a reasonable price.

The costs were estimated as follows, falling just within the limit.

Land	4,974	£11 12s. 5d. per house
Development	23,000	£53 15s. 0d.
Building	278,200	£650
Wiring	6,741	£15 15s.
Architect	4,697	£10 10s.
Quantity Surveyor	1,512	£3 10s. 8d.
Clerk of Works	684	£1 10s. 3d.
Total	**319,808**	**£747 2s. 4d.**

This required a government grant of £213,205 with a loan of £79,952 and a Housing Rate of £26,651.

While the Corporation had some preference for direct labour, the Minister preferred contracts with commercial builders. The Corporation was prepared to concede the point in relation to roadways and voted so in 22 January 1923 but the Minister ultimately had his way and the entire scheme went to tender. He also had his way in terms of the specifications of the houses.

They decided to proceed by means of contracts for individual sections, with an underlying principle that contracts should last no more than a year because of a belief that building costs were on a downward trend. This limited contracts to about 200 houses. Four major contractors emerged from the various tendering opportunities over the next few years – H. & J. Martin, G. & T. Crampton, John Kenny and Paul Kossel, a German firm.

For the first phase, the Corporation decided to proceed by way of two tenders, one for 231 houses and one for 197 houses but when they came to examine the 10 tenders received, they decided to award both to John Kenny of Harcourt Road. His overall price was £640 3s. 6d. with £645 0s. 7d. for the 231 houses and £634 9s. 0d. for the second tranche (Report 267/1923). He came second in the completion for the roadways but was given the contract on the basis that he would be on site. However, the Minister believed that prices were still falling and he did not think it wise to commit beyond what could be built in a year; 200 houses. Kenny committed to build 231 in a year and was awarded the contract in 1923.

The price was fiercely negotiated, at the insistence of the Department of Local

Government, and the first contract worked out at £589 19s. 5d. per house. Concrete or tiles were substituted for granite sills, breeze concrete was used for party walls and breasts, skirting was made smaller. The second contract also went to Kenny, largely because he was on-site and this time was price was down to £550. However, the biggest saving was a dramatic one. The specifications included a bathroom with a hot and cold water system. This was now dropped, as happened in other schemes. It was soon realised that this was a step too far but not before the houses were completed. There was a retro-fitting project in 1926, which resulted in an additional cost to the tenants who wanted it of 10d. per week (Report 205/1926).

During 1924 Dublin Corporation was abolished by order of the Minister for Local Government and the Commissioners completed the project.

Marino Housing Scheme Reductions per house (Type A)

1	Substituting breeze concrete for brickwork in party walls and breasts	£6 7s. 0d.
2	Substituting tile or concrete window sills for granite window sills	£18 10s. 0d.
3	Substituting concrete slab lining for 4½-inch stock brick lining in cavity·walls	£3 12s. 4d.
4	Substituting 4-inch breeze concrete slabs for 4½-inch partitions	£1 15s. 7d.
5	Omission of flue linings from parlour and bedroom fireplaces	£0 15s. 6d.
5a	Substituting Portland cement plastering for white glazed tiles at sinks	£0 12s. 0d.
6	Substituting poilite ceilings for fibrous plaster slabs	£2 10s. 0d.
7	Omission of cupboards throughout, except food cupboards	£1 5s. 0d.
8	Omission of picture rail	£1 1s. 3d.
9	Omission of clothes racks	£0 11s. 0d.
10	Substituting granite door sills worked in quarry for granite door sills worked in the City of Dublin	£0 5s. 3d.
11	Reduction on P.C.'s	£8 14s. 2d.
12	Omission of hearth curbs	£0 15s. 0d.
13	Reduction in size of skirtings	£7 17s. 9d.
14	Substituting steel sashes for wood sashes and frames	
15	Omission of ventilators	£0 8s. 0d.
16	Substituting Solignum for three coats of paint	£0 18s. 8d.
		£55 18s. 6d.
Less 3 per cent. allowance		£1 13s. 6d.
		£54 5s. 0d.
The foregoing reductions when applied to the other effect an average saving of		£47 17s. 7d.

At a subsequent conference between Mr T. J. Byrne (L G. Housing Dept.),
Mr Hicks, and the Contractor, Mr Kenny, the following further reductions
were agreed to:

17	Alteration in types. Changing Type F into F1, 40 houses, equivalent to per house divided over the entire scheme	£2 3s. 1d.
18	Reduce surface excavation from 9-inch to 3-inch, equivalent to per house	£1 8s. 9d.
19	Reduction in filling consequent on last, equivalent to per house	£0 12s. 8d.
20	Rising walls in concrete instead of brick, equivalent to per house	£1 1s. 8d.
21	Reduce contingencies from £500 to £250, equivalent to per house	£0 4s. 8d.
22	Reduce steel reinforcement by 12½ per cent., equivalent to per house	£0 11s. 6d.
23	Omit trap doors in ceilings, equivalent to per house	£3 8s. 1d.

Additions

1	Wall tiles at sinks, per house	£0 12s. 0d.
2	Two coats paint instead of Solignum, per house.	£0 10s. 0d.
3	Felting under tiled roofs, per house	£1 4s. 10d.

Nett reduction (per house)	£55 1s. 2d.

Original tender for 231 houses	£645 0s. 7d.
Deduct as above	£55 1s. 2d.
Agreed price per house	£589 19s. 5d.

Thomas Farren, Chairman
4 September 1923 (Report 267/1923).

[Nobody would have realised the implications at the time but substituting Poilite ceilings for fibrous plaster board introduced asbestos into the houses].

Mr Farren complained at the time about how the Corporation had been treated by the Department during this process. The cost cutting seems to have had a quality impact, recognised in the Minutes of 27 November 1926. These noted that numerous complaints had been made about the houses built by Messrs Kenny in the first phase of Marino. The Commissioners accepted that there were many serious defects in the houses which should have been put right before the purchase process was concluded. Messrs Kenny had not proved co-operative and had argued that improper specifications were to blame and that they were not liable because the complaints had not been made during the maintenance period. A compromise proved necessary which involved Kenny making a payment which, in the opinion of the Commissioners did not come close to the cost of rectification of the issues.

The Corporation would bear the remaining costs. The justification was that litigation would have been necessary to prove the case and the view of the Corporation was that it would cost more than they would recover. However, in informing the Minister, the Commissioners 'fully recognise how unsatisfactorily these contracts have been carried out, and do not wish to conceal the fact that their decision now is merely to conclude the matter with the least possible cost to the Corporation'.

By the end of 1925 it was time to proceed with the Croydon Park extension. Arbitration had been required to determine a price and this worked out well from the Corporation's point of view. The award was £18,200 for the land but £49,000 had been claimed (Report 19/1926). The plans provided for 918 houses on approximately 90 acres with the price renegotiated down to £550. The houses would have five rooms with a variety of elevations and contain a parlour, living room and scullery on ground floor, and three bedrooms and bathroom on upper floor.

The elevations were grouped in types but all houses had rough cast on concrete to rear.

A   Stock brick facing with slated roof

B   Concrete block facing with Du Nord or other approved clay tiles

C   Stock brick facing to ground floor, with rough cast facing to upper floor, and slated roof.

D   Rough cast facing with red tiled roof.

In a lengthy memorandum of notes upon the plans, the Ministry made a number of suggestions, e.g., the desirability of providing a proportion of four-roomed houses containing living-room and three bedrooms, the provision of hot water services, the reservation of space for places of Divine Worship, schools, shops, and other public buildings, etc. Ever alert to the need to heed the State, the Commissioners agreed, though they did not always follow through.

> It has been decided to set apart portion of the site for 50 four-roomed houses according the plans and specification furnished by the Ministry. The large circus in the centre of the area is to be reserved for public buildings. His Grace the Most Rev. Dr Byrne, Archbishop of Dublin, has selected a site on the City Estate to the North of the 100 foot trunk road

for a church and schools. The circus adjoining Philipsburgh Avenue has been allotted as a playground. Hot water systems are to be installed in the houses. The effect of the re-arrangement of the plan to have it conform with the suggestions of the Ministry is to reduce the number of houses on the area to 856 (Report 105/1925). The overall cost was estimated at £435,436 0s. 0d.

Tenders were invited for 200 houses with the stipulation that a contract should be completed within six months and with penalties for lateness and bonuses for early completion. They received the following tenders including one from Paul Kossel, whose method of construction was new to them.

	Section I. 100 houses	Section II. 100 houses	Section III. 100 houses
H. & J. Martin	£52,184 5s. 3d.	£51,902 10s. 0d.	£51,975 13s. 6d.
G. & T. Crampton	£55,096 0s. 0d.	£54,555 0s. 0d.	£54,882 0s. 0d.
John Kenny	£55,733 0s. 0d.	£55,553 0s. 0d.	£55,524 0s. 0d.
Meagher & Hayes	£57,453 2s. 0d.	£57,145 10s. 2d.	£57,030 1s. 8d.
Paul Kossel	£58,700 0s. 0d.	£58,250 0s. 0d.	£58,250 0s. 0d.

Neither Meagher & Hayes nor Kossel provided for boundary walls.

The tender from Kossel generated a lot of interest. This was a German firm, based in Bremen and there was some surprise that a contract would be given to a non-national. These houses would be built using poured concrete using 'special' sand imported from Germany, rather than bricks and it was claimed that a considerable time saving would result. The *Evening Herald* reported that 'Houses, comportable *(sic)* five-roomed houses, will spring up like mushrooms. You may pass a field today and if you return the same way next day you will find it covered with houses with painters and paperhangers busily engaged giving the finishing touches (*Evening Herald*, 19 September 1925, p.1).

While Martin produced the best estimate, they suggested that they would complete their allocation in eighteen months. Since the Commissioner did not want a contract to last more than a year, it was agreed that some reorganisation of the building plots would take place to allow Martin to complete two 100-house sections within one year. This produced a contract for them of £105,612 9s. 9d. (Report 105/1925). The acquisition of a small parcel of land, just over 2 acres, from the CYMS allowed some additional building on the Philipsburgh Avenue side of the development and this was split on a pro-rata basis between H. & J. Martin and G. & T. Crampton (Report 271/1925). A second contract for 216 houses was soon offered and Kossel again tendered. This time, the contract went to G. & T. Crampton who offered to use poured concrete (Report 126/1925). The Commissioners continued with poured concrete for the next contract for 230 but it went to Kossel on this occasion and his tender was approved on 29 August 1925 (Report 192/1925). The final contract in the scheme also went to Kossel. This was for 104 houses and was approved on 29 May 1926 (Report 106/1926).

By now, the Corporation had decided on tenant purchase and the first houses in the Marino scheme houses were sold in 1925 for between £400 and £440 with a term of 40 years at 5 per cent per annum, the price depending on the type and situation of the house. No deposit was required but fixed amounts could be set either against the purchase price or to reduce the term of the loan. Those who had the funds could pay for the property outright. The leases were for 99 years and there were

Mr. Kossel has a few sand castles constructed for his children at the rate of ten per hour.

114. Mr Kossel's building technique as seen by *Dublin Opinion*, July 1926, p.141.

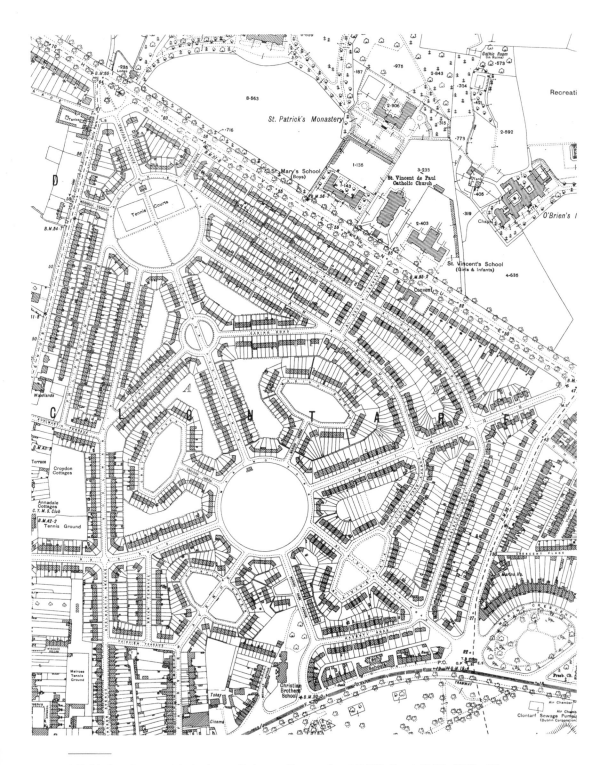

115. Marino, the completed scheme. Ordnance Survey plan, 1:2,500, Sheet 18 (IV), 1938 edition.

116. Houses (front) in the Croydon part of Marino (Casino Road), built by G.&T. Crampton, 1925–6. G.&T. Crampton photo archive, UCD.

117. Houses (rear) in the Croydon part of Marino, built by G.&T. Crampton, 1925–6. G.&T. Crampton photo archive, UCD.

118. Houses at the junction of Shelmartin Avenue and Casino Road, built by Crampton 1925–6. G.&T. Crampton photo archive, UCD.

119. Kitchen in the Croydon part of Marino, built by Crampton, 1925–6. G.&T. Crampton photo archive, UCD.

120. Aerial image of Marino. Note the different roof colours and the amount of green space.

conditions in relation to use and resale but nothing particularly onerous (Report 133/1925). This was an excellent price for the times. A private house in nearby Drumcondra would have cost in the region of £750. Even allowing for higher specifications in the private house, the value-for-money in Marino is evident.

The first 248 houses were allocated following public advertisement (see *Irish Times*, 8 June 1925, p. 7) and an application process which attracted over 4,400 responses. Large families were given priority and all tenants had households with at least 8 persons. This time a public draw was not used but rather the system set out in Report 162/1923 where the Superintendent of Housing made recommendations having considered the size of family, income and current housing circumstances. This resulted in 414 families being selected for further consideration.

Families with 12 persons and upwards	21
Families with 11 persons and upwards	40
Families with 10 persons and upwards	76
Families with 9 persons and upwards	117
Families with 8 persons and upwards	160

121. Housing on St Declan's Terrace, Marino.

122. Housing on Brian Road, Marino.

Sale price and annuity charges for the Marino scheme, derived from Report 133/1925.

Class	Price	Annual Payment (40 yrs)	Ground Rent (Min.)	Type of house
Class A	£440	£26	£2 10s.	All Semi-detached, end houses of blocks of three and end houses of blocks overlooking ornamental grounds.
Class B	£420	£25	£2 10s.	Blocks of three built on an angle. Centre houses of blocks of three built in a straight line, and intermediate houses of blocks overlooking ornamental grounds. Also houses of all blocks built in terraces.
Class C	£400	£24	£2 10s.	Intermediate houses of all blocks in terraces.

The sale arrangements allowed for purchasers to be 'admitted into occupation of the houses as soon as possible after they are selected, and from the date of entry up to the 1st April, 1926, they will be regarded as tenants at a rent equivalent to the weekly payments set out hereunder. No legal costs will be charged to the purchaser, save and except stamp duty, which must be paid on signing the lease' (Report 133/1925). The names of the streets needed to be decided before the leases were issued and the following were chosen in July 1925 (Report 163/1925).

- Marino Park
- Marino Park Avenue
- Haverty Road
- St Aiden Park
- St Aiden Park Avenue
- Carleton Road
- Brian Road
- Brian Terrace
- St Declan Avenue

By July 1926, it was time to allocate the houses in the Croydon Park element of the development. There were three classes of houses, differentiated much as previously

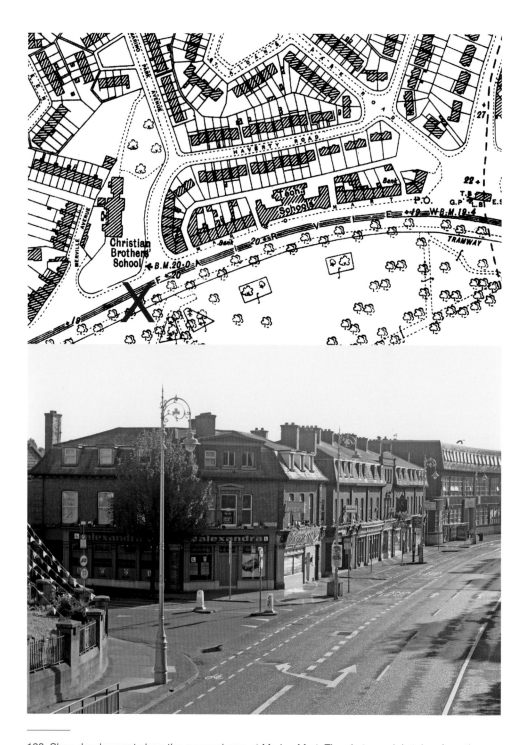

123. Shop development along the reserved area at Marino Mart. The photograph is taken from the position marked X. Ordnance Survey plan, 1:2,500, Sheet 18 (IV), 1938 edition.

124. Shopping
provision in
the reserved
area along
Marino Mart,
built by G.&T.
Crampton,1926.
G.&T. Crampton
photo archive,
UCD.

and on sale for the slightly increased price of £460, £440 and £420 respectively but all houses had a bath and a circulating hot water system. It was also reported that the 431 houses from the first phase (the 50-acre plot) were now occupied as were 284 houses in Croydon Park with the remaining 568 in the hands of the contractor, giving a grand total for Marino of 1,283 five-roomed houses – there was no mention of four-roomed houses (Report 161/1926).

There was a great deal of open space in Marino. Not only were there substantial gardens, there was space behind many of the houses for allotments. This left the question of the management of the two large circular parks. It was decided that they should be used for recreational purposes and they were fenced with pitches, tennis courts and pavilions at a cost of £3,100, of which £1,200 came from the Carnegie United Kingdom Trust. While the Corporation would retain control of the parks via the Housing Superintendent, it was agreed with Fr Flanagan, the local parish priest, that the management would be done in co-operation with a local committee. Regulations were approved in summer 1930 (Report 163/1930).

125. Dublin Commercial Public Utility Society houses along Malahide Road reserved area, Marino.

126. 'Warden' houses at the junction of Philipsburgh Avenue and Griffith Avenue.

Most of the general regulations were what might be normally expected but it is interesting that no public meetings or public addresses were permitted nor was anyone to drill, use weapons or give military evolutions. The use of catapults was also forbidden. Marino Park was not a public park. The local committee controlled access within the general framework of the regulations, though the Corporation could permit other groups to use it. Croydon Park (the more northerly of the two) was open to the general public but not before noon nor later than sunset. It had a particular focus on tennis and football was not permitted there. The charge was 6*d*. per person per hour but locals could get a book of 7 tickets for 2*s*. 6*d*. Racquets, balls and shoes were available for hire. There was no guarantee that people could get more than an hour's play. This was at the discretion of the groundsman and dependent on demand (Report 163/1930).

Reserved Areas

A reserved area was a portion of a suburban housing development which was reserved for private ownership, facilitated by a variety of measures that included the provision of a serviced site and privileged access to funding. Reserved areas continued to be part of Dublin Corporation's approach to housing provision even after they had shifted their focus away from tenant purchase to rental. It might seem odd, therefore, that they continued to support private ownership when they had determined that tenant purchase was not the best policy approach to deal with the housing crisis.

The beginnings were accidental. Dublin Corporation members and officials, in common with many others, were impressed with model towns and the garden city movement in the early years of the twentieth century. The hugely popular 1914 Civic Exhibition and the associated international competition for a town plan, which resulted in Patrick Abercrombie's *Dublin of the Future* (1921) was but one manifestation of that interest. In their early consideration of their model development in Marino around 1911, they had the idea that better quality houses should be built around the edges of the development to improve the overall 'look'. When the opportunity came in 1919 to begin the development, the idea of using more expensive houses to improve the image was maintained through the various versions of the plans. Unfortunately just at the time came to begin, a decision by the new Irish government upset these plans. The difficulty was that while the new

State was happy to continue with the new practice of supporting local authorities by means of grant-in-aid, the Minister put a cap on the amount he was prepared to pay per house. This was significantly below what the Corporation expected to pay to build its edging houses and it left them with a dilemma. They could wait until housing costs fell below the threshold set; a not entirely unreasonable position as building costs were falling from their post-war heights. They could scale back the specifications for these houses. They could meet the additional costs themselves, putting the cost onto the rates. None of these solutions appealed. Some creative thinking was needed and the solution that emerged was that they would develop what would now be called public-private partnerships. They would incentivise the private sector to build these houses and so they would get the finish they wanted for the development. It did not really matter that these houses would be sold in the private sector, since they would have been for tenant purchase anyway and would have gone to the better-off 'working' class. As a refinement, they maximized the effects of any subsidies by removing the profit element from the private development. This was done by facilitating public utility societies.

By 1920, public utility societies were well-known in the UK and had been endorsed by the Tudor Walters report as being suitable partners for local authorities in housing developments but they were not used in Dublin. They had developed in the latter decades of the nineteenth century as co-partnership co-operative societies which allowed people to combine their resources and build and own their own houses. The model was a simple one. The initial resources of the group, which included personal savings and shares bought by supporters, permitted the construction of a number of houses for members of the group. These people then repaid the purchase price to the group, allowing more houses to be built and so on until all of the group had been housed. The society continued in existence until all of the houses had been paid for.

It was not until the concept was applied by Canon David Hall in a small but innovative housing development in the East Wall docklands in 1919 that their value was brought to the attention of policy makers (McManus, 1999). Quite quickly it was seen that they could make a contribution to the housing crisis by facilitating people who had the income to support house purchase but who did not have access to the necessary credit. The new State was also convinced that such societies would be useful and enhanced government grants were made available. In 1925, a private individual purchasing a five-roomed house for £600 could expect grants totalling £150 and access to a loan of £150 but a utility society member would receive grants of £200 and access to a loan of £200. The better houses the Corporation hoped for could be built at lower cost and the supports would encourage people to buy who might otherwise not be wholly enthusiastic about living close to a council estate.

Report 64/1925 noted that 'in connection with the Marino Housing Area it has been decided, with the sanction of the Minister for Local Government and Public Health, to reserve the main frontages for better-class residences and business premises'. The first step was the advertisement of plots along Fairview Strand/ Marino Mart in February 1925 for 36 residential shops. This was a controlled development and those building had to build to the specifications of H.T. O'Rourke who was anxious to ensure a uniform appearance for this edge development.

Among the first developers was Keatinge (of Grafton Street) who offered to take up and develop the western corner of the site. By September he was back for an additional four sites (Report 283/1925) and by early the following year it was reported that he had sold three shops with a three-bedroomed dwelling above in the same block (*Irish Times*, 14 January 1926, p.4). The same report noted that the corner block would be occupied by Johnson, Mooney and O'Brien, the bakers. In that same month Mr. Thomas C. O'Leary, 10 Iona Crescent, Glasnevin applied for and was granted a site (Report 21/1926). By April a total of eighteen sites had been disposed of, mostly to individual purchasers (Report 74/1926). After that the pace of development was steady but the frontage was not complete until the commissioning of the vocational school in June 1934. Thom's Directory for 1929 shows eight vacant sites but a good mix of uses that included a bank (Bank of Ireland), a branch of the Monument Creamery, a number of butchers (including Youkstetter) and grocers together with a post office, chemist, tobacconist, newsagent, draper, outfitter and the branch of Johnston, Mooney and O'Brien.

The other frontages were reserved for housing and Report 255/1925 noted a proposal from the Dublin Commercial Public Utility Society Ltd., 9 Cavendish Row, to build twelve houses on Malahide Road at an average cost of *not less* than £750 a house, for sale to the members of the Society. The frontage was 35 feet (with a depth of approximately 100 feet) with a ground rent of £6 per annum and

127. Houses in the reserved area on Philipsburgh Avenue, built by G.&T. Crampton, 1926.
G.&T. Crampton photo archive, UCD.

a lease of 150 years. The usual leasehold conditions stipulated that the houses were to be used as residences, and for no other purpose whatever. There would be no ground rent for the first year but the houses needed to be completed within a year. In approving the report, it was taken as a template for any subsequent proposals to build on Malahide Road. This indeed did happen and the DCPUS were soon back for an additional four sites (Report 283/1925) and a further twelve (Report 21/1926). That left a small site leading to the junction with St Declan's Road and the DCPUS were allocated this in 1928 for six semi-detached houses of a design similar to those they had already built (Report 196/1928).

The Guild of Building Workers also became developers as they asked for (and got) two sites on the developing 100-foot road, near the junction with St Declan Terrace (Report 7/1927). The plot was 97' deep with a frontage of 34' 9" with a requirement that they build semi-detached houses. The 100-foot road was now tentatively called Griffith Road (Report 17/1927) but formally named Griffith Avenue in April 1927.

By now, the Corporation had begun to understand that they had hit on a good approach. By designating part of their development for private housing, they improved the socio-economic profile of the area and the higher average income was seen to be important in sustaining the shops, which were also provided as part of this approach. It also had the less tangible effect of promoting good civic values amongst the tenants who had little prior experience of ownership. Thus was born the 'reserved area' policy. When they came to plan the Croydon Park phase of the Marino scheme, the Commissioners, with the agreement of the Minister, were prepared to reduce the number of houses from 918 to 856 to allow for this and for improved amenity. They noted that: 'Agreeably with the policy already adopted for the first section of the housing scheme, it was decided to reserve the frontages to Philipsburgh Avenue and the new 100-foot thoroughfare for better-class residential or business premises'.

It seems that the Philipsburgh Avenue frontage was not as attractive a prospect and it proved impossible to get developers. So, in September 1926, the Commissioners decided to become their own developers but with Crampton (who had the nearby contract) to do the building. The motivation was the same as before. It was important that the estate would look well and that 'it was highly desirable to have the frontage covered without delay and so obviate the objection of having the reres of the houses in the Scheme exposed to view from the main thoroughfare. (Report 1926/191). The houses were to be on the same plan as Crampton were building but with increased dimensions and more embellishment such as improved elevations and bay windows (Report 1926/191). The frontage was increased by 2 feet compared to the scheme houses, the depth by 6 feet and the height of the external walls by 2 feet. There were 28 houses in the scheme at a cost of £18,200. The total area of each house within external walls for the buildings in the scheme was 844 square feet compared to 996 square feet in these houses. A comparison was offered.

	Frontage	Living room	Parlour	First bedroom	Second bedroom	Cubicle	Scullery	Bath room
Housing Scheme	End House, Intermediate House 19' 5" 19' 9".	157	130	139	112	66	41	40
Frontage Houses	End House, 21' 9". Intermediate House 21' 5"	190	163	150	134	80	57	60

Note: All capacities are 'superfoot' – a measure of capacity equal to one-foot length of a board one foot wide and one inch thick.

The Philipsburgh Avenue Reserved area houses were ready for sale in 1927 at a purchase price of £650 with ground rent of £4 and a 99 year lease. The Commissioners decided that 'applications will be considered from persons, resident or employed in the city, who can put up a deposit of £200 to get a loan of the remainder over 40 years at 5¾% interest'. This came to £49 11s. 0d. per annum (Report 94/1927).

The City Commissioners were also responsible for the erection of some 32 houses between St Declan Terrace and Torlogh Parade. Derryquin Castle, Sneem, Co. Kerry was burned by the IRA in 1922 and Colonel Warden, the owner, was awarded damages of just under £23,000 under the Damage to Property (Compensation) Act, 1923. He chose not to rebuild and in an unusual transaction, the Commissioners bought the award for just under £19,000 (Report 143/1928). With this money from the award, they obtained the permission of the Minister to build not less than 26 houses in the Marino development. They chose to do in the reserved area in the space between St Declan Terrace and Torlogh Parade. This time they felt that it would be important to provide an opportunity for the small-scale speculative builder so they invited tenders for 8 houses, 16 houses or 32 houses. In the event, all of the tenders were for the full 32 houses and H. & J. Martin were given the contract. Though there was not enough money to build with brick and the houses are terrraced, the Commissioners stated that these houses offered the best accommodation and design of all the houses built to that date (Report 178/1928). The sale price was £700 for intermediate houses and £725 for the end houses. Applications were invited from persons resident or employed in the city, and 'in the case of those who are unable to pay the purchase price in full, but are prepared to make a deposit of not less than £100, the repayment of the balance shall be by equal annual instalments over a period of 40 years, at 5¾ per cent interest. Preference, and where possible selection of house will be given to persons offering the largest deposits (Report 88/1929). The Commissioners were so pleased with the results that they decided in March 1929 to extend the development to Philipsburgh Avenue and to complete the unbuilt frontage on that avenue by building an additional 17 houses in the same style and using the same contractor (Report 68/1929).

The 100-foot road was gradually developed and extended westward over the next number of years with the DCPUS being given 43 sites on the north side of Griffith

Avenue between Upper Drumcondra Road and Goosegreen Avenue (Gracepark Terrace) in December 1927. The plots were 200 feet deep and 35 feet wide, at a ground rent of £7 5s. per annum and the houses were to cost £1,000 (Report 3/1928). The Saorstát Civil Service Public Utility Society were given a plot that stretched for 650 feet east from Upper Drumcondra Road on the southern site of the avenue in August 1928 on condition that they built 19 semi-detached houses, which would also cost no less than £1,000 (Report 172/1928).

The housing component on Griffith Avenue was now taking shape but there was still the question of a church and schools. The Parish Priest of Fairview, Canon Pettit wrote asking for space for a church and a boys and girls school. As was usual, the Commissioners were supportive and they offered a site, part of the city estate, on the north side of Griffith Avenue, between the Christian Brothers property and the O'Brien Institute, giving that side of the avenue an institutional character. The price agreed for the 8.75 acre site was £325 per acre, mid way between the Corporation's own valuation and the first offer (Report 285/1925). By now it was a joint venture with the Christian Brothers but it resulted in a very fine complex of buildings of a school on either side of the parish church.

Drumcondra

While the Marino scheme was being developed, plans were being formed for a scheme in Upper Drumcondra and Glasnevin. The Corporation long had plans for what they had called the Millbourne Avenue scheme in Drumcondra. The first plan, made in Spring 1915, envisaged two sections, the first provided for 42 four-roomed cottages, 70 three-roomed cottages and 50 two-roomed cottages, a total of 162 dwellings. In the second section, they anticipated building 186 four-roomed cottages, 249 three-roomed cottages and 148 two-roomed, giving a total for this section of 583 dwellings and a grand total of 785 (Report 195/1915). The LGB in their informal advice to the Corporation in 1919 were very enthusiastic about what they described as a 'magnificent' 35-acre site with good subsoil and aspect and just at the end of the penny stage of Nelson Pillar tram. The proposal at that point was for 420 houses and the LGB had only minor suggestions for improvement. The Corporation was encouraged to acquire the site as soon as possible and to extend it to the east in so far as possible. This could be done by acquiring 45 acres of the Butterly estate.

On that basis, the selected architects, McDonnell and Dixon, prepared plans in 1920 for 836 houses at a density of twelve to the acre. They suggested 362 two-bedroomed houses (type A and B) of which 96 would have a parlour (type B), 180 three-bedroomed houses (type C) and 394 four-bedroomed houses (type E and F), of which 118 would have a parlour (type F). These early plans were much modified in later discussions (Report 110/1920) and the scheme came to be known as the Drumcondra scheme.

It was mid-decade before the Drumcondra scheme was realised at a time when there were still 22,000 families living in single-room tenements in the city. Those earning less than £8 a week were unable to afford a house and questions were being raised about whether the strategy of building five-roomed houses, as in Marino, was the best approach. For the moment, the Corporation took the view that it was. By taking these people out of the tenement market, it freed up houses which could be taken up by those with lower incomes. This was the argument put by the Town Clerk, John J. Murphy, at the Local Government Inquiry at City Hall at the beginning of September 1926 into the request by the City Commissioners for sanction for a loan

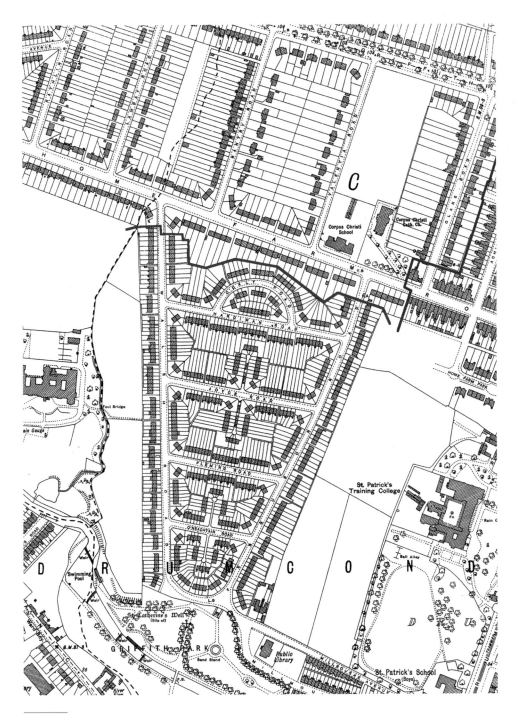

128. The Drumcondra scheme with the Reserved area on Home Farm Road and the area to the north. Ordnance Survey plan, 1:2,500, Sheets 14 (XV) and 18 (III), 1938 edition.

129. Ferguson Road, Drumcondra scheme, shortly after completion.

130. Houses in the Dublin Corporation part of Drumcondra, built by G.&T. Crampton, 1928.
G.&T. Crampton photo archive, UCD.

131. Reserved area housing on Bantry Road for the Civil Service Housing Association. Contrast with the Kinlen houses on the other side of the street.

132. Reserved area housing on Bantry Road built by Kinlen.

of £684,787 17s. 0d. for their new scheme. He was asked if in fact they were building for the lower middle classes and he agreed with that suggestion.

The plan was now for 1,060 houses on a site of 158 acres and 10 perches of lands (64 ha) with seven acres left for churches and schools. This time they would build some four-roomed houses but two-thirds of the houses would have five rooms with a bathroom, lavatory and hot and cold water. In addition, there would be allotments available of one eighth of an acre each at a rent of £1 per annum. The cost of the houses would be 15s. 10d. per week for the five room and 13s. 2d. for the four roomed houses, with ground rent additional, on a lease of 99 years.

The report of the Local Government Inspector was favourable but not all parties were happy with the resulting compulsory purchase order and they appealed through the courts, slowing the process up. It was decided to proceed on part of the site which was already in Corporation possession. The 'Butterly' segment was 32 acres (13ha) and they proceeded to put in services and foundations for 176 five-roomed, 143 four-roomed and 215 three-roomed houses. The Commissioners explained that the five roomed houses reflected the fact that larger families needed to be accommodated. While they agreed that they had not completely satisfied demand in that regard, they had made sufficient progress to allow them to begin to house smaller families. The two or three roomed houses comprised a living room and two or three bedrooms. Adjacent to the living room was a scullery with a bath and copper boiler, said to be capable of heating the water for the bath in twenty minutes. The arrangement in the larger houses was for the water to be heated by the range but this seemed not to be possible in the smaller ones. The layout of the scheme bears more than a passing resemblance to what was being built in places such as Becontree for London County Council.

The building involved two tenders, one for 266 houses which went to G. & T. Crampton and the other for 269 houses which was given to H. & J. Martin. While each submitted the lowest tenders, the Commissioners placed a great deal of store on the fact that they had positive experience of working with both firms. This was only in June of 1927 and by November of the same year, it was noted that houses were nearing completion and names were chosen for eleven of the roads in the area.

Advertisements were placed in the newspapers on 23 November 1927 inviting

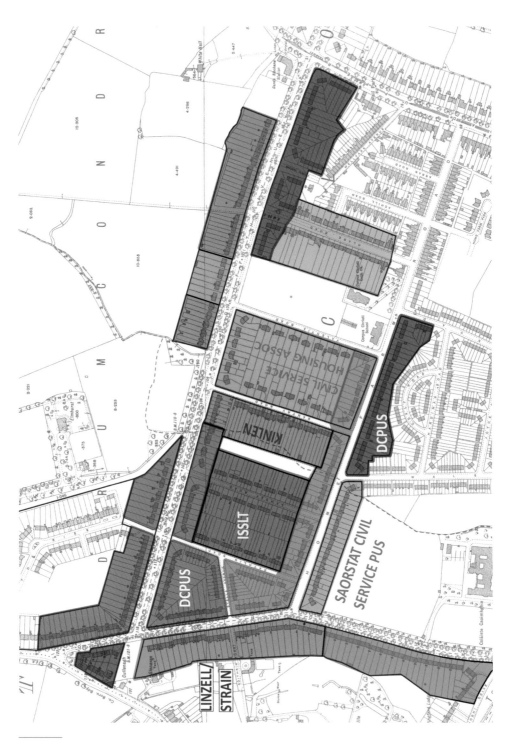

133. Drumcondra, Reserved area and major developers. Ordnance Survey plan, 1:2,500, Sheet 14 (XV) and 18 (III), 1938 edition.

134. Reserved area housing on Home Farm Road, built by G.&T. Crampton, 1928-29. G.&T. Crampton Photo Archive, UCD.

applications from people resident in Dublin for the three, four and five roomed houses. The cut-off date for applications was 6 December (*Evening Herald*, 23 November 1927, p.4). It was reported that over 3,000 applications were received for the houses, each applicant was required to have at least two children under 21 years of age (*Irish Independent*, 8 December 1927, p.8). As before, the sale price reflected the size and location of the houses with a lease of 99 years from 1 April 1929 and an interest rate on loans of 5¾ per cent (Report 26/1928). The total cost included the annuity charge, annual rates, ground rent, fire insurance plus a collection charge (which got significantly higher the more frequent were the payments – those who could pay half yearly were charged 2*s*. per annum compared to £2 8*s*. 0*d*. for those who paid weekly).

	Sale Price	Total per annum	Weekly Charge
5 Roomed Houses			
24 Semi Detached	£460	£45 10s. 10d.	£0 17s. 7d.
58 end of terrace	£440	£43 17s. 4d.	£0 16s. 11d.
98 Intermediate	£420	£41 13s. 9d.	£0 16s. 1d.
4 Roomed Houses			
18 Semi Detached	£350	£37 8s. 11d.	£0 14s. 5d.
44 end of terrace	£340	£35 0s. 7d.	£0 13s. 6d.
82 Intermediate	£330	£32 19s. 11d.	£0 12s. 9d.
3 Roomed Houses			
8 Semi Detached	£250	£29 16s. 11d.	£0 11s. 6d.
70 end of terrace	£240	£26 6s. 3d.	£0 10s. 2d.
133 Intermediate	£230	£24 0s. 8d.	£0 9s. 3d.

The Ordnance Survey plan shows that a geometric layout was favoured once again. Aligned with the slope of the site, it took the shape of a parabola with the apex restated by a circular feature at the north of the scheme. Cross roads joined the outer roads – the arms of the ellipse – to create the individual blocks which increased in area to the north. Terraces of six houses or less were used with setbacks but semi-detached houses were used only at road junctions to soften the angles. The plan shows that gardens varied in extent but were substantial to the rear of houses though more modest to the front. A variety of materials was used to add interest but most houses had a cement mortar finish and there was less variety than in Marino. Culs de sac were included forming almost a central spine but they are narrow and more on the model of Becontree in London than the design used in Marino.

Reserved Area

The reserved area concept was further developed in the Drumcondra scheme and it seems that the Commissioners were so enthusiastic about the concept that they might have lost sight of their real mission. They could have built upwards of 1,000 houses directly on the site but they decided to forego this and instead to give 85 acres (34ha) for the reserved area where they hoped to get approximately 450 superior houses. The reserved area was the upper and higher part of the site and it was developed largely by public utility societies though the Irish Sailors' and Soldiers' Land Trust was also involved. Interestingly though the Keogh Square/Emmet Road development was under construction at the same time, no reserved area was included, which is odd given what was being contemplated in Drumcondra. What is odder is that there was no discussion either. It may be that the area was not seen as being suitable in that it was not quite suburban and there was more pressure on land.

The Saorstát Civil Service Public Utility Society was one of the first to express an interest and they were given sites for 19 houses on Clare Road (Report 230/1926). Another body that responded was the Irish Sailors' and Soldiers' Land Trust. The Commissioners felt that these were particularly suitable because of the number of ex-servicemen (550) who were in Corporation housing and the large number still awaiting housing. This led to a decision in September 1927 (Report 194/1927) that a plot of about 4¼ acres be sold to the Trust on a fee-simple basis to permit the erection of about 40 houses. An additional site of 2 acres to the east on which they proposed to build 20 houses was provided in February 1928 (Report 49/1928). As with other developers the Corporation provided considerable help.

- Home Farm Road was to be extended as far as may be necessary, and the Corporation would make two new side roads on either side of the plot, connecting this extension with the new main road.

- The sewers would be extended so far as may necessary to serve the houses, free of cost to the Trust.

- Water supply and public lighting services would also be provide free of charge to the Trust

This was a good arrangement, but one which was extended to other developers too. This report is interesting in that it now explicitly refers to 'reserved land'. Development continued from 1928 into 1930. The Commissioners advertised the land in relatively small plot sizes, probably with a view to attracting a range of developers If they did, they were disappointed. While a number of public utility societies became involved, the Dublin Commercial Public Utility Society dominated building by a considerable margin and was often the only bidder. Even then, it operated on a scale different to others and it can hardly have been much of a surprise when it transformed into a limited company (but with a social mandate) in the early 1930s. Only two private builders sought plots, Louis P. Kinlen and

Strain / Linzell. This made particular sense in the latter case since they were local but needed building land. The pace of building varied from year to year but 1928 was a busy year. Plots were allocated to Kinlen, the DCPUS and the Civil Service Housing Association, whose low density development stands in marked contrast to the adjacent Kinlen development (see the reserved area map).

It was good year and a good deal for all concerned. The houses came within the terms of the Housing Acts, 1925–26 as extended and modified by subsequent legislation. Report 219/1926 dealt with enhanced supports for individuals or public utility society who built under the provisions of that 1925 Act.

	Grant Payable for dwellings of		
	3 rooms	4 rooms	5 or more rooms
Any person	45	55	65
Public Utility Society	60	80	100

In addition, the Corporation agreed to construct the roads and underground services free of charge. That left the purchasers liable just for stamp duty, the cost of connections of light, water and sewerage to the main services and out of pocket expenses. The purchasers were eligible for Small Dwellings Acquisition Act (SDAA) loans, equivalent to 75 per cent of the accepted tender, provided the market value of the houses came within its limit (Report 86/1928).

The importance of the grants was pointed up when Kinlen asked the Corporation to swap land he had been previously allocated. Report 41/1928 had allocated the plots to the Civil Service Housing Association and Kinlen. However a portion of Kinlen's plot was outside the Borough Boundary at the time and houses built on it would not be eligible for local grants or Corporation assistance under the SDAA legislation. He reckoned that he would have built 10 houses on the site so he asked for and was given an equivalent plot of ground on the north side of Griffith Avenue to the right of the Eustace reserve (Report 14/1929).

A comparison of the plot sizes on the reserved area compared to those in the Corporation housing area shows that the utility societies built at low density with semi-detached houses being the norm on large plots. The one exception, and this bears out the original contention that public utility societies were more suited to realize the

Corporation's vision, was the plot given to Kinlen, a private builder. In comparison to the low density semi-detached houses directly across the road on Bantry Road, his commercial reality required that he build high density terraced houses, though they were five roomed and priced competitively at £600. These and other houses on Griffith Avenue prompted a complaint from the Whitehall and Glasnevin Residents' Association. They saw this as a deviation from the policy of building only superior types of houses on the reserved lands. The annoyance extended to getting J.J. Byrne, a Cumann na nGaedhael TD, to ask a question in the Dáil on 31 March 1928. General Mulcahy, Minister for Local Government and Public Health, was able to reassure him that 'the types of houses now proposed to be erected in the area cannot be regarded as detrimental to the amenities of other ratepayers in the district'. Though an impressive urban landscape was produced on the reserved area, it must be seen as being somewhat removed from the urgent needs of the city at the time. The map provided shows where each of the builders was active. The importance of the DCPUS in creating the main roads and thus the frontage of the scheme can clearly be seen.

There must have been a realisation that the Reserved Area in Drumcondra had taken a good idea too far because never again was such a large proportion of a development devoted to a reserved area.

Concluding Comments

By the time the future owners were moving into their houses in Drumcondra, Dublin Corporation had truly become a major force in house building. The Marino scheme was larger than anything built previously in the private or public sectors in sheer scale, while it was innovative both in planning and in policy. Private builders were now coming to rely on the large contracts which the Corporation made available and home ownership was now within reach for a group who never believed it would be possible. Yet, there were major problems still to be solved. Though the scale of building was impressive, there remained a huge and constantly renewing demand; it was rather like trying to empty a bath while the taps were still running. The owner occupancy approach had solved the problem of the Corporation's (and the State's) balance sheet in that they could build without incurring continuing debt. But it was clear to all that this approach was never going to provide high quality housing to many, perhaps the majority, of those in need. The best that could be hoped for was that they would come to occupy the better-quality tenements, something made possible by falling rents as a result of declining demand. The approach of the 1920s had served a particular need but by the end of the decade it was time to reconsider. That time would come when the Corporation was restored in 1930 and both major political parties came to the view that it was now possible (and high time) to tackle the slums.

Reading

The readings listed here will provide added detail to the text and develop additional lines of inquiry. This text relied heavily on the published and unpublished research of the authors and that drew greatly on the excellent resources of the City Archive. One of those resources is the collection of minutes, reports and documents presented to the City Council. A reference to Report xx/yyyy is a reference to report number xx produced in year yyyy. While the reports are a wonderful source of data, it must be remembered that they were often produced to very tight deadlines. There are sometimes small differences and inconsistencies in the statistical data from report to report. Sometimes this is due to changes being made to housing schemes on site but sometimes this is no more than a minor error. The data have been presented here as published.

Abercrombie, Patrick. *Dublin of the Future*. Dublin: Civic Trust, 1922.

Affleck Greeves, T. *Bedford Park – The First Garden Suburb*. London: The Bedford Park Society, 1975.

Bannon, Michael, J. ed. *The emergence of Irish planning*, 1880–1920. Dublin: Turoe Press, 1985.

Bannon, Michael, J. ed. *Planning: the Irish experience*, 1920–1988. Dublin: Turoe Press, 1989.

Bolton, Albert. *The Housing of the Working Classes (Ireland) Acts 1890 to 1908*. Dublin: Falconer.

Boyd, Gary. *Dublin, 1745–1922 – Hospitals, spectacle & vice*. Dublin: Four Courts Press, 2005.

Brady, Joseph and Anngret Simms. eds. *Dublin through Space and Time*. Dublin: Four Courts Press, 2001.

Brady, Joseph. Dublin 1930–1950 – *The Emergence of the Modern City*. Dublin: Four Courts Press, 2014.

Brady, Joseph. "Dublin – A City of Contrasts". In *Voices on Joyce*, edited by Anne Fogarty and Fran O'Rourke, 77–96. Dublin: UCD Press, 2015.

Brady, Joseph. *Dublin 1950–1970 – Houses, Flats and High Rise*. Dublin: Four Courts Press, 2016.

Brady, Joseph. *Dublin in the 1950s and 1960s: cars, shops and suburbs*. Dublin: Four Courts Press, 2017.

Brady, Joseph and Ruth McManus. "Marino at 100 – a suburb of lasting importance". *Irish Geography*, 51, no. 1 (2018): 1–24.

Brady, Joseph and Ruth McManus. "Dublin's twentieth-century social housing policies: tenure, 'reserved areas' and housing type". *Planning Perspectives '35, Issue 6 (2020): 1005–1030'.* https://doi.org/10.1080/02665433.2019.1662833

Cameron, Charles. *Lectures on the Preservation of Health.* London and New York: Cassell, Petter and Galpin, 1868.

Cameron, Charles. *Reminiscences of Sir Charles A. Cameron, C.B.* Dublin: Hodges Figgis, 1913.

Carroll, Lydia. *In the Fever King's Preserves: Sir Charles Cameron and the Dublin Slums.* Dublin: A&A Farmar, 2011.

Flinn, D. Edgar. *Report of the Sanitary Circumstances and Administration of the City of Dublin with special reference to the causes of the high-death rate.* London: HMSO, 1906.

Hall, Mr and Mrs S.C. *Ireland: Its Scenery, Character, &c.* 3 Volumes. London: How & Parsons, 1841–3.

HM Stationery Office. *Housing of the Working Classes in Ireland.* Dublin: Stationery Office, 1919.

Howard, Ebenezer. *Tomorrow: a peaceful path to real reform.* London, Swan Sonnenschein, 1898.

Howard, Ebenezer. *Garden Cities of Tomorrow.* London: Swan Sonnenschein, 1902.

Hubbard, E. and M. Shippobottom. *A guide to Port Sunlight.* Liverpool, Liverpool University Press, 1988.

Local Government Board for Ireland. *Report of the Committee appointed by the Local Government Board for Ireland to inquire into the public health of the city of Dublin.* Dublin: HM Stationery Office, Thom and Co., 1900.

Local Government Board for Ireland. *Report of the departmental committee appointed by the Local Government Board for Ireland to inquire into the housing conditions of the working classes in the city of Dublin.* British Parliamentary Papers, 19, 1914, cd.7272/7317–xix. Dublin: Local Government Board for Ireland, 1914.

Local Government Board UK. *Manual on the preparation of state-aided housing schemes. Local Government Board.* UK: HM Stationery Office, 1919.

Mapother, Edward, Dillon. *Report on the Health of Dublin for the year 1865.* Dublin: Dollard, 1866.

McManus, Ruth. *"Public Utility Societies, Dublin Corporation and the development of Dublin, 1920–1940."* Irish Geography, 29, no. 1 (1996): 27–37.

McManus, Ruth. "The 'Building Parson' – the role of Reverend David Hall in the solution of Ireland's early twentieth-century housing problems." *Irish Geography,* 32, no. 2(1999): 87–98.

McManus, Ruth. *Dublin 1910–1940: shaping the city and suburbs*. Dublin: Four Courts Press, 2002.

McManus, Ruth. "The role of public utility societies in Ireland, 1919–40". In *Surveying Ireland's past, multidisciplinary essays in honour of Anngret Simms*, edited by Howard Clarke, Jacinta Prunty and Mark Hennessy, 613–38. Dublin: Geography Publications, 2004.

McManus, Ruth. "Tackling the urban housing problem in the Irish Free State, 1922–1940." *Urban History*, 46 no. 1 (2019): 62–81. https://doi.org/10.1017/S0963926818000214

O'Brien, Joseph V. *Dear dirty Dublin, a city in distress, 1899–1916*. Berkeley: University of California Press, 1982.

Ó Gráda, Diarmuid. *Georgian Dublin – the forces that shaped the city*. Cork: Cork University Press, 2015.

Prunty, Jacinta. *Dublin slums 1800–1925, a study in urban geography*. Ireland: Irish Academic Press, 1998.

Prunty, Jacinta. "Improving the urban environment". In *Dublin through space and time*, edited by Joseph Brady and Anngret Simms, 166–220. Dublin: Four Courts Press, 2001.

Rowley, Ellen. ed. *More than concrete blocks: Dublin's twentieth century buildings and their story. Volume 1 – 1900–1940*. Dublin: Four Courts Press, 2016.

Rowley, Ellen. ed. *More than concrete blocks: Dublin's twentieth century buildings and their story. Volume 2 – 1940–1972*. Dublin: Four Courts Press, 2019.

Royal Commission. *Report of the Royal commission appointed to inquire into the housing of the working classes. Minutes of evidence etc.*, Ireland, British Parliamentary Papers, cd. 4547. London: Eyre and Spottiswoode, 1885.

Stationery Office. *Report of inquiry into the housing of the working classes of the city of Dublin, 1939–43*. Dublin: Stationery Office, 1944.

Tudor Walters, John. *Report of the committee appointed by the President of the Local Government Board and the Secretary for Scotland to consider questions of building construction in connection with the provision of dwellings for the working classes in England, Wales and Scotland*. London: HMSO, 1918.

Unwin, Raymond. *Nothing gained by overcrowding*. Garden Cities and Town and Country Planning Association. London: King and Sons, 1912.

Whitelaw, James. *An essay on the population of Dublin*, being the result of an actual survey taken in 1798 with great care and precision, to which is added the general return of the district committee in 1804, with a comparative statement of the two surveys, also several observations on the present state of the poorer parts of the city of Dublin, 1805. Dublin. Reprinted as *Slum conditions in London and Dublin*. Farnborough, Hants: Gregg International, 1974.

List of Images

Index

A

Abbey Street Upper, 214
Abercrombie, Patrick, 127, 149, 201
Aberdeen, 131
accommodating, 85, 210
accommodation, 33, 37–38, 46, 49, 63, 78, 82, 86, 105, 109, 122, 124, 126, 132–34, 146, 222, 224–25
    sanitary, 44, 92
    shop, 162
    unhealthy, 196
accusations, 137, 184
acquirement, 65, 89
acres, 29, 32, 65, 114–15, 118–19, 144, 159, 174, 188, 202–3, 209, 212–13, 233, 236, 238, 244–45, 250, 257, 279–80, 284, 287–88
Act of Parliament, 34
Acts of Union, 11
adoption, 31, 42, 160–61
agenda, 127, 152, 240
air, 15, 19, 22, 37–38, 43–44, 65, 72, 92, 99, 108, 110, 114, 146, 148, 157, 181, 183
air space, 37, 45, 63, 208
air temperature, 19
Alderman Corrigan, 135
Alderman Hubbard Clark, 233
Alderman Kelly, 183, 185
Alderman McCarthy, 94
Alderman O'Connor, 135
Alderman O'Reilly, 135
Alderman Thomas Kelly, 141
Alderman Tom Kelly, 256
Alderman Vance, 118
alleys, 65, 86, 157, 176
allotments, 213, 233, 245, 271, 284
altruistic motives, 185
amendments, 133, 160–61, 230, 235
amenities, 159, 290
angles, 158, 166, 269, 287
annoyance, 69, 133, 290

annuity, 230–31, 269, 286
apartments, 44, 181
applicants, 232, 235, 286
applications, 30, 35, 50, 66, 89, 118, 133, 154–55, 178, 191, 230, 239, 278, 286
arbitrator, 35, 89, 154, 184
Arbour Hill, 85
Archbishop of Dublin, 96, 153, 171–72, 233, 260–1
Archdiocese, 171
architects, 32, 36, 72, 205–6, 212–13, 221, 233, 258
    appointed city, 40
    selected, 280
Ardee Street, 218, 227
area
    cleared, 74
    communal, 257
    congested, 149–50
    designated, 158, 198
    insanitary, 35, 41
    slum, 106, 162, 217
    unhealthy, 13, 30, 66, 82, 101, 103, 181
Arran Street East, 173
artisans, 13, 24–25, 28, 30, 34, 48, 57–8, 72, 91, 93, 115–16, 228, 238, 240, 244
Artisans' Dwellings Committee, 35, 44–45, 47–48, 50–52, 55–56, 69, 73
Artizans' and Labourers' Dwellings Act 1875, 13, 32
Ash Street, 86, 127, 144, 152, 181
assessment, 84, 128, 133, 142, 157
Assistant City Architect, 40, 250
Aungier Court, 86
Aungier Place, 194
authorities
    local, 25, 30, 87, 139, 210, 223, 232, 240, 274
    local sanitary, 33
avenue, 44–46, 49, 67, 246, 278–79
awards, 35, 184, 258, 261, 278